# LIFE
## IN
# ABUNDANCE

*To Nancy –*

# LIFE
# IN
# ABUNDANCE

## A CONTEMPORARY SPIRITUALITY

*With Hopes for Much Abundance –*

*Francis Baur*

*Francis Baur, O.F.M.*

PAULIST PRESS
*New York/Ramsey*

Library of Congress
Catalog Card Number: 82-60745

ISBN: 0-8091-2507-2

Published by Paulist Press
545 Island Road, Ramsey, N.J. 07446

Printed and bound in the
United States of America

# Contents

# Dedication

With gratitude
this book is dedicated to the memory of
*Pierre Etchelecu, O.F.M.*
who would have enjoyed it
had he not already lived it to the full

# Preface

This work is undertaken in the spirit of an exploration. It is not meant to be a handbook of the spiritual life nor a guide-book of steps to spiritual perfection. The reason for this is quite straightforward. I am convinced that the very notion of life is too large to be confined by the logic of structures or restricted by directives. Life, like love, is a difficult topic to speak about; the spiritual life, which encompasses supreme love, com-pounds these difficulties beyond imagination.

What is presented here is offered as the first-fruits of a personal search, a search which has been made possible and accompanied by a vast confederacy of friends and loved ones, students and teachers, women and men. All of us are still on the way and not a one of us knows for certain where this journey ends, if it ends at all.

What is presented here is simply the invitation to join this company of those who are seeking to discern the way and, as the Gospel invites us, discovering that we may yet have the eyes to see. The only forewarning is that what is offered contains very little in the way of answers, if anything; what is offered is but an approach to looking in new ways as we strive to search out the meaning of spirituality and, possibly, the meaning of our lives.

I wish to confess at the outset, however, that I write not so much out of the experience of what I have already been in my own life; I write, rather, out of a vision of what I would yet like to become and of how I would yet like my life to be lived. I am convinced that I and my entire believing community can become better than we are. In this work I try to lay out the contours of this vision and show how our lived commitment to such a vision is the full content of our spiritual endeavor. I believe that we are called to adventure beyond our wildest imagining, and I offer here a proposal as to why such a risk is not only worthwhile but also the only proper response to the call of Jesus, "Follow me."

What I write here has come to me gradually out of my life with a Franciscan community and a larger community of faith which surround and support me. Even though I write out of deep conviction and with a certain degree of passion, I wish to say clearly that what I present here is offered with great hesitation and a goodly degree of tentativeness. The fruits of these reflections will be the abundant lives of those who live by them, and I have already seen such lived abundance in my faith-community.

Because I live in an academic environment, I have over the years absorbed ideas from my confreres, my colleagues, and my students, as well as from a wide range of reading. And because I am a teacher of theology I find that I readily incorporate these ideas from others into my teaching. I am now at that point where I find it difficult to determine where many ideas, now blended into my own thinking, first originated. If I do not always pay proper due to the author or originator of a particular notion, I wish to apologize and express my gratitude. Much of this material, however, is the product of my own reflection on these matters and represents my own personal vision of the spiritual life. Thus, if any fault is found with the presentation of this material, the fault lies with me.

After each chapter I give a short list of readings. I mention here only those selections which I have found personally fruitful and enriching, and I hope they can be so for others. This list is by no means intended to cover the broad range and complexity of the topic under discussion. Ideas, I think, are much like seeds, and it is our own spiritual environment which will allow them to blossom within ourselves into something we had never clearly envisioned or even expected. I lay great trust in this inner process, and I ask you to do so also.

I owe a great debt to Professor Bernard Loomer who first introduced me to the religious beauty of process modes of thought. I wish most especially to express my gratitude to my Franciscan community in Berkeley; these confreres with whom I have lived and prayed for the past several years have been my most persuasive example of faithfulness and commitment. Kenan Osborne, O.F.M., president of the Franciscan School of Theology, has for many years quietly encouraged me to write. Joseph Chinnici, O.F.M. perhaps unwittingly convinced me that my ideas should be expressed to a larger public. Michael Guinan, O.F.M. first suggested that we together teach a course in Contemporary Spirituality; in that course many of my seminal ideas first took flesh. A multitude of students in their response to this material have encouraged me more than they will ever know. A few close friends, too dear to be mentioned here but who know who they are, have made my life an abundant one, and this book is but a token of my thanks to them.

*Francis Baur, O.F.M.*
*Berkeley, California*
*December 1981*

# The Vision of Spirituality

## The Meaning of Spirituality

Undoubtedly the term "spirituality" has a large variety of meanings, and each of us who uses this term brings a certain personal interpretation to it. One common thread, however, must necessarily run through the entire spectrum of meanings associated with this term. That one common understanding is that the concept of spirituality has something to do with the living of our lives. This is almost too obvious in the saying, but let us consider this point. We are interested in spirituality precisely because it has a direct effect on the value of our lives, because it will make an effective difference in terms of our final fulfillment, because it will somehow enable us to achieve the perfection of life willed by God.

The aim of our spiritual quest is the fulfillment of our own lives, and it makes no difference whether we are referring to our lives in the future or our lives here and now. The approach to spirituality here proposed will be the attempt to take with utmost seriousness this notion of life as the controlling concern of our spiritual quest. How we concretely live our lives here and now in this world and what values will provide an ultimate motivation for our striving are the basic themes of this work.

Reluctant as I am to offer a definition of spirituality which could hope to capture the inherent inexpressibility of our deepest values and the darksome ambiguity of our vague but powerful longings for some sense of fulfillment, I would like to suggest as an appropriate description the haunting title of one of St. Bonaventure's most mystical and lyrical works: *Itinerarium Mentis in Deum*—the journey of the soul into God. The tale of the lives of each of us is the unique and individual story of a life journey which receives both its direction and its end in union with God. To what extent each of us travels the span of life, illumined not by a light at the end of the tunnel, but rather by that which has already lightened up within ourselves, will be the story of our personal spirituality. The degree of that spirituality will finally be gauged by that same light which will seem to consume us to the extent that we finally, also, appear as light. This is Bonaventure's vision, as it is the vision of this work.

What we mean by spirituality, therefore, is not so much a matter of method and technique, nor something which can be achieved by the persistent adherence to certain disciplines. Our spirituality is more a matter of attitude and conviction which is reflected not first of all in our actions, but rather primarily in our stance toward the world. The first impact of spirituality will be upon how we appreciate what it is to be human and how we evaluate the goals and ends which demand our energetic cooperation.

## A Matter of Vision

In this sense, spirituality describes first of all our way of seeing reality and ourselves as part of reality, a way of looking at the world and the relationships which afford the context for our lives. This fundamental evaluation of ourselves, our lives, and our world is not pre-established or pre-ordained in such wise that every right thinking human being will have the identical appreciation of the proper scale of values which accrue both to the universe and to human striving. On the contrary, skeptic, atheist, and believer alike construe their world according to the contours of a personal vision. Unproved and unprovable, such a vision sets out the framework through which the world is received according to orderly patterns and because of which meaning is possible.

Our interest in spirituality is driven by just this sort of

vision, and it differs from the faith of every human being only in that it understands the self and the world in the ultimate context of God. Since it is the size and shape of this vision which will determine the size and shape of our lives, it is well worth exploring that particular vision which informs our lives with transcendent value and shapes our striving by transcendent ends.

We are fortunate in that we stand with a large company of those who have embarked on this spiritual quest guided by this same vision. We have received their record of this journey over the long years in our sacred book which we call our Scriptures. More important than the story of their struggles is the delineation of the vision which lured them into such remarkable adventures. We have the luxury of being able to comb these Scriptures for the formative intuitions which serve to encapsulate their ultimate concern. The major theme of this work will be but a concentration on two of these fundamental and essential intuitions.

### The First Intuition: Life In Abundance

The first of these intuitions is readily discernible in the very shape of the content of our Scriptures. By far the greater part of our Scriptures is in the form of stories, and these stories portray the life-struggle of a people deeply involved in establishing the meaning of their lives before their God. They are the stories of a people fully implicated in the struggle for the fullness of life, and as such they show forth the passion and intensity which this venture demands.

The intuition reflected here is that the passion and intensity of life is the supreme value of life itself, so that whatever energy or sacrifice is demanded is a fair price for the abundance of life itself. The one who enfleshed this intuition most beautifully is the Jesus of our Gospels, who has left to us the everlasting challenge of that awesome paradox: this crucified Jesus proclaims to us, "I have come that you may have life, and have it more abundantly" (Jn 10:10). This is one of the central Gospel intuitions which is the theme of this book.

### The Second Intuition: God Is Love

This intuition of the inestimable value of the quality of life itself takes the depth of its meaning completely from an allied intuition concerning the nature of God. During the long years of those trying times it would have been easy to assimilate the gods of the tribes—power, fate, capriciousness, vengeance. Can we ever repay the debt we owe to that faithful remnant who, in the face of mounting evidence which seemed so clearly to contradict them, would not forego their tenacious hold of a God whose nature it was to love them? This intuition received its supreme exemplification in the crucified Jesus who insisted with his life, "God is love" (1 Jn 4:8). It is suggested here that this twofold intuition is both the motivation and the content of our spiritual quest. We are pursuing the perfection of our own lives in the confidence that our living is precious and valuable to the God who holds all things in love.

### Two Misconceptions

There are two misconceptions which can be both troublesome and destructive to our spiritual striving. The first has to do with an approach to spirituality which places great emphasis on spiritual exercises, practices, or disciplines. The peculiar danger here is of relying on a thinly-disguised form of magic. The impression can easily be given that the perfection of such disciplines by dint of hard practice or the persistent repetition of certain exercises can be taken as a guarantee of spiritual development. To be spiritual, it is assumed, is to be engaged in methods and techniques which have as their effect the spiritual quality of the person.

### Mastering The Disciplines

The underlying assumption which is being challenged here is that spirituality primarily refers to practices or disciplines, activities in which we can be engaged. In this sense, one could become spiritual almost in the same sense that one could become an engineer or a plumber—by mastering certain disciplines. This analogy, however, is completely false and misleading. It would indeed be magic if the mastery of certain techniques could have a spiritual effect. The above assumption works in exactly the wrong direction. It is not our practices and our disciplines which have the effect of making us spiritual; on the contrary, it is our spirituality which gives meaning and value to our practices and disciplines. The reason for this is that our spirituality is not primarily a matter of what we do; fundamentally it is who we are in our relationships before God that gives value to all of our doings.

The first move of spirituality is inward, where we change our hearts and set ourselves right as far as this is possible. Only then will our outward actions take on new meaning and new value. This turn inward, however, does not have the effect of making us spiritual; it simply sets us out in a direction and orders our lives on a spiritual quest. Whatever we choose to utilize in the way of exercises, practices or disciplines simply has the nature of an instrument for achieving a heightened spiritual life. All of our practices are but means and can never be canonized to the status of ends. The end of our spirituality is not the mastery of practices but the quality of our very existence, and such quality is more a function of our faith and conviction than of any outward activity.

## Special Expertise

A second and associated misconception concerning the nature of spirituality would present spirituality as a subtle form of Gnosticism. Gnosticism has always referred to that view which would make salvation a matter of special knowledge; fortunately this has been condemned as a heresy. The Gnostic approach to the spiritual life would place undue emphasis on the spiritual expertise required in order to be truly holy—the mastery of the great spiritual writers, knowledge of the spiritual paths outlined by the great mystics, and adept facility with the intricate methods of prayer.

What is especially troublesome about this approach is its tendency to reserve the perfection of spirituality to that elite few who have the patience and leisure to master these secrets. Spirituality thus becomes esoteric and removed from the lives of the majority of the faithful. It surely seems contrary to our Gospel to assume that while salvation may be intended for all, the perfection of spirituality is destined for an elite few. It does not seem that the fullness of the Gospel promise is intended only for specialists. Our basic intuition concerning the God who is love and who wills the abundance of life must present a possibility within the means of even the least of us.

## The Perfection of Life

The aim of all our spiritual striving, the goal of our heartiest endeavors, and the purpose of whatever practices serve our intentions is the fullness and perfection of our own lives. The purpose of our religious existence cannot be viewed as some reward tacked on to the end of our lives. We are religious, rather, because the religious mode of being is the most satisfying to the yearnings of our lives here and now.

We have a variety of ways to speak about our religious motivations and intentions and we must be careful that a style of language does not misguide us needlessly. Our religious language is composed entirely out of rather homey and earthy words derived from the ordinary context of our everyday lives; these are then invoked for religious purposes but they do not escape the homeliness of their origins.

When we call upon our religious words to describe the purpose of our religious living we tend to invoke the language of salvation, redemption, healing, or ransom. In spite of the hallowed usage of these terms within our tradition, the aim of religion is not that we be *rescued.* When we use terms like saved, redeemed, ransomed, or healed, the model employed invokes an image somewhat like that of going to a doctor. We go to a doctor when we have something wrong with us, some illness or malfunction; and we go to the doctor precisely because it is thought that he can do something for us that we cannot do for ourselves. We look to the efficacy of an external agency to remedy an internal difficulty. Thus our healing in this case is caused by an agency from the outside; we, literally, must be patient and receptive to the workings of this external agent. We are healed when something external—a medicine or a chemical—performs something within us which we cannot do for ourselves.

When we invoke the religious language of salvation and healing, it is exactly this model which determines how we think about the processes of spirituality. This is why it is so easy to view religion as a rescuing agency which comes to us from the outside. If, however, we pay close heed to our Gospels we will see that the end of our religious living is the abundance of life itself.

Just as "health" refers to the harmonious functioning of the entire body and is not something superadded to bodily life, so also "abundance" refers to the passion and intensity of life itself and not to something tacked on. Both health and abundance are a quality of our internal functioning and internal relationships; they are, thus, something we create for ourselves out of the earthy and fleshly context of our existence; in no way can they be something which is done to us. No one can impose health, happiness or love upon us from the outside. These are qualities which we ourselves fashion from the stuff of our lives, and whether we do it badly or well, the fault or the enjoyment is due to our own inner workings.

## Life in a Cosmic Context

We see, then, that life and its qualities become the fundamental category by which we explain the import of our striving and our values, then we may view our spiritual striving in a new light. If the abundance of life is both our human and our religious aim, then we find that we are straightforwardly concerned about discovering the possibilities of life in abundance, pursuing the conditions for abundant life, and seeking to experience for ourselves the qualities of abundant life. How do we grow, how do we enjoy, how do we fulfill ourselves in some abundant form of life? In similar fashion we discover that we alone are the agents responsible for our own lives, that we alone have control over the quality of our experiencing, that we alone determine what life will mean for us. No doctor and no salvation can perform something which we have not already undertaken ourselves.

If we begin to search out the quality of our own lives we will come to see that our first worth is our own self-worth, our first value is our value to ourselves, and our first and last goal is self-fulfillment. A first response may be that this is selfish and individualistic in the extreme, and if such a thing as independent and individual existence were possible this objection would be serious. If, however, we view ourselves in the concrete context of the universe we will see that the matter is otherwise.

## The Individual Is Social

It is precisely our presupposition that we are individual and independent that leads us astray spiritually. So much of our traditional spirituality is based on the relationship between the soul and God, the individual and the Creator. This surely gives the impression that the focus of the relationship of God to the world is primarily and essentially to individual persons. A spirituality which begins with this premise will ultimately be selfish, because whether we place the reward within this life or in some other life, it is the individual soul's well-being that is at stake.

This inherent selfishness may be avoided if the individual soul's relationship to God is not taken as the starting point for spirituality. The individual person belongs to the world, the world belongs to the universe, and the universe is part of the total cosmos. The first question of spirituality should concern not the nature of the individual person, but the very nature of reality itself. Too long have we spoken of human beings as if they were mere visitors to the universe, transients who pass some time here en route to another world. We are now keenly aware that we are not so much *in* the universe as we are a part *of* it.

The entire cosmos is held together in a vast and complex

structure of relationships which allow this earth to be what it is and, by virtue of this earth, these bodies are possible which enable us to be human selves. The matter which constitutes our bodies was spun out eons ago in some stellar cycle and eventually may well return to the stars. We humans are part and parcel of the web of reality and hence cannot be rightly understood in separation from it. We humans are the late-comers to the universe and, for all we know, we may be some of the earliest to depart forever. What we do know, however, is that the grandeur of this cosmos is that it is the furnace of infinite creativity which thus far has proved inexhaustible in its production of novel wonders, including ourselves.

To attempt to understand the individual personal self in isolation from the boundlessly tender cosmos which has spawned us is not to hold us apart as special but to completely misconstrue the allegiance we owe to this cosmos which has allowed us a special birth. If we are seeking to discern the import and meaning of the human, should it not be important to seek also to come to some understanding of what kind of God would be involved with a cosmos of such unimaginable size and infinite complexity, and why? As human beings we will only give ourselves due credit if we have a passionate sympathy for the elegance of the cosmos with which we are allied and without which we would have no being. The infinite mystery of the self is but a reflection of the infinite elegance of the universe.

## What Is This God Like?

From the opening page of Genesis it has been consistently asserted that the only God we know is the Creator-God who does all things well and fashions all things beautifully. What would this Creator-God be like that has fashioned a cosmos of such exquisite intricacy that we, in our own eyes the focal point, have not even yet begun to plumb the inestimable mysteries of its depths? Whatever we are as humans, we are part of this cosmic mystery and hence whatever we are can only be understood in necessary relationship to this first mystery which gives us birth and sustains us with its food and air. And is this cosmos but a tinker-toy production of the Creator-God which can be dismantled once we humans have run our allotted course? Or is there perhaps some necessary and intimate connection between the cosmos and this Creator-God such that they do not and cannot exist apart?

Such questions as these must be at least looked at before we can begin to come to any understanding of the magnificence of what it means to be human. In this same fashion, only as we grow in our sympathetic awareness of the elegance of the cosmos which is our home do we begin to have a glimmer of the awesome size and splendid wonder of that one who is Creator-God. Thus it is that our search for spirituality must begin in the wider quest of the search for self-understanding in relationship to the entirety of reality. Only this appreciation of the broader context of reality itself will give us a proper foothold for the endless search into who and what we are, where we are going and how we should get there.

Our human consciousness is irretrievably locked into the limits of its own experiential borders, so that we must live with the unresolvable paradox that our very knowing of the world is shaped and patterned by our human ways and means of knowing; all of our human knowing is a reflection of ourselves. With this in mind we should be cautioned by the fact that the way we perceive and evaluate our world will inform the way we speak about God. If, for example, we perceive the world as orderly, machine-like and law-governed, then our God will evince these same qualities of law, order, mechanical structure. We might recall the great Watchmaker God of the nineteenth century.

On the other hand, the way we speak about our God will influence and shape the way we perceive our own world. If God is conceived as righteous, authoritarian and vengeful, then these same qualities will be sanctified in human use. With this in mind, we dare not let our God be too small, too narrow, too restrictive, or too jealous, for the entire universe is at stake, not just ourselves. When in our day the simplest schoolboy can casually speak of a universe millions of light-years in expanse, billions of years in age, spinning out hundreds of millions of galaxies containing stars by the billions, we must be cautious indeed in our speech about God. If the awesome surprises which our universe has been revealing to us are any indication, then the incredible mystery of God has yet much to reveal about our own splendid selves. Let us willingly explore the unfathomable secrets of the universe, both to enjoy its beauteous elegance and to appreciate the wealth of our own being. It is quite possible that in this quest of discovery we will come to know our God.

## Theology of the Fall

Fortunately there is ample scriptural warrant to support such an approach. Even when we ponder our Scriptures, however, we read out of our own habitual preconceptions. When we reflect on the first chapters of Genesis we tend to read there the story of failure, of sin, of death and corruption. Genesis is for us the sad tale of human fallibility and weakness which have brought us to depravity and betrayal. We see the story of humankind as the sorry tale of a curse which inflicts us still. Out of this reading of Genesis we perceive ourselves as fallen, sinful, depraved and lost, and it is precisely because of this violent alienation that we are compelled to cry out for salvation, to relate to the only power that can redeem such corruption.

Thus the fundamental motivation for our relationship to God is that of weakness and need, and the God who can right us is the God of judgment, righteousness, wrath and punishment. Our saving grace was God's infinite mercy. A religious consciousness based upon such a reading cannot but help to perceive our human existence as darksome and awful, this world but the loathsome realm of death and corruption to be abandoned like an ill-used way-station. The spiritual task is to placate this fearsome God whose anger is infinite and whose vengeance is eternal. We hold our very lives in fear and trembling, and use our flesh but as the earthen vessel which, if unchecked, will contaminate the soul. Our Scriptures serve as the melancholy record of how tenacious we are in our perversity, how irreversibly prone to sell out to the flesh-pots of the world. These are stories of betrayal, individual and social, and of sin, personal and corporate. So it is that this world is but a vale of tears, and for those of us who see rightly we can be but ill at ease and tearful.

## A Spirituality of Fallenness

The attitude here described is simply an elaboration of a theology of the fall where the fundamental category for understanding both the Old Testament itself as well as our own lives in relationship to God is that of original sin. The Old Testament is not only a record; it stands as a warning of somber import. If we are to know ourselves rightly we must hearken back to our forebears through whose agency we are conceived in sin and doomed to corruption. The evidence is too repetitious and consistent for us to deny that our human touch is indeed the touch of death; we betray, violate, sully and kill the best and finest in all of our relationships. We surely are not to be trusted, nor should we be allowed to trust ourselves. We inhabit bodies of flesh which are prone to passion, concupiscence and gross unruliness. Trapped in our own blindness and embalmed in the evil bias of our own will, our drift toward sin and death is as sure as gravity.

If, however, we perceive ourselves in this fashion, then our spiritual quest will bear the earmarks of this struggle with fallenness. Spirituality will include those things which will discipline our waywardness, punish our unruliness, warn us against temptation and threaten us with consequences. Such a spirituality will be serious and somber, often morose. More than likely it will also be dreadfully pessimistic about our chances, especially if left to our own devices. Worst of all, life within this world is the enemy, to be tamed and denied and finally left behind.

## Theology of Creation

It is fortunate that what has been here described as the theology of the fall is not the whole story of Genesis nor of the rest of the Scriptures. Since our eyes tend to sort out anything that we choose to focus on, let us shift our gaze and concentrate in a new direction. Contrary to our assumption, the story of the fall is neither the opening nor the central story in the Genesis account. Rather, the opening proclamation of Genesis is the story of the creation, and every detail here portrayed is a strong affirmation that God knew well exactly what he was doing, and everything he did was done well.

This positive evaluation of the created order is affirmed by the description of the orderly sequence in which God called forth the various items of creation with the fivefold refrain, "God saw that it was good," followed by the climactic affirmation, "He saw that it was very good." God's invitation to our progenitors, Adam and Eve, is to enjoy this world as if it were a garden fashioned only for their delight. The undeniable thrust of the Genesis account is toward the hospitality of this world for its inhabitants; the earth was a home, sustaining and life-giving and capable of affording immense satisfaction. Formed out of the dust of the earth, our parents were allied with the nature of the cosmos itself, fashioned from the same stuff, feeding off the world and returning their gracious control in orderly and beneficent use.

The primordial theology of our scriptural heritage is a theology of creation in which a positive affirmation of this world and life within this world is the central and essential claim. The entire world, exemplified supremely by our human forebears, existed in a living relationship to God—not a relationship of antagonism, but a harmonious relationship of compatibility and mutual gift.

The fullness of human life was to be achieved within the garden of this created realm, in harmony with all the members of the created realm itself. God, however, was not the silent partner or the unconcerned spectator; God was the one who walked with us in the cool of the evening, who shared our thoughts and enjoyed our pleasures. To be human was to be of the earth and of God at the same time, to be of supreme value to life in the world and equally to be of supreme value to the life of God. This is the gracious vision of the Genesis account.

Assuredly, the beauty of this primordial interrelationship was ruptured by the choice of sin. But the story of the fall is only the sub-story which has its meaning solely in relationship to the main plot, the story of creation. The rest of the scriptural account is not primarily the story of human irretrievability and recalcitrance; it is, rather, the kindly tale of the promise of the human return to the harmonious and gracious relationships from which we had our origin and which are still our final end. Instead of describing the struggle of our human lives in terms of a battle against sin, a war against evil, a ceaseless conflict with depravity, the Scriptures describe the human struggle for goodness, the efforts to achieve value, the imposing of order over chaos, and the relentless quest for supreme value—all in relation to that elusive God who will alone satisfy our hearts' desire. That shadowy figure is seen in various guises and appears in striking forms—fiery bush, cloud of dust, shepherd—until that special one who had reclaimed intimacy with the divine as our natural right spoke clearly something we had always known but perhaps had half-forgotten: God is love.

## A Spirituality of Goodness

If we place our spiritual quest within the context of the creation theology of the Scriptures, then we have neither the need nor the right to base our spirituality on sin, depravity and curse. Spirituality can be neither a mode of doing penance nor an escape from a world of sin. The primal intuition of creation theology is the affirmation of the goodness of the world and the most excellent goodness of human life precisely because this world and this life are God-related, essentially and necessarily—so much so that this gifted relationship cannot be ruptured or lost at all. It may, of course, be disfigured, defaced, neglected or half-forgotten, but never destroyed.

If we but pay regard to those heroes of the Scriptures we will see that their persistent message is that we may yet achieve good, that life can yet be enhanced, that God can yet be found in the secret places of the garden. The struggle of our life is not to leave it, but rather to regain our rightful inheritance of goodness, beauty, and harmony within the gracious relationships of this lovely and tender earth, our home. If we are to find our God, we will find him here. It is we who have walked away from God and his garden; the gracious indulgence of our Scriptures is that this world is full enough with clues and occasions that those who seek with a pure and bold heart may find their way back home.

The saving grace offered by our Scriptures is that our God is a God of life and his inmost nature is nothing else but love. The boundaries of life and love set out the expanse of infinite possibility in which our freedom can be exercised. The awful burden of our freedom is that we may choose rightly or wrongly, well or poorly, toward life or death. The comfort of our freedom is that God will accept with gratitude whatever we accomplish and will not reject us for what we fail in accomplishing. The love of God is such that it desires only what is freely offered and cannot be satisfied by obligation and debt.

The terrible beauty of our love is that it cannot be demanded nor required but only freely given, so this God of infinite patience will not forsake us, because we have within us always the power to turn to him in love. God surely does not thrive on our weakness; he thrives only on the strength of our love. Our spiritual journey will be the story of our quest for ways of responding to a love which has created us and which will never forsake us.

## Why Be Religious?

Fortunately much of this awareness is already a fruitful part of our religious tradition and hence it is mostly a matter of emphasis. Why is it that we should want to be religious and live our lives religiously? Since we are accustomed to our religious way of viewing our lives, we rarely reflect on the role of religion in the concrete everydayness of our living. The only concern of religion is with the values that inform our lives and give meaning to our striving.

We do not live neutrally in a neutral world; rather we are always enmeshed in an ongoing web of relationships which we shape and reshape in order to accommodate ourselves. Every breathing moment is a series of choices by which we try to create a semblance of harmony and satisfaction within our own experience. It is our choices which are highly instrumental in determining the qualities of our experience, and hence these choices, in spite of all appearances, are not made randomly and casually. Every choice is a selection made from a spectrum of alternatives, and this selection is decided out of a perceived sense of value. We move toward values and struggle toward the achievement of values because these contribute to the qualities of our self-experience.

These values which direct our striving, however, are not all equal and are not sought with equal intensity. Although the variety of possible values is nearly infinite, in the concrete context of our own lives there is a definite hierarchy of values which both defines the limits of the range of our possible and ideal choices and also establishes their order of importance. Although, for example, money may be precious to us, when given the choice of losing the money in our wallet or losing our life we need no time at all to come to a decision. The pattern of our lives is structured along this organization of choices, so much so that our own self-identity can be fairly evaluated in terms of the values which determine our life-choices.

## Religion: The Values of Our Decision-Making

In view of this it is easy to recognize how religion functions as the primary agent in our decision-making. Religion's total concern is with the values which determine our choices, not primarily about the ordinary and everyday, but fundamentally about the long-term choices which shape our character and organize the lesser choices into manageable systems of order. All lesser choices are structured into a hierarchy in terms of their relationship to the first and final choice that outweighs all the others. In the midst of a plethora of competing and conflicting values endless in their variety and bewildering in their multiplicity, we perceive a single value which is final or supreme.

This supreme value is ultimate in the sense that there is no value which is greater or more important, and hence it is this ultimate value which gives meaning and importance to all lesser values. Thus our striving after lesser values is always in a pattern that will contribute to the achievement of the ultimate value. This may perhaps explain why religion is inevitably concerned with ethics and morals; this is the attempt to insure the choices which will lead to the ultimate value. The unforgettable and lovely Gospel image for this supreme value is "the pearl of great price."

It is a very simple matter to think of our values in terms of something external to us, something which can give us satisfaction by mere addition or by usefulness. Things like money, material possessions, power and even a good reputation appear to fit this model. And yet if we reflect carefully on how such items actually function in our lives, we will see that items which are external to us are perceived as valuable because their possession enhances the quality of our own experience. Such experience is internal to us and is a quality we create within our own experience by the utilization of something external. Thus it is that the only real value is internal and personal in that it is the passion and intensity of our own qualitative self-experience.

It is how we experience ourselves in our world that gives us meaning and purpose, and consequently our pursuit of values is the pursuit of our own identity and our own enhanced experience. We should notice that in our serious and reflective moments we do not define ourselves by objects which accrue to us, nor by the accumulation of any sort of item, nor in any quantitative fashion whatsoever. Rather, when we probe for our deepest self-awareness we point to our valuing, our choosing, our striving, our loving, for these are the agents of meaning and purpose in our lives, since they create the very qualities of our experience.

Equally important, all of these activities serve to point out our various relationships to a reality beyond ourselves which somehow is also constitutive of our very selves. To value, to choose, to love—these are the ways in which a reality beyond us is appropriated within in order to qualify our own self-experience. This leads us to the paradox which lies at the heart of reality: our striving for value is finally the struggle for self-value, and our self-value is only possible because we create ourselves out of our relationships to a world beyond ourselves.

This murky interplay of values may be more easily envisioned if we but focus on the model of the love-relationship. Have we failed to notice, especially within ourselves, that the very first effect of love is *the lover?* The qualitative experience of identity, affirmation, emotional strength and beauty takes place within the lover first of all. Nonetheless, this passionate intensity is made possible by the presence of the beloved to and within the lover, and the same effects occur within the beloved. We have but edgy and flimsy words to point to that Gospel mystery that only in losing our hearts will we ever truly find them.

## The Ultimate Value of Our Life: God

Our spiritual quest, therefore, is the unquenchable desire for the enhancement of our own experience and the perfection of our own self; our ultimate desire is to live our lives as richly and fully and intensely as is possible. On the other hand, the enrichment of our lives is a product of the relationships available to us and out of which our experience emerges. Thus it is that our ultimate concern is for the abundance of our own lives, and this abundance is made possible solely by that ultimate value which both outweighs and orders all lesser values.

Religiously we call this ultimate value our God and the religious purpose of our lives is to live in such relationship to this God that the full meaning and value of our lives abides in the depths of this creative relationship and in no other. The religious problem which determines the nature of our spiritual quest is inexorably related to the structure of our choices: What should I value? How should I choose? What is worth pursuing?

The religious answer to such questions is never in terms of objects or possessions or items which can be gained or lost. The religious answer will always be in terms of those relationships which most enhance our being and those qualities of experience which most satisfy our passionate desire. Our abundance of life is not in our possessions but in our relationships, not in what we own but in how we love. The full abundance of our lives will be in our relationship to that ultimate beauty and ultimate good which we call the God of love.

## Abundance Is Love

On the one hand, therefore, our religious quest is internal to ourselves, our own life-experience of abundance and satisfaction; on the other hand, our spirituality relates us to the wealth of reality which transcends us and which affords us the possibility of learning how to love. Our spiritual question concerns how we shall become, how we shall select those relationships which are most growthful, how we shall fashion in ourselves the image of the God who is love.

Our spiritual journey will not be an obstacle course in which we are tested to show our strength of sacrifice; rather it will be the journey of a life which must cope with the everyday and the ordinary with the saving assurance that this is the stuff of everlasting life. Our spiritual endeavor is not judged by the fact that we have failed in our choices, or that we have chosen badly and poorly. Our spirituality will be judged, rather, by the passion of our quest for that ultimate value and our perseverance, in the face of all odds, in the quest for abundant life.

Our perseverance is but our fundamental faithfulness to the vision of what we may yet be and what we may yet experience. Why is it that we remain faithful and why should such faithfulness be worthwhile? The reason is simple; we are not faithful first of all to something outside of ourselves. Our first faithfulness is to our own integrity, our own authenticity. It is our struggle to be whole and fulfilled which demands our faithfulness to the vision which informs us and the values which shape us. Our struggle is not a competition for objects or prestige; it is, rather, the struggle for the quality of life itself. We are committed to the fullness of our own being, and the lesson of reality is that we are undeniably intermeshed within relationships which stretch across the cosmos itself.

## Faithfulness to the God of Love

The faithfulness of the spiritual quest is defined by our loyalty to that One who is origin and end of all that is, whom we call the God of love. We are faithful because we are captivated by the faith which claims that to a God of love nothing, absolutely nothing, can be unimportant and nothing can be lost. We are faithful because those gracious and tender loves of our lives have shown us that we can never be satisfied without that full and final love which is the very meaning of our lives. We are faithful because we are unafraid to admit the beautiful value of our own being since we are precious to the God of love. Thus it is that the spiritual quest is finally the quest for beauty and goodness, the striving for love—for these things alone can lead us to fullness and these things alone are the gifts we can proffer to the God of love.

## The Pursuit of the Vision

The spirituality presented here is but the attempt to pursue this particular vision. The themes introduced here will each be developed in an effort to flesh out the contours of a vision of wholeness, a vision of abundant life with deep satisfaction, a vision of God who has both infinite passion and infinite compassion because his nature is love. Such a vision cannot be designated as true or false, since we have nothing but our intuitions to go on and nothing but our own lives to offer as evidence. A vision can only be judged as worthwhile or useless, as more or less adequate.

Such a vision is worthwhile if it enables us to achieve what it is pointing at, if it provides the inspiration to renew our energies, if it lures us into the adventure of our own lives when we would have preferred to stay put, if it allows us to experience our own lives with an abundance and richness which we had thought belonged to another world. Such a vision is worthwhile if it encourages us to trust our own deepest intuitions about the God of our lives, if it emboldens our hearts to believe, perhaps for the first time, that God is indeed love and all of his relationships are loving and nothing else. Such a vision is worth pursuing if it heartens us to reaffirm and enjoy our own loveliness because the tender companion of all our strivings and all our doings is the God of love.

The strength of this vision is that it rests on the magnificent intuitions gleaned from the religious experience extending over thousands of years of those people passionately involved in the struggle for the meaning of their own lives and who always found their God in the very midst of their struggle for life. We could do worse than to join their company and hear their words. We could do worse than make our own the complex anguish of their struggle and the single-minded passion of their search. We might have their good sense to be gracefully puzzled by our uneasy mix of good and bad. We might have their conviction that we may yet piece our lives together out of eloquently disparate materials if we can but set our hearts on that persistent but elusive Beauty which charms us always but never lets us rest in peace.

## The Abundant Life

If we are to take seriously the good news of the abundant life revealed by Jesus as the will of God for all, then it is important that we search out for ourselves what this abundant life would in fact mean for us here and now. It is all too easy to view this notion of abundant life as if it were a reward which is to come to us after the inexorable course of this earthly life. The very frailty and imperfection of our worldly existence inspires us to yearn for a life freed from pain and failure, from ambiguity and tragedy, and freed also from risk. The struggles and hardships of our present existence can become bearable if we are assured that they will eventually be left behind in some future and better life.

Our Western patrimony of Greek thought has been in large part responsible for bequeathing us with a deep-rooted dualism which is part and parcel of our awareness of the world and our understanding of ourselves. We readily invoke the terminology of body and soul, matter and spirit, earth and heaven, as we attempt to place ourselves within a context of ultimate meaning. With this dualistic apparatus of explanation, it is both simple and understandable that the abundant life be considered as a matter of deferred value—a fuller and better life in some future time and in some other place. Within this same context of dualism, the concept of spirituality referred primarily to those qualities and conditions which served to relate one to the enhanced life of the future.

### This World: God Saw That It Was Good

In contrast to this other-worldly bias engendered by a body/spirit dualism, we cannot overlook the consistent Old Testament theme of the primacy of shared life made available in and through this world. The opening story of Genesis pictures God calling the human world into being in orderly stages. For each of the five successive days there is the lyrical repetition, "God saw that it was good." This culminates on the sixth day with the creation of Adam and Eve and the unparalleled claim, "God saw that it was very good." This image of God's own wonder at the beauty of what had come to be at his instigation should at least generate an awesome wonder in ourselves, the same thrilled enjoyment of the sheer goodness and loveliness of this earth, our home, and of the singularly precious life we share.

The recurring theme of the Old Testament is the challenge to struggle mightily to bring life to the fullness of its goodness in the face of repeated fallenness and failure. The way of life is the way of wholeness, the sharing of the abundance which is God's grace made available through the medium of this earth. The only denial in the Old Testament concerns that which is humanly destructive and death-dealing, and anything whatsoever that is life-denying can only be taken as an affront to this Creator-God of goodness and life.

Let us not overlook the fact that for the Scriptures the

primordial setting for human life is the garden in which all created beings coexisted in mutual harmony and support. As Scripture would have it, God's intention for humankind was sheer enjoyment and delight, while the arena for this enjoyment was this earth itself and the instruments for delight were the beneficent fruits afforded by the world.

As was noted earlier, the story of the fall is a second and derivative story and is illegitimately read as the central message of the Old Testament. To allow the story of the fall to dictate our understanding of the spiritual life is to allow ourselves to be defined by sin rather than by grace. The primordial message of the Scriptures is not that we are hated by God because of our sin, but rather that we are unremittingly graced by God with love.

## The Worthwhileness of the Present

The very tone of our spiritual quest will be subtly modulated by the personal emphasis which we superimpose, perhaps unconsciously, on grace or sin, creation or fall. The mighty struggles of the Old Testament people are motivated by the worthwhileness of this present existence in which the fullness of life is both the promise and the will of their God. It is for this reason that their struggle is always shaped by their resistance to bondage, oppression, injustice, and poverty. It is the overcoming of these negativities which is the content of God's active will for them as well as their own achievement of abundant life. Their special claim to an intimate presence of God to them was justified by the activities and qualities of their lives—on the one hand their championship of the claims of justice, and on the other hand their own satisfaction in the life-giving integrity of just relationships. Both the battleground and the paradise of their passionate intensity was this earth with its concrete limitations and beckoning opportunities.

These Old Testament people had the uncommon good sense to realize that whatever God was about, he was about here and now, this time and this place. Whatever the will of their demanding and luring God might be, it had to do with these concrete relationships, these experienced conditions, these trying times, and these available possibilities. The challenge of their demanding God was not to lay away insurance for some future life, but rather to take hold boldly of the conditions of their own lives that they might suitably tabernacle the Holy One who longed to reside in their midst.

## The Significance of the Incarnation

Equally important is our Christian rootage in the New Testament. And what precisely is the primary and essential claim of New Testament Christianity, the claim which sets it off from everything which had come before? While in the Old Testament the Creator-God was one who would walk with Adam in the cool of the evening, the New Testament claim is almost literally beyond belief. That crucial claim centers on Jesus Christ, and we have selected a special word to denote the unique relationship embodied in him; that word is *incarnation.*

We dare not overlook the inexplicable genius of the unique phraseology of John's Gospel Prologue. When pointing out the supreme mystery of our Christian faith, the Prologue does not state that the Word became human or that the Word became man, nor does it state that the Word assumed a human nature. No, on the contrary, the unique phrasing of the Prologue is, "The Word became *flesh.*" Not human being, not even human person; rather, the record claims quite starkly and quite simply that the Word became flesh. In the eyes of John's Prologue the greatest compliment we can pay to Jesus Christ is to realize and admit that he joined our flesh, became a living being of flesh and blood just as we are, lived in and experienced a life in the flesh.

And this incarnation, this entrance into the flesh, was something which would never be reversed and never denied. The Word was thenceforth to be identified with and discovered within this bodiliness, this materiality, this fleshiness— with all the implications of passion and sensuality, of worldliness and bodily delight that cannot be dismissed. It is suggested here that it is misleading to interpret our record to mean that the Word became flesh in order that we might leave the flesh for another existence; the more straightforward interpretation surely appears to be that the Word became flesh because this world and this flesh are peculiarly the intimate habitat of God.

The pivotal claim of our Christian faith is not that Jesus Christ came to show us how to escape our bodies and our world; no, the message is rather that he became flesh in order to show us how to live in our bodies and in our world. Far from relegating life in this world to a second-rate adventure in the service of another world, the incarnation demands a recognition of the inherent value of our embodied earthly life. If Jesus Christ is God-flesh, then all life and all flesh are indeed sacramental by virtue of this primordial sacrament of God-flesh in Christ. All life is indeed holy and the body is indeed the temple of the spirit. Dare we deny or devalue the flesh that embodied God and the earth which was his home?

### Embodied Selves

Thus scriptural theology seems to reinforce a distinctly modern sensibility—the rediscovery of the value of human feelings and the undeniable import of our bodily feelings. A renewed awareness of our times is that as humans we are perhaps rational, but we are many other things besides; thinking is indeed an essential human quality, but even our thinking is laden with emotional tones which carry their own passions and inform our coolest thoughts with felt desire. Where, finally, do we live? We live in our bodies. How do we meet the world? We meet always first the physical world of our own bodies and through this precious instrument the greater universe beyond us. The body is the origin and locus of our experience such that both our world and our thinking are mediated to us in relationship to the experience of the body. For this reason, a dualism which devalues the experience of the body sets us in opposition against ourselves and sets in conflict our passionate struggle for the fullness of life.

If we take the Gospel as the necessary inspiration of our spirituality, then we pledge ourselves to the reality of the incarnation, not only of Jesus, but also of ourselves. The Gospel promise is that we too might become godly if we learn to live in faithfulness to the will of the God who is love. The possibility for each and every one of us to become the son or daughter of the gracious Father is the revealed promise of Jesus. Hence it is not so much that in our spiritual journey we draw close to God; it is rather that by our Gospel lives we give flesh to the love of God in our time and in our place. Even the least of us are in our finest moments the incarnation of God in the world, and thus our spiritual challenge is that we make these finest moments the norm of our lives rather than the exception.

### Jesus: The Presence of God

For those of us who walk the way of spirituality as charted by the Jesus of the Gospels, we willingly look to his life for whatever clues we may discover as to the quality of our life journey and the nature of our spirituality. Since the Gospels portray Jesus as the full revelation of the nature and activity of God, we rightly look to Jesus as the model of the spiritual person. What is supremely attractive to us is that neither Jesus nor the Gospels present an abstract theory of spirituality; on the contrary, what attracts us most by the Gospel stories is that concrete particularity and specific individuality of earthly detail.

Perhaps we do not always realize to what extent the greater part of Jesus' life was concerned with ordinary and homey detail. Both his actions and his words seem to indicate that the concerns of God are not primarily revealed in the spectacular or the extraordinary; his own stories more than hint that the pervasive activity of God is as subtle as seed and as unobtrusive as a soft breeze. More remarkable, perhaps, is that those natural things to which Jesus spontaneously points are not meant to be seen as signs of the activity of God; for Jesus they are, rather, the very activity of God beyond which there is no other. We are enchanted by the unique vision of this man who saw everything in his world not merely as the revelation but as the actual presence of the God whom he called Father.

Thus it is, Jesus reminds us, that the sure fall of the rain on the just and the unjust without favor is not a mere sign of the graciousness of God; it is the very graciousness of God infallibly operative in this most earthly of situations. The quiet and slow transformation of the seemingly dead seed into the largest of sheltering plants is not to be taken as a metaphor for the unobtrusive activity of God; the creative transformation of the seed is exactly what the patient activity of God effects in our midst. That the lilies of the field exhibit their own unparalled beauty does not point to anything beyond by which we should be instructed; the lilies themselves are the straightforward evidence for the beauteous working of God in all things, even the least. The fig tree which fails to produce fruit stands as a natural example of the strange intransigence of the creature before which even God is powerless.

We see that Jesus was captivated by the earthly and palpable detail of his physical environment since it was here that he rooted his deepest personal intuition of the pervasive and even obvious—for those with eyes to see—presence of God. To stand in the presence of God, Jesus had but to stand in the presence of the everyday world whose elegance and grace spoke to his spirit with the voice of God.

### The Stories of Jesus

If we attend to the stories which Jesus spins out, we will notice that he peoples them with an unlikely mix of characters with seemingly little in common—a king, a farmer, a fisherman, a husband, a widow, a father. We should notice, however, that in each case it is not the main character who bears a resemblance to God that we should emulate. On the contrary, these main characters are invoked simply to embody those types of relationships which occur every day in our own lives and in the lives all around us; it is in these quite ordinary relationships between persons that we realize for ourselves the activity of God. A farmer's providential care for the condition of his fields and the growth of his crop; a father's response to his child even in the middle of the night; a widow's concern for something as small as a mite; a shepherd who calls each of his sheep by name—the point of these tales is the easy ordinariness of the relationships which are not singular or spectacular, but available to all of us.

Important to note is that it is not really the father or the widow or the shepherd who is like God; it is, rather, that the relationships of care, concern, compassion, and justice are the godly activities possible to each of us. We need not become someone special or someone remarkable to host the spirit of God within our lives, Jesus assures us; the given and present relationships which form the web of our lives are sufficient to be taken seriously as the only context which will ever be necessary for our meeting with God.

## The Verbs of Jesus

In our spiritual quest, however, perhaps we can be most assured by the singular insight of Jesus concerning those activities which are the work of God. We become Godlike, Jesus promises, when we do those things which are the special concern of the love of God for all. Most consoling of all, for these activities we need not be specialists or professionals or people set apart. For this reason, Jesus enjoins upon all who will hear him those ordinary and unremarkable activities which are available to all and possible to each. We need but advert to that long chain of verbs scattered like seed throughout the Gospels: show mercy, offer forgiveness, search out justice, respond with compassion, live in trust, tender food and drink, listen for the cry of need or pain. No expertise is demanded here, but only our sincerity and wholeness of heart.

Our doing of such things will be the practical and concrete working of our love in those situations and toward those persons for whom it is most required. That God is love is a revelation aimed immediately at us, and perhaps the first burden of every serious believer is to become inwardly convinced that such a marvel can be true—for all of us, deep within, best know ourselves, and know also how unlovely we can be. The greater revelation well might be that if each of us is loved by this God, then all others are loved also—even those others we may deliberately fail to love, even those we actively despise.

To love with the love of God does not require of us a special heroism reserved to the saints; it requires only the good will to be attentive to the need and hunger and pain which lurk in every nook and cranny of our most intimate and our most casual relationships. Perhaps what is so easily overlooked here is that when we speak of such responses as compassion, mercy, or forgiveness we tend to focus on the effects such activities will have on their recipients. We must attend also, however, to their effects upon those who perform them—we the doers of such deeds ourselves become compassionate and merciful and forgiving. Need we be reminded that such qualities most rightly describe our God, and if they can be used also to rightly describe ourselves then indeed we are becoming godly?

The strange paradox of the Gospel is that the first effect of God's love is our own self, and our transformed self is God's love made present to all whom we encounter. It takes no small faith on our part to rest content with the awful fact that the only assurance of God's love we will ever have is our own patience, our own compassion, our own love. But if such qualities do form the pervasive texture of our lives, then we indeed will be transformed and made anew, for we will have a taste of that passionate intensity which is at the heart of the God who is love.

What Jesus urgently wishes us to see is that this gracious world is the chalice of God and that the transformation of the simple bread of our everyday lives into the presence of godliness is the lovely miracle to which each of us is called. If our God is love, then the only proper response to such love is to be loving; and the quality of our loving, Jesus insists, is as obvious and discernible as the growth of a seed or the flowering of a lily.

## The Metaphor of the Journey

In conclusion, it is worth reflecting on the fact that one of the most recurrent and intriguing metaphors for the spiritual life is the theme of enduring the journey. The Old Testament is dominated by the exodus theme—the journey out of Egypt toward the promised land, with forty years of trial and wandering. Paul Bunyan's *Pilgrim's Progress* charts the journey of the pilgrim Christian through the snares and traps of life; Bonaventure's *Itinerarium Mentis in Deum, The Journey of the Soul into God,* maps the soul's perfection in terms of the spiritual journey. This theme of the pilgrim, the wayfarer, the traveler on a search, the knight on a quest, is a constantly recurring image of the spiritual life.

The elements of the journey invariably include trials, temptations, conflicts, doubts, dangers and even failures. Always these tribulations must be countered with loyalty, commitment, perseverance, trust and faith. The trials of the journey, in fact, serve as the testing ground for these most human of virtues, virtues which are portrayed as the essence of the spiritual life. Parallel to these spiritual journeys, however, we discover a whole array of secular journeys—Ulysses and the travails he endures throughout his voyage in the *Odyssey,* Huckleberry Finn and his raft trip down the Mississippi, Tolkien's *Ring* trilogy with the hobbits on a fearsome search, and even the knights of the Round Table in their quest for the holy grail.

I would suggest that the point of the secular journey is exactly the same as that of the spiritual journey—the human virtues, often heroic but never exceptional, which give to life its meaning and depth and value in any context and within any community, are neither spectacular nor impossible. They are the almost homely virtues which characterize our most basic and our most intimate relationships—faith and trust, honesty and perseverance, love and commitment—virtues almost prosaic in their commonness yet sacred in their ability to produce passion and intensity in the most ordinary of lives. Both the sacred and secular journey stories are meant to inform us that the dignity and value of our lives lie in our own hands, and the means of achievement are available to all though practiced by few.

Those who persevere in the undistinguished but demanding virtues of loyalty and commitment, love and concern in spite of the temptations to dismiss their hard demands are few enough to appear heroic to us of lesser will and smaller desire, so much so that we list them in our catalogue of saints, sacred and secular: Moses, Jesus, Francis, Gandhi, Martin Luther King, Jr. They are our heroes and our saints because we would like to have their stature, and deep down we know that it is indeed possible to have it.

## A Journey With No End

It is most remarkable that with this constant metaphor of the journey rarely is there an end to the journey; in the language of the cliché, there is no "there" there. The point of the journey is not really to arrive at another place, to find the grail, to discover the pot of gold. Rather, the point of the journey is the journeying itself.

Always the journey is a metaphor for life, and the point of life is not to find its end but to discover how to live it well. All the adventures of the journey—the conflicts, the battles, the trials and the threats—are simply the episodes of the maturation process out of which we weave the meaningful experiences of our lives. The point of the journey is not to find a place nor to find an object; it is, rather, to find our home. Always our life is a journey in which we struggle to be at home in the world, and the quality of our struggle is the only quality of our lives we will ever know.

To read the journey metaphor as if it meant that we are to travel from this earth to heaven is to both misread the metaphor and to deny its insistent injunction to passionate commitment now, in this living present. There is no grail to find, no city to discover. There is only this life and its commitments, and no matter how common or ordinary we may be, as the Gospels insist, we have a right to a life of passion and a gracious home in the kingdom which is already in our midst. Our instruments are the commonplace virtues of all humane life—faith and trust, truth-telling and love, loyalty and perseverance. These things we can do, though we may find them difficult. But the Gospels insist that they are not impossible, as they also insist that those who do them will become godly. Is this not sufficient for a spiritual life?

## Follow Me

When Jesus called to those strangers working at the seashore and invited them to follow him, they rightly wanted to know where they were going. To this reasonable inquiry, Jesus offered the paradoxical answer which is still ours to puzzle out: "Come and see." Equally puzzling is that these unexceptional fisherfolk, with names like Peter and Andrew, James and John, with almost remarkable quirkiness leave their nets and their boats and their fathers to take up this following of Jesus. Are we not surprised that our records are almost innocently vague and silent as to the time and place of the deaths of these first followers? Evidently, where they ended up was not at all important.

The story of their following portrays without shame the almost infinite variety of human failure and personal obtuseness. Of extraordinary import to us is the fact that, not just up to the death of Jesus, but during the death and even after the death, they exhibit those faults and failures, from casual to grievous, which plague all of us to the moment of our death—selfishness, lack of understanding, petty jealousy, fear, cowardice, and even betrayal. Of such was the uneasy personal mix which Jesus chose to be the leaven of his good news. The point of their story is not that they became perfect in any humanly understandable sense; the point is, rather, that in their following of Jesus they were better than they ever would have been—better only in the sense that gradually they felt them-selves driven by the same unquenchable thirst and the same passionate commitment to the cause of life which brought this Jesus to death on a cross.

Those of us who respond to the lure of the spirit set out on a life journey equipped only with our personal miscellany of strengths and weaknesses, vices and virtues. Perhaps our char-acter will undergo heroic transformation, but we seriously doubt this. The transformation which we seek is that of our fractured and dissonant hearts. How can we feel comfortable with our striving and motivated for our struggles? What is worth our dearest energies and where is our passion rightly directed? Where will we ever discover something lovely enough that, at last, we might love fully and well?

Not even the Gospels give us a clear and straightforward answer to these heartrending questions. We have, rather, the kindly invitation, "Follow me." We have also that gracious communion of saints who have found such following worth-while. For the abundance of life and the fullness of love, we have nothing to lose, finally, but our own half-hearted lives. We would like to be better than we are; we would like to heal our hearts with wholeness. And so, with eyes like question marks, we set out on the following of Jesus.

### Selected Readings

In *Building the Human* Robert O. Johann offers a collec-tion of essays written over the years. His approach to spiritual matters is wholesome and humane, deeply encouraging to those of us who feel ordinary and unexceptional in our spiritual endeavors. (New York: Herder and Herder, 1968)

*Discerning the Way* by Paul van Buren is a sustained exposition of the Christian life under the image of "a people on the way." It is concrete and earthy, and a healthy reminder of the ordinary practicality of the demands of our spiritual quest. (New York: The Seabury Press, 1980)

In a warm and charming book, *To a Dancing God,* Sam Keen explores his own personal odyssey of religious self-discovery. His reflections on the meaning of his deepest religious aspirations have applications for all of us. See especially Chapter One, "Exile and Homecoming." (New York: Harper & Row, 1970)

Although Alfred North Whitehead is known primarily as a philosopher, his small volume, *Religion in the Making,* is a profound and moving analysis of the depths of our religious ideals and their effect on our character. See especially Chapter Three, "Body and Spirit." (New York and Cleveland: The World Publishing Company, 1971)

*Scripture Reading*
The First Letter of John

# 2

# The Final End of Our Lives

The fact that so much of our ordinary religious thinking seems to rely on an implicit dualism must be faced squarely, for such a view will have definite consequences on our vision of spirituality. For this reason it is important to understand how such a theory could have an enduring and persuasive hold on the mind and heart of the West over a period of almost two thousand years. In this chapter I will develop two main themes. First, I will present an explanation of the philosophical basis which supported traditional dualism for so long. This philosophical basis will be called the substance-theory of reality. Secondly, I will elaborate some of the implications of the substance-theory in relationship to our views on spirituality.

## The Substance Worldview

Since our worldview provides the framework out of which we do our thinking and speaking about the world, rarely do we have either the occasion or the ability to step back, as it were, to view the framework itself. The philosophical basis which has informed and shaped our worldview is called a substance-theory of reality, and though the terms may be unfamiliar to us the concepts and realities to which they point serve as the bread and butter of our everyday experience. Our consciousness is so totally informed by the concept of substance that it dictates the way we perceive our world and consequently the way we think and speak about it. In fact we are so accustomed to this way of perceiving and speaking that it strikes us as completely natural; we are quite easily led to believe that there is no other adequate way to construe reality. For this reason, the philosophical presuppositions of our worldview strike us with a certain obviousness; this obviousness, however, is due to the taken-for-granted character of these presuppositions which serves to put them beyond our direct questioning.

## A Language of Nouns

If we are native speakers of English we share in a Western language-structure. If we wish to speak a coherent sentence in English we must search for a particular type of word, as every schoolteacher knows. In English, we must always begin a sentence with a noun, and a sentence which contains no noun cannot be a sentence. Almost unconsciously we look for a noun if we wish to speak a sentence: the house, the hat, the car, the tree, the teacher. We know that grammatically a noun is the name of a person, place, or thing. But what exactly do we do when we name with a noun a person, place, or thing? What we are doing with our use of nouns is pointing out some item of our universe which is enduring, repeatable in our experience, and hence reliable. Nouns name the stable and predictable parts of our reality.

Once we have named a noun, we can then proceed to point to something which need not be stable or predictable, something which quite easily perhaps comes and goes. For example, once we name "the boy," then we can say, "is hungry," "is sick" or "is running." Any of these qualities can be different and in this sense are incidental to the enduring reality which is the boy. Linguistically, nouns are the primary realities of our universe of discourse because nouns name the things which comprise our reality. In the world of science, scientific investigation is concerned with the world of objects. Whether investigating atoms, mountains or galaxies, the scientist is studying the things which comprise our universe and his ideal is to study these with complete objectivity. The objects of science are the nouns of grammar.

## A World of Things

At the everyday level of our casual speech we do not use the term "substance" very often nor do we much use the term "object" unless we are being technical. The most commonplace and homely word in our language is "thing," and it can be used to refer to literally anything at all. If an item we wish to refer to is not a thing, then it is quite literally "no-thing"—nothing—and there is nothing we can point to or say about nothing. Thus the world of our experience is a world of things, and the linguistic things which we name and describe are the real things we touch and use. In philosophy, the nouns, objects and things of our experience are called "substance." A substance is simply an item which has real existence and thus has reliability and endurance. Things, nouns, objects, and substances are all the same category, and they simply show how we choose to divide up our universe. They all serve as a very broad category which allows us to sort and organize the complex multiplicity of our experiencing.

Finally, we have another term which sounds a bit more educated than the unsophisticated "thing," and this term is "being." We use "being" in exactly the same way that we use "thing," and like "thing" it is the broadest and most general word in our language. Anything at all which exists in any way has to be some sort of being; if it cannot be described as some sort of being then it is literally non-being, which is identical with nothing. This broadest of all categories, being, stretches across the entirety of our universe so that any item whatsoever that can be spoken of at all must be referred to as some sort of being. It is important to notice that we even include God in this universal category so that we must refer to God's reality as "Supreme Being." If we could not use the term "being" of God we would somehow seem to be saying that God is non-being, which we would understand as nothing.

Now the whole point of this rather abstract exercise is simply to point out something that we all take for granted: our worldview presents to us a reality which is finally a universe of things or beings, separate, independent items with endurance, reliability, repeatability and self-identity. To really know ourselves and our universe, then, is to be "objective"—to have a reliable and true knowledge of the objects which exist. If any of us were to question this rather obvious and straightforward approach to reality we would probably be thought rather silly.

When it comes to dividing up the various types of being we immediately notice that the existing substances of our world exhibit an almost endless variety; we have trees, rocks, animals, houses, water, human beings—our list could run for several pages, but each item exists as a particular type of being. To account for the sometimes radically different types of beings we encounter, philosophy postulated two separate factors or principles. On the one hand, every real substance in our universe was some form of matter, whether a rock, a tree, an atom, or a human body. To account for the material aspect of real substances there was postulated a principle called "prime matter," and this is what every real being in the universe shares in common. Notice how casually we can speak of our material universe, the matter of the stars, or a material body.

On the other hand, however, why is it that matter can be so different? Why is it that the human material body is so different from the material rock, and the rock so different from the material tree? One way to answer this is to say that the difference is a difference of form; a rock has a different form than a tree and the human body has a different form than a chair. The principle of form is introduced to account for the differences that matter exhibits in existing substances, so that the form is the principle which "informs" prime matter, giving it not just its physical shape, but its metaphysical shape as well. Thus a tree is a tree because the form of tree constitutes the prime matter into treeness, and the form of humanness constitutes prime matter into a human being. When we look at a real material substance and ask what it is, the answer to this "what" question will always be the form which specifies matter to take the form of that particular type of being.

## Metaphysical Dualism

Since this system of explanation postulates two fundamental principles to constitute a real being, it is consequently a system of metaphysical dualism. On the face of it, a dualistic system is a legitimate way of explaining things. But let us pursue some of the implications of this dualism.

All of us are aware that the matter which constitutes our human bodies comes and goes; we are told that the matter of our body completely replaces itself every seven years. We notice also that any physical substance of our universe will change over a period of time—metal rusts, wood rots, mountains and atoms decay. All the material objects of our universe undergo changes, and over the course of time enough changes can take place that the original substance is completely corrupted, as, for example, when uranium turns to lead, or when a human body dies. Obviously matter is a transient factor because it is corruptible, so that a sufficient degree of change can corrupt the substance completely. An essential characteristic of matter is that it can both change and corrupt.

Since it is the form, however, that shapes the matter into a self-identified being, it is the form which never changes. A chair will be a chair, no matter what condition its material may be in, as long as it is informed by the form "chair." Since the form is always permanent and identical it is that principle which perdures throughout all changes and which maintains the self-identity of the particular being. So we now have matter as a principle of change, corruptibility and impermanence, and form as a principle of identity, incorruptibility and permanence.

## Dualism and the Human Person

When we apply this division to human beings we will see immediately where much of our traditional language has its roots. The material element of human beings is obviously the human body, and it is this material element of our body which can change in a variety of ways—it can increase, decrease, age, wrinkle, and eventually die. On the other hand, the principle which makes this matter the body of a human being is the form, and traditionally we have called the human form the "soul."

It is only because matter has been informed or ensouled that the result is a human being; the matter otherwise could have been formed into something completely different. But the life-giving form, the soul, is always exactly that and nothing else. It can now be seen that this dualism forces us to view ourselves as human beings essentially constituted out of two radically distinct factors, one of them transient and corruptible and the other permanent and incorruptible. While this is not the scriptural view of humanness which in no way sees the person as divided but only as a single unified whole, this is nonetheless a way of thinking about ourselves that we are quite accustomed to.

### The Body as Dispensable

One striking result of this matter/form split, which translates into body/soul, is that because matter is transient and corruptible, the body finally is dispensable. Since our real identity resides in our soul, the flesh is seen as merely instrumental to maintaining our life in a worldly context; in another context, however, the body can be done away with and we can exist as pure spirit, or soul. Our traditional religious language has referred to the spiritual task as "saving your soul," with the implication that saving your body was neither necessary nor important. Such a view produces an instrumental cosmology in the sense that the material items of the universe, our human body together with the world and the environment it affords, are merely instruments for the more spiritual process of saving the soul. While we may use our bodies and use our world, these are finally unimportant since they will all be left behind when the spiritual soul moves to another realm.

As a result of this dualism, then, the magnificent splendor

of the cosmos with its billions of galaxies and millions of light years of expanse simply provides the instrumental context in which we work out the salvation of the soul. To take such an attitude is to deny the inherent value of the God-created cosmos and to denigrate the incalculable richness and beauty of the entire created order along with the myriad of astonishing life-forms it has produced. The universe just happens to be the place where we humans live, and once human history has run its course the cosmos can be closed up and abandoned like the shutting down of a used-up coal mine.

Since matter is corruptible and transient and only form is enduring, there is absolutely no compelling motive to be loyal to this universe, our home, and to the near-infinite expanse of time and space which surely hides more richness and wonder than we in our dreadfully narrow and limited expanse of time and space could possibly even imagine. This astonishing lack of world-loyalty is a serious neglect of our scriptural heritage where we find that even the Creator-God marveled in wonder when he saw "that it was good." This casual dismissal of the infinite elegance of our inexplicable cosmos and the equal dismissal of the loveliness of our own bodies seems to pay no serious heed to the Word who became flesh to dwell among us, here, in this cosmos, this world, this flesh. Can any theology seriously claim that this human flesh was a mere instrument for the Word, to be easily dismissed into nothingness once the redemptive task had been performed? As we will show later, such a view surely denies the resurrection of the body of Christ, so crucial to our own faith.

## Individualism and Independence

This dualism of the substance theory also tends to overemphasize the extreme individualism and high independence of any existing object of reality. The really existing items, which are substances, are individual and specific and hold their existence independently of other substances. The traditional definition of a substance was "that which exists in its own right and needs nothing else in order to exist." Such a definition identifies a substance as something which is self-existent and independent, something which can exist in isolation and can hold its identity in total separation from the rest of reality. Such a theory of individual self-existence supports quite readily an attitude of high individualism. At the human level, persons are individual and separate, independent of the human community and independent of the conditions of both the society and the cosmos which hold them in being. A moment's reflection will reveal that this notion of independent, self-existing individuality is high fiction and in no way corresponds to our real world. We will develop this point later.

### The Effect of Individualism on Spirituality

This high individualism has had a serious influence on traditional spirituality. The constant insistence that the spiritual task is to "save one's soul" puts the obligation completely on the individual person, since the person alone is responsible for one's spiritual well-being. Crassly put, spirituality becomes highly self-centered since my soul can be saved in total disregard of the community in which I live and the world in which I have my being. Whether the other members of my human community are saved or not is finally of no importance since I hold my individuality and self-identity independently of one and all. The social groupings which support and enable my humane existence—for example, family, church, religious community, civil society—were mere convenience at best and obstacle at worst. I would not be saved because of my communities nor because of my relationships to these communities; salvation was something I worked out between myself and God. My family or church or religious community might support me or direct me or even challenge me, but the responsibility was finally my own, as was the salvation.

This high individualism made possible by the substance theory generates a version of reality in which existence is seen as ultimately non-relational and the self is viewed finally as non-social. The social relationships out of which and through which I experience my selfhood—my self as friend, my self as lover, my self as parent and so on—are basically accidental and finally incidental. Although these relations serve to shape the quality and form of my life, they somehow do not touch or affect my true selfhood. If this non-relational version is indeed correct, then my family, my friends, my dearly loved ones are not in any real sense part of the depths of my being without whom I simply could not be myself. Experientially we need only consider what we mean by being in love, whether with husband, wife, parent or child, and we realize that the unique particularity of that specific relationship not only creates an invaluable quality in our lives but at the same time quite literally touches the very depths of our being; without that particular love-relationship we would most surely be a different person.

It is perhaps quite demeaning, to ourselves and to others, to consider other persons, no matter how close to us in love, as mere vehicles or impediments to our individualized activity of saving the soul. That haunting Gospel injunction of Jesus to love our neighbor even as we love ourselves points to a personal interrelational community in which we are enmeshed in each other's salvation and can ill afford to stand idly by as disinterested spectators.

## Antagonism Between Body and Soul

Besides the devaluation of matter and the high individualism produced by the substance theory, a third ramification can be discerned. When matter and form are translated into body and soul the resulting union of the two, rather than being cohesive and creative, becomes an antagonistic relationship. Rather than working together for the well-being and fulfillment of the whole person, the body and soul work against each other, the "lower faculties" of the body pulling against the "higher faculties" of the soul in ceaseless struggle for dominance.

Traditional spirituality constantly opposes the spirit against the flesh, and our life process is portrayed as a continual conflict fought within the battleground of our own selves. Not only is there an inexorable anatagonism between the strivings of my soul and those of my body, but there is an equally cruel antagonism between myself and my world, myself and other people. The entire cosmos and all those who people it stand as a vast conspiracy to lure me from my true perfection, which is the pursuit of God alone. To enter wholeheartedly into the workings of the world and to respond freely to its attractions is to degrade oneself by succumbing to delights which can finally only distract us from the one true beauty which is God.

The deep-lying pessimism enshrined in such a view is reflected in many popular prayers and devotions. In the traditional "Salve Regina," for example, we are spoken of as *gementes et flentes in hac lacrimarum valle* (groaning and weeping in this valley of tears). Our lives must be lived in sadness bordering on despair because we are engaged in a battle which will never cease, and those things and persons closest to our experience must in fact be considered as the enemy, always held at bay and looked upon with distrust. The only world which we know and in which we lead our lives, the world which triggers our passionate involvement and through which we have experienced indescribable satisfaction, is finally not our home and we have no right to feel at home within it. Such spiritual pessimism does much to instill a grim determination to undergo struggle but does little to promote that magnificent Gospel wonder which proclaims the almost incredible good news that God so loved this world that he sent his only-begotten Son to inhabit its earth and dwell in its flesh.

## The Danger of Rigid Moralism

A fourth consequence made possible by the dualism of the substance view is that the entire religious enterprise becomes thoroughly moralistic. Since the world is so fraught with temptations and dangers, lurking even in quiet corners where we do not even think to look, the moral soul must be protected within a secure wall of restrictions. We are all already too familiar with the "do's" and "dont's" of our religious moral codes. Ranging from "Do not drink" to "Do not commit adultery," they set rigid boundaries to the possibilities of our experience and severely delimit the road to self-discovery. It is said that the medieval cartographers, when they had charted on their maps those parts of the earth which they knew, would draw at the edges of the map, where there was nothing but the unknown boundaries of the ocean, sea-monsters of frightful mien with the brooding legend, *Hic sunt monstra* (Here lie monsters).

The unknown and the untried would ever remain so if fear and dread could hold back our relentless drive for exploration and discovery. The greater part of the traditional moral codes, rooted in an anti-worldly bias and steeped in a pessimistic distrust of human nature, held its own dooming legend, "Here lies hellfire." When we consider that the spiritual quest is surely the most vital and consuming drive of our being, which will enable us to enter into depths of passionate intensity and love that we cannot yet even imagine, it is somewhat disheartening to think that such struggle and such commitment can actually be reduced to the simple but silly morality of drinking, gambling and attending church on Sunday. While a rigid moralism may serve well those faint of heart willing to settle for the pale fervor of abiding by the rules or the cold comfort of never having transgressed a law, there will always be that small band of bold ones who, driven by a passion for life in its intensity, will see the moral enterprise as a challenge to be like their God. These will use the moral codes as guidelines as they venture into the heart of their own darkness and into the teeth of their own dragons where they may face the all-consuming fire who is their God and the source of their own best self.

## God as Pure Form

Let us look at one last corollary of the theory of matter and form which applies to God rather than to ourselves. It was seen that it was obviously false to construe God on the model of a material object; whatever God was like, he was not like a tree or a rock or a human body. For this reason, God could in no way be constituted out of matter and hence only the category of form could be applied to God. Thus God becomes "pure form." Such a move surely protects God from the corruptibility and decay linked with matter, but when it is recognized that our appetites and passions, all those qualities which instill our striving with zest and adventure and emotional strength, are products of the intricate workings of our bodies rather than of our minds, we should instinctively know that those emotionally qualitative and passionate tones of feelings are the hallmarks of anything we seize upon as distinctively human.

The concept of pure form has very little to do with emotional intensity, passionate involvement and qualitative enhancement of feeling, and yet these are the qualities which are the full meaning of our experience and serve to drive the fierce struggle for self-worth. The wonder of our existence is that marvelous complex of feelings, emotions and passions which both originate within our bodies and resound throughout them as we grasp the world and others into the felt heart of our own being. Even though we may often talk a bit too glibly about being in love, our actual being in love contains a bodily involvement and emotional interchange which rises above our words and yet gives depth of meaning to what we mean by love.

If, then, God is disembodied he will also be, as traditional theology has long claimed, passionless—impassive and devoid of passion, appetite and emotion. Such a move does in fact remove God from the irrationality of our deep lying and darksome emotional drives, but at the very same time it makes of God an unspeakable being, cold as marble, passionless as a corpse, bereft of driving appetite and irresistible desire. Such a

Pure Form ill accords with that awesome figure of the Old Testament who rails with anger, cries in compassion, and pleads in love. The Scriptures, at least, indicate that these powerful emotions which enkindle our desire and fire our strivings are not just the creation but the very image of the passion of God. The adscription of pure form to God does defend God's inexplicable majesty, but at the same time does little to explain an infinite love which would create us, humans in our bodies, and strive ever after that we become one with that very Godhead.

## An Alternative View: The Final End

We have spent a good deal of time analyzing how a metaphysical/cosmological dualism supports most of our commonly accepted notions of the spiritual life—the notions of the soul, of saving the soul, of getting to heaven. Such a dualism puts the end of our spiritual quest in another realm, in a new type of existence, achievable by a power which must be supernatural because it is not contained within the natural order. While there is a great deal of persuasiveness about this view, as evidenced by the fact that it has held sway for so long, it is purchased at a fairly steep price: a denial of the inherent value of the cosmos, a devaluation of the importance of the flesh, and a rejection of physical passions. Let us see if there is perhaps an alternative way of looking at the ultimate concerns of our spiritual quest which may empower us with the same ultimate motivation and yet avoid the weaknesses of a dualistic theory.

A somewhat different approach might be suggested if we were to ask ourselves anew: What are we about in this world? What are we really striving for? What is it that gives meaning to our conflicts and energy to our struggles? Exactly who, finally, are we trying to be? To get at this type of question which attempts to suggest a "why" to explain the things we do, the traditional category of the "final end" is remarkably helpful.

## Striving After Ends

In ordinary language we call an "end" anything that we are striving to achieve (and hence it is not to be understood in a temporal sense, as the end of a timespan or the end, i.e., the finish, of our life). What we define as a particular end simply specifies the purpose for which we are acting. For example, if someone, seeing me peruse a book, were to say: "Why are you doing that?" and my reply was "Because I want to pass the exam," the other would immediately know that the purpose of my studying was that I might achieve the end of passing the exam. It should be obvious that we have a countless number of ends and a myriad of purposes in our everyday lives. We choose all sorts of things for all kinds of reasons. What is it that gives a semblance of order to our choosing, that somehow we know what is more important and what is less important, what more valuable and what less—since we will often be in conflict where we must make a choice between two good things we want? What we would like to discover is what is the most important end of all, that purpose which dominates all our other purposes, that choice which will control many lesser choices. Here we have the traditional notion of the *final end*.

## The Final End

A final end is an end or a value to be achieved which lies beyond all other ends and values; hence there is nothing we can strive for beyond the final end, and this is why it is final. Notice, however, that the final end is at the same time the end which gives meaning and value to all the lesser ends. Many of the things we do are only partial ends, and we do them solely because of their relationship to the final end. For example, if my final end (relatively speaking) is to get to New Orleans, then I will find myself doing all sorts of things which I ordinarily would not be choosing to do: going to the travel agency, arranging for a ticket, obtaining a map of the city, packing my suitcase, and eventually boarding the plane. It is the final end, being in New Orleans, which makes sense out of and gives meaning to these lesser ends.

It can be surprising to look at our lives to see how many of the choices we make on a day-to-day basis are only made in the light of some larger end still in the future. Set in our life-context, the true final end is that end which stands beyond all our other purposes and gives meaning to and explains all the lesser ends and choices of our daily living. All of our strivings, all the other purposes for our choices, all the other values we seek, take their meaning and their value in accordance with their relationship to that end which is final and unsurpassable. Paul Tillich's marvelous phrase, the "ultimate concern," perhaps best encapsulates the meaning of the final end. If we can come to a clear understanding of what is indeed the final end of our lives, that is, what concerns us ultimately, then we will be in a much firmer position to make decisions about the purposes and values which are enmeshed in the complexity of our everyday worldly lives.

### Saving the Soul

In the traditional religious language of spirituality, the most commonly used phrase to designate the final end of our spiritual life was to save the soul. It was the weight of a dualistic theory, as we have seen, which translated the saving of the soul into the notion of the priority of the soul over the body with the transference of the soul from this realm to another realm. Consequently, in view of the importance of everlasting spiritual life in another realm, any sacrifice made in this worldly realm was well worth the price. Part of the end of our worldly striving, therefore, was precisely to escape this earth and all else with which we are here so familiar.

Saving the soul, however, was not the only term used to designate the final end. In fact, there exists for our use a whole cluster of terms which we tend to use almost casually and interchangeably to point to our final end. Thus it is that we talk quite easily about desiring to "get to heaven"; we speak of working out our "salvation"; we refer to our desire for "union with God"; we look forward to enjoying the "beatific vision"; our strongest yearning is for final "perfection." I would suggest that all of these phrases which are so common to us are designed to point to the selfsame identical reality of what we mean by our final end. They are simply diverse ways of speaking about our ultimate desire and our final purpose. These are the most meaningful words we have to describe the relentlessness of our striving, the demands of our moral energy, and the continual sacrifice of lesser goods. Saving the soul, union with God, beatific vision, perfection—these are unsophisticated but serious pointers to that reality, however understood, which will be the fulfillment of our being and thus the guide of our lives.

### Reappropriating Our Spiritual Language

Because these terms used to designate our final end are tattered and frayed by our casual usage, it is important that we probe beyond their obviousness to search out that deep-lying spiritual base upon which they rest. Getting to heaven, for example, is both a spatial and a spiritual metaphor, but we surely mean more than just moving from one place to another like changing one's apartment for a high-rise condo. What is it about heaven that it should be so desirable? Or what will the soul be doing once it has been saved? Such questions may sound naive, perhaps facetious, but let them be the beginning of a serious attempt on our part to clarify for ourselves, in this matter of ultimate importance, exactly what we are about in this business of our life's final goal and the human commerce whereby we lay purchase on that pearl of great price without which we are condemned to eat the dust from which we came.

On the one hand, these notions have been much contaminated by the vulgarizations that become debased coinage when religion slips into being crassly popular rather than thoughtfully sublime. I refer here to those crude versions which would reduce the life of heaven to a happy hunting-ground or refer to our redeemed activity as everlastingly playing the harp; even a paradise-regained is too romantic to claim our serious commitment. On the other hand, there is a kernel of religious truth hidden away within these coarse nuggets, layered over by rude usage but somehow still glimmering with a hint of elegance. So, once again, what could we possibly mean when we speak of salvation and perfection and union with God?

## Human Fulfillment

The suggestion here is that whatever else may have been included in the understanding of these notions of ultimacy, each of them singly and all of them collectively point to one obvious, though unmanageable, reality: they all point to some notion of human fulfillment. In the parlance of the day which has become so popular as to be prosaic, personal human fulfillment is the end and the goal which drives our strivings and fires our energies. In this life of conflict and struggle, of attempt and failure, of temptation and sin, of suffering and pain, we find ourselves submerged in the morass of our own imperfection, dragged deeper by the frustrations of our own culpable failures, half-choked on the evils we have spawned with even our well-intended attempts at good. This experiential defectiveness of our failed selves is the rooting-point wherein a creative vision of that same self, freed from the gravity of weakness and blindness and endemic lack of will, can break forth into faultless functioning like a well-tuned machine freed at last from the grind of friction. It is indeed human perfection we dream about and human perfection we seek.

Note the weight of the word "perfect." It is our experience of struggle and loss, both partial; striving and failure, both partial; good intention and poor deed, both partial; brilliant ideal and pedestrian achievement, both partial. Such experiences of partiality and fragmentation supply the festering but creative source from which we, at a level too deep and primordial to be called rational perhaps, spawn an inarticulate but compulsive ideal of perfection. *If only*—if only all my parts could work in complete coordination, if only my vision were clear enough to see beyond the trivialities which hang on my life like barnacles, if only my will were firm enough to hold in balanced order the many pearls which take their precious shine only from the pearl of great price. *If only* ... If only all things worked together unto good as the Gospel had promised. Perfect coordination, perfect functioning, perfect vision, perfect achievement and perfect satisfaction—this is the ideal state which lures us to gather up the fragmented pieces of our imperfection in the irrepressible hope that somehow we can achieve wholeness, and in wholeness satisfaction at last.

Perhaps this version of the final end strikes us as too mundane, too natural to have any serious truck with the supernatural. But lest we be too quickly derailed by the impact of the word "supernatural," let us think again. What else could we possibly wish to be if we did not wish to be humanly perfect? What other sort of perfection is even vaguely within our ken? What else could we possibly wish to be if we did not wish to be humanly fulfilled? What other fulfillment, besides human, could be open to us? What else could we possibly wish to be if we did not wish to be humanly satisfied? Could any non-human satisfaction give anything but ersatz joy? If "supernatural" by virtue of its dualistic bias must mean "non-natural" as well as "beyond the natural" then let us openly admit we do not know what that could mean. We do not seek to be unnaturally fulfilled nor unnaturally perfect.

## Jesus Christ: Perfectly Human

Let us hearken back to our good news which cries with such staunch conviction: "The Word became flesh." The home of the supernatural is the flesh; the message is no less than this. What Jesus Christ became—the challenge is flung at us—let us strive to the death also to become. It was not by accident that one of the earliest of the councils was compelled to insist: Jesus Christ became truly human and shared fully in the flesh. If "supernatural" is to mean that we must leave the natural, then we deny not just our world, we deny our Christ. Jesus Christ is for us the living symbol of the perfection of the human. We dare seek no less than the perfection of the human. We become Christlike or we are indeed damned.

If, then, our final end can be conceived as the full and final perfection of our humanness, as the perfection of our being so that we finally become what God has willed us to be, as the fulfillment of our ideal image as envisioned by God, how may we rightly think about the actual process of such achievement? Need it be a state irretrievably beyond our knowing here and now, or could it perhaps be a process and a state of which we have already tasted? The message of the Incarnation surely seems to suggest that the process of human fulfillment begins within this world where the material of our perfection is the everyday and ordinary commerce of our fleshed lives within the context of those human communities which set the patterns of our choice-making. We learn about the intimate grandeur of love only from the highly particular earthly and fleshly loves which lure us out of our selfishness into that broader community of life which Paul has called the body of Christ.

## Other and Different

On the one hand, a dualistic understanding tends to view ultimate human perfection as something that is *other* and *different* than anything now within our experience. It transfers this experience to another realm and translates it into a new kind of experiencing beyond both present capacity and present knowledge. Perhaps it is this view that produces what can be pejoratively referred to as the happy-hunting-ground theory. Since our human perfection was so totally divorced from present experience and meaning, the poetry of the concretely actual was pressed to do a service it could ill perform. If our perfected reality will truly be *other* and *different* than our present reality, then what finally is the purpose of this present reality which is not just all that we know, but all that we are?

## More and Fuller

On the other hand, an alternative to the view of our ultimate human perfection as something *other* and *different* is so obviously available in our scriptural tradition that our dualistically jaundiced eyes easily overlook it. Is it possible that the full perfection of our lives refers to, not something *other* and *different*, but rather to that which is *more* and *fuller?* It may be the case that our concept of final perfection is not pointing to the abolition of our existence and the destruction of life as we know it in order to enter into an entirely new form of existence. On the contrary, the concept of final perfection may mean precisely what it says: the perfection of everything which is now contained in our human existence.

We should notice that the phrase "human existence" is fairly abstract and consequently disconcertingly vacuous. By "human existence" we can only concretely mean "human life," and "human life" refers simply and solely to my life and your life, concrete and earthly, here and now, heady and fleshy. "Existence" is too vague a category to be of much help, for rocks and mountains and galaxies exist but we are not immediately concerned about their final end. Our primordial experience of ourselves is that we are alive; we are *living* creatures. All of the qualitative distinctions between thinking, loving, willing, valuing and the like are simply diverse and oblique ways of pointing to the ineffable variety and richness of being alive. The overarching category that best embraces what it means to each of us to be human is to say that we have life.

## The Purpose of Life Is Life

Viewed in this light, the perfection of life should not mean the cessation of life or the shift to a different kind of existence. The perfection of life is simply—*more life.* What is here being suggested is that our vision of the final end as the ideal perfection which we will achieve in union with God is our intuitively indestructible sense that what we are living our lives for is the fullness and richness of life itself. What is the end of life (not in a temporal sense, as in death), or, put otherwise, what is life for? Life is for life—the living of life for the intensity and depth of life itself. Our final end, therefore, as perfection, or heaven, or union with God, is nothing else than our very lives, freed from the crippling grasp of selfishness and blindness and sin, plunged to depths and raised to heights of intensity and fullness approaching the fullness of the life of God, the eternally living One. In this sense, then, we do not become other than what we are; we become rather more of what we already are (and here, surely, hangs that terrifying threat that what we will become *then* depends so infallibly on what we become *now)*. We do not transfer to another type of life but rather blossom into fullness those qualities which we have zealously nurtured as the values of our life now.

## Life More Abundantly

The case presented here can be argued on firm and secure grounds. If life is taken as the primary explanatory category of our final end, then the goal of life can only be the fullness of life itself. Can we still be so casual with our Gospel origins that we refuse to hear that haunting promise of Jesus, "I have come that you may have life, and have it abundantly" (Jn 10:10)? The language of Jesus does not say that he has come to take us to heaven, or to save our souls, or to bring us to the beatific vision. The language of the claim is overwhelming in its directness: I have come that you may have the abundance of life. One can hardly appreciate the Jesus of the Gospels until one sees that he was one enchanted by life; his stories, his parables, those things he solemnly enjoins upon us—all have to do with the possibilities and conditions by which even the least of us might enjoy what the Creator of life intended—the abundance of life itself. One could do worse than read the story of the crucifixion as stark testimony to the intractable conviction of Jesus that the only thing worth dying for was life itself.

## Resurrection: The Fullness of Life

The second argument is simply an extension of the first. The central and essential symbol of the Christian faith is the resurrection of Jesus Christ. Although we tend to focus on the death of Jesus in order to plumb the meaning of the stunning fact that he died for us and for our sins, it would be unfaithful to the Gospels themselves to establish this as the central or ultimate reference point for the relationship of Jesus to ourselves. For the end of the crucifixion story is not death; it is resurrection. And can we be deluded into thinking that the risen Jesus is but an immortal soul that our dualistic vision would want us to see?

Embodied and worldly as we are, cannot we but be enamored of that puzzling net of earthly detail which does not simply remind us but *demands* that we believe that this Jesus was recognizably alive, with an earthiness and bodiliness that were unmistakable? Jesus asks for something to eat; he eats fish and honeycomb; he fries fish on the beach in the early morning; he breaks bread with his friends; he pleads that Thomas place his hand in the wounded side that he and we may finally believe beyond all doubting that this Jesus is alive in his body. There is no spirit here, no disembodied soul—only the living embodied Jesus. The resurrection of Jesus in its starkest and most undeniable form is this: the ultimate and final judgment is not death; the final word is life, always life. The symbols surrounding the resurrection are the concrete poetry proclaiming what we have always known: the end of life is life, life in its fullness, life in its richness, life in abundance.

## The Pervasiveness of Evil

But for those of us who firmly believe in the abundance of life, where are the signs of it now? We dare not spin tales that do not root on reality. Life as lived by us does contain enough heartbreak to establish a vale of tears. Never dare the believer deny the gross and intractable reality of evil in our world. We need not be especially alert to be aware of the pervasive presence of evil, starvation, cruelty, pain and death not just out there in a world beyond us, but here in our midst, and, unfortunately, in our own lives. Each of us has had perhaps more than our share of pain and suffering; each of us has been sorely grieved by the death of a loved one.

More than this, each of us has had a personal role in the inflicting of suffering and hurt on those around us. Our deepest sense of guilt is no "trip" as the faddist would have us believe; we feel guilty because we *are* guilty—who of us has not sinned? When we focus on the inexorable presence of evil in even the most commonplace corners of our lives, it is difficult to trust our claim that life in abundance was bestowed upon us by God through Christ.

A traditional answer to this problem was to assert that this evil was precisely what we would leave behind in our journey to heaven. Our sojourn here in this valley of tears provides a testing ground wherein we are challenged to prove that we can endure. But once our mettle has been tested, we move on to a more peaceful realm. An alternative way of viewing the matter of evil, however, is closer to the clues left us by the Gospels. In the Old Testament the Ten Commandments demand that we dare not commit evil. In the New Testament, on the contrary, we find the Jesus of the Beatitudes where there is no threat and no recrimination. The Beatitudes are simply a plea to our own intuitive self-awareness that the best we can do is to do good. We fulfill ourselves, that gentle man assures us, by being makers of peace, by hungering and thirsting for justice, by feeding the hungry, by simply being meek in the face of violence.

Surely we cannot be so dense as to think that Jesus counseled that we flee evil and its world and its effects. Not only his words but his very life give unmistakable testimony that the quality and meaning of life derived, not from fleeing evil, but in the overcoming of evil. The challenge of the Gospel is to live by the faith that our never-ending involvement in the struggle against the evil, which, like a continuous drip of water or like a roaring wave, threatens to erode and demolish the only life we have, is to be full partners in the work of God who will never be satisfied with less than the fullness of life. Do we doubt for the briefest of moments that we are called to be yeast, salt, light, so that it is not the magnitude of the task but the intensity of the commitment which will finally win the day? Our failure is perhaps a failure of nerve: we want the assurance of an afterlife, but the only guarantee left by Jesus is the workings of this life.

## Conclusion: An Alternative Worldview

We have now come a long way in our investigation of the philosophical theory of substance as a dominant part of the presuppositional base supporting our traditional anthropology as well as our spirituality. The point of the argument has been that from our present-day view of the historical spectrum it may be possible to discern that some of the basic tenets of our traditional worldview have seen their day and are no longer serviceable. If the discussion so far has been reasonable, it points to the fact that a reformulation of some of the basic notions of spirituality is a legitimate enterprise which demands both our serious attention and our sincere commitment. To round out this critique of the substance view of reality, let us examine one final point.

The construction of a comprehensive worldview as described in the previous chapter is never an overtly self-conscious operation guided by clear vision and hard choices. On the contrary, a worldview evolves only slowly, in bits and pieces, with trial and error. The analogy is not that of a sea-conch in which a bit of living tissue gradually works through the intricacies of a programmed plan to arrive at an exquisitely structured and perfectly designed spiral shell. The analogy would perhaps be closer to that of a sponge, which grows randomly and without seeming direction, with no final form to give it shape; eventually it is just there with *that* particular shape because of *those* particular circumstances surrounding its growth. So with a worldview. What this means, then, is that elements will eventually be an important part of a worldview simply because originally they just happened to be there, at the right time and in the right place. Such items were incorporated into the worldview because they were the best available.

Because we are so inveterately accustomed to construing our universe by utilizing the category of objects, we find it difficult to conceive what a "non-objective" universe might be. But objects and substances are simply the categories given to us, and so these are the categories we invoke to explain everything from rocks to galaxies, from human persons to God. Do we ever stop to consider that it is somewhat awkward to reconcile the Supreme Being of Western theology with the Loving Father of Jesus, the one he called endearingly Abba?

One of the discoveries of the modern world is that there exists not one single worldview, but a host of competing worldviews: for example, the worldview of the West, of the East, of the Native American, of the Muslim. These worldviews differ radically from one another and cannot be judged as true or false. They are meant to be serviceable, and as long as they perform their function of creating a cosmos, a meaningful world, for those who hold them and live within their frameworks, they are adequate and trustworthy. With this in mind, it becomes much easier to recognize that the basic explanatory category, such as being or object, is in fact fairly arbitrary—in the sense that it could have been otherwise. The primary explanatory category of the Eastern worldview, for example, is not that of object. What actually occurs is that a specific historical context of human experience allows a particular facet to be sorted out and utilized as a clue. This clue functions as a hint, or even a key, along the path of discovery. If the clue proves fruitful it will become a formative part of the worldview.

The concept of object or being has functioned as such a clue for the unveiling of the structures of the cosmos. As such it has served well. But even with this compliment, it must be immediately added that this notion of object has been responsible for some villainous duty as well, and the reason is quite simple. By approaching reality first of all in terms of its objectivity we are compelled to concentrate on its materiality. The material objects of the cosmos, however, were seen as inert, lacking inherent power, inanimate and non-personal. It was their very objectivity and patent reliability which made them stand out as important.

## Persons as Subjects

When the theory of matter and form is applied to explain the human persons, serious problems arise. Even though we can look upon our own bodies as objects, as things which can be weighed and measured, this type of objectivity is not the primary characteristic of human persons. On the contrary, our intuitive claim is that we as human are not mere objects, and to consider us as mere objects is to defile our very being. We are, rather, subjects, and it is our inherent and essential subjectivity that constitutes our very humanness. We humans are not inanimate, we are not impersonal, we do not lack inherent power. Whatever reliability and stability we may show is more a matter of choice than of determination. Our claim to sacredness lies in our free subjectivity, the very image of God. The outcome of this crucial difference is that human persons stand out as the supreme exception to the objectivity of the cosmos.

In the midst of this near inestimable expanse of objects scattered through the millions of light years of cosmic space, on this tiny earth there resides a small, short-historied cluster of subjects—ourselves. This would mean—dare we face the awful fact—that we few subjects are somehow the freaks of the universe. We are unlike everything else in this galactic infinitude. The categories of explanation which so ably handle the universe do poorly when applied to us. We the cosmic freaks, the only self-consciously aware and deliberately striving creatures in this massive cosmos of still undiscovered creativity and elegance, are distinguished primarily because we are aliens, destined to be lost forever and never at home within a universe in which nothing is like ourselves. Is it any wonder that we were driven to postulate another world, a new realm, that finally we, the aliens born into a home not our own where we feed the experience of our lives from things foreign to our substance, might finally, as the saying goes, rest in peace?

## The Word Became Flesh

No wonder, then, that our spirituality has been a spirituality of alienation. Foreigners to this earth, our very bodies the prison-house of the soul, the world itself simply the stamping ground of the devil and his minions, our fierce passions somehow sabotaging our true self—the spiritual-minded must perforce be other-worldly with spiritual growth measured by removal from and antipathy toward this world, this body, this imprisoned life. There could be no heart for this world, no loyalty to this life. Flying in the face of the one unrefusable Gospel command that we love one another even as Jesus has loved us, we moved in the terrifying fear that our deep and almost unwilled love for another could somehow deter, and perhaps disbar, us from the kingdom yet to come. And yet because we root ourselves on the indubitable conviction that the Word did indeed become flesh and move among us with passionate love, we, often unadmittedly, are fired to experience deeper intensity than we ever thought possible by the pervasive, inexpressible intuition that this flesh is very good, this earth our true home, that we are—yes, we are, here and now the image of God.

Our spiritual life, therefore, cannot be the denial of life as we know it. If we cultivate a spirituality of alienation, then we can only be diseased aliens. A spirituality of wholeness, so beautifully rooted in Scripture, would have us take hold of our lives as our most prized possession; it would have us seize upon whatever passion and intensity is within our power in the commitment to, and the advancing of, the peaceable kingdom. It challenges us to gaze upon the gracious courtliness of this universe which allows us to be and to say with the mind and the heart of our Christ: "You are my friends."

## Selected Readings

One of the most penetrating analyses of the dehumanizing effects of an objective worldview has been written by Theodore Roszak in *Where the Wasteland Ends* (Garden City, New York: Doubleday and Company, Inc., 1972). Most pertinent to this chapter is Part Two, "Single Vision and Newton's Sleep: The Strange Interplay of Objectivity and Alienation."

Modern physics, with its startling and almost incredible discoveries at the subatomic level, has been the dominant factor in forcing a rethinking of our traditional worldview. Gary Zukav offers a fascinating and intelligible account of the discoveries of physics in the last one-hundred years in *The Dancing Wu Li Masters: An Overview of the New Physics* (New York: Bantam Books, Inc. & William Morrow & Company, Inc., 1979).

In *The Grammar of Faith,* Paul Holmer works to remove the concept from the realm of the abstract and to give it renewed life in the practical experiences of our daily living. See especially Chapter 4, "Scientific Language and the Language of Faith" (San Francisco: Harper and Row, 1978).

Sam Keen's *Apology for Wonder* is a most artful remedy for our tendency to take our universe and ourselves for granted. His claim that wonder is the basic religious emotion throws a new and charming light on the marvels of our spiritual life. See especially Chapter Six, "Wonder and Authentic Life" (New York: Harper and Row, 1969).

*Stories of God* by John Shea takes seriously the scriptural affirmations about the activity of God and thus presents a moving and convincing view of our spiritual life. See especially Chapter Three, "Stories of Hope and Justice" (Chicago: The Thomas More Press, 1978).

A thorough investigation of the place of the body and embodied life in the writings of the early Christian authors is done by Margaret Miles in *Fullness of Life: Historical Foundations of a New Asceticism* (Philadelphia: The Westminster Press, 1981). There is solid agreement that belief in the incarnation and the resurrection entails the fullness of bodily life here and hereafter.

*Scripture Reading*
The Letter to the Philippians Chapter 2:1–11

# 3

# God Is Love:
# An Alternative Model
# For Spirituality

It is important that we examine for a moment the consequences of our traditional worldview for our understanding of God. Once we have reviewed some serious problems presented to our notion of spirituality by a substance-informed concept of God, we will be in a position to strike out into a completely new path. The burden of the second part of this chapter will be to lay out the foundational guidelines to an alternative model of reality, of human personhood, of God, and, finally, of spirituality. In a certain sense, this alternative model is not really new at all; the concept of reality and of God here proposed is simply the systematic development of the religious content of our Scriptures.

For the most part we rarely advert to the fact that so much of our accepted language about God is not at all scriptural language; it is, on the contrary, highly developed and systematic philosophical language. The reason for this is both simple and obvious: those categories which are employed by the worldview and its philosophy to describe the ultimate nature of whatever exists are the broadest and most universal categories available. Therefore, when we come to speak about and point to that One who is source and end of all that is and hence who is ultimately significant, we find that the only meaningful and intelligible categories afforded to us are those of the dominant worldview. Since all theology speaks systematically and coherently only by utilizing the comprehensive categories of the worldview, theology itself will take its contours and shape from the cut of the philosophical configurations.

### God Within a Substance View: Supreme Being

In a world of substances and beings, what word would be used to most aptly describe the greatest of all beings who is the source of all? Notice how easily the phrase comes to our lips: God is the *Supreme Being*. The well-used category of being is simply applied to God as the supreme case. But obviously the being of God differs radically from the being of all the creatures. To account for this radical difference of the being of God, it was asserted that the essential characteristic of God was God's *aseity*.

In the Latin terminology of traditional theology, it was said that God existed *in se* and *a se*—that is, God existed in himself and of himself. The aseity of God points to his uncaused existence and his absolute independence of being. God exists completely on his own right and quite literally needs nothing else in order to exist. God is totally independent—independent in his own existence and independent of any other existences. This is surely serious testimony to the awesome incomprehensibility of God. It portrays God as existing from all eternity in himself and of himself, with no need for anything else to qualify his existence. Since God is totally self-subsistent and self-sufficient, God is supremely independent and essentially isolated. God enjoys his existence completely within his own being; this was the case from all eternity, and he could go on in splendid isolation for the rest of all eternity.

This high metaphysical compliment to the nature of God, however, demands a price. If God so exists in independence and self-sufficiency, then in an absolute sense God has no need of anything else at all. Whatever may be said of beings existing outside of God it can surely be claimed that God has no need of them. The religious implications of this view will be developed later.

## God as Infinite

The meaning of this notion of aseity is amplified by the addition of the essential attribute of infinity. To say that God is infinite is to say that God is completely beyond limits, beyond limitations of any sort. Within the being of God there is no such thing as a limited quality. If God is thus unlimited in his being it is required that God contain within his own existence the sum total of all perfections. Whatever perfection we can possibly conceive of, that perfection exists infinitely in the nature of God. If this is so, however, then it would be contradictory to think that anything could ever be added to God. God exists in such consummate fullness that no addition is possible, nor, by the same token, is any diminution possible. Nothing could possibly be taken away from God; God can in no way become less. God is always the absolute fullness of being, being in its plenitude and finality.

Such a view surely makes God incomparable and incommensurable in the light of our existence in finitude and imperfection. If God is infinite in the sense that he is the fullness of being and contains the sum of all perfection, then it must truly follow that God needs nothing and that nothing can be added to God. Nothing outside of God can give an increase to the infinite perfection which is God. With inexorable logic, then, this further claim must also be true: if God in fact needs nothing, then God does not need me, nor you, nor all of us together. God does not need our virtue, nor our goodness, nor our prayers, nor, finally, our lives.

## Do We Give to God?

Let us not tread casually here, for there is too much at stake for all of us. Resplendent in the fullness of infinity, God cannot be added to. Let us not be too dull of mind to perceive the consequence of what is being claimed here. If God cannot be added to, then we, you and I, can *give nothing* to God. You and I can *do nothing* for God. We cannot affect the quality of the experience of God. Is it true, then, and dare we shout this from the rooftops: that our struggling and our suffering, our moral striving and our heroic sacrifice, our patience and for-bearance—the sum and substance of those things which give meaning and depth to our lives—not only do not, they cannot, affect God?

To a God infinite in his fullness, nothing, nothing at all, can make a difference. Put this way, do we not hear the echoes of a subtle blasphemy: nothing makes a difference to God—not you, nor I, nor all of us together? I would simply here suggest that with our high proclamation of infinity in orthodox chorus, we do not really believe it, you and I. Why dare we challenge this hallowed metaphysical orthodoxy? *Because we pray, you and I. And when we pray we mean it.* And deep within those dark recesses of the spirit which give us whatever hold we have on meaningful life, we know, you and I, that our prayer does mean something to God.

## God Beyond Change

To further complicate this religious matter at the center of our spiritual lives, this infinite Supreme Being is of necessity immutable—incapable of change in any fashion or form. Such changelessness flows relentlessly from infinity and perfection and insures that God will remain the selfsame within himself no matter what may occur outside or beyond. Immutability, like infinity, allows of no increase or decrease within God. God's self-enclosed being is not changed by any vicissitude nor moved by freakish chance, no swaying of emotion nor nudging by passion. Such portentous claims, metaphysically based, serve to isolate God into a majestic self-enclosure of sameless-ness, a being unaffected and unaffectable by anything but its own inner and secret workings.

## The God to Whom We Pray

Bow our heads as we may to the fearsome sovereignty of such unimaginable infinity and immobile immutability, we do not have it within our religious hearts to keep faith with such sophisticated speech. It is not our philosophy but our own inner voices which urge with incessant throbbing like the beat of our own hearts that we are the creatures of the Creator-God and as such are enclosed in his being as assuredly as his own inner heart. We do not need a theology to tell us, for our Scriptures have spoken, long before theology was born, that *we count* before this God, that we the creatures make a difference to this God, that this Creator-God would not be the same without us because he has created us and shares our presence.

The God to whom we pray in our anguish and pain is not the unmoved mover of philosophy; no, the God to whom we pray is moved to heal our wounds and is affected by our painful cries. In defiance of our received philosophy and theology we have always clung, beyond argument and beyond reason, to that unquenchable conviction that the wealth and the weakness of the life we hold so fragilely offer something of inestimable worth to this Creator-God who saw that we were very good. No theology can ever take this from us, and if there were burnings at the stake today, this conviction would be well worth dying for.

Furthermore, infinity and immutability as ascribed to God in the traditional sense do violence to our estimation, not just of ourselves, but of our world and the entire cosmos, the unfathomable wealth of which we are not yet fully aware. If it were true that nothing outside of God could make a difference to God, if nothing external to God could add something to God, if human life itself could mark no change in its Creator, then we are driven to that strange impasse whereby we are forced to deny the intrinsic value of the universe and the inherent value of human life itself. Ultimately and finally the entire cosmos could be extinguished like a recalcitrant spark and the Supreme Being would remain uninvolved and unruffled by our passage. This is to assert that there is no value within the cosmos itself, there is no value within life itself, there is no value to the moral striving which provides both challenge and strength to the direction of our lives.

### Precious Before God

But once again, our hearts refuse to keep pace with our heads. No dose of philosophy, no matter how severe, can infect us to the degree that we doubt for a moment our own self-worth, or doubt the value of the moral enterprise which engages our very souls in committed moral struggle, or doubt the inexpressible value and dignity of those we love. Our unshakable faith is that we are indeed created in the image and likeness of God, and this image reflects but the surface of a value too rich and too everlasting ever to be lost by God. The sheer loveliness and grandeur of the world around us should, and in our better moments does, give us pause to wonder at the sheer beauty and awesome glory of the plain and simple fact that such marvelous things as trees and flowers and human persons exist. This is not to be romantic; this is, rather, the religious sense of the infinite value of all that is, the unexpressed but felt awareness that we are very, very precious before this God.

Need we be reminded that the Creator-God of our Scriptures can hardly be said to have the mien of a Supreme Being or an Unmoved Mover? As we chart the course of those Bible stories which are the mined gold of our religious tradition we are confronted here and now by the almost terrifying revelation that our Creator-God is a God who cares, a God who is passionately concerned about the quality of our lives, a God so involved in the comings and goings of his sons and daughters than even the hairs of their heads are numbered. The good sense of our untaught faith will not dismiss as mere metaphor those ancient stories of the God who suffers; it is this unschooled assurance like a rock in our heart of solid gold which can never be dissolved or eroded, of the suffering of this God which compels us to hold till death that dreadsome conviction: to this God nothing will be lost—not the sparrows, not the foxes, not the lilies of the field, not you or I or our least-recognized brothers and sisters.

Our spiritual life is not the struggle to escape a world denied by its Creator; it is rather the co-creation of a world fit

to be God's home. If a substance worldview could so far misguide us that we find ourselves no longer trusting our theological ears, then perhaps the time is ripe for us to rethink our
speech about God. Let us return to our Scriptures and speak
with those ancient, hallowed voices who claimed to their dying
breath that they spoke with the voice of God.

## A Fitting Language for God

Most of our language about God is something that we have
inherited, and we have received it as part and parcel of our
lives in exactly the same way that we received the human
language which we speak—from our families, from our schools,
from our churches, from our textbooks. Just as we imbibe our
human language from the social context which surrounds us
and then use it on our own to discover that it works, so also we
imbibe our theological language from our social milieu and
then proceed to use it in our prayers, our liturgies, even in our
private aspirations. But merely because a language is inherited
does not prescribe that this is the only possible language or the
only correct language. Many of us go on to learn other lan-
guages, and sometimes we feel more at home with a language
not natively our own.

In much the same way, our inherited theological language
seems to have a natural fit to it and seems to work well enough
in those places where we must use it. But even a theological
language has its alternatives. Let us seriously investigate one of
these theological alternatives which has at least the merit of
being much more ancient and much longer used in a bewildering variety of circumstances than our current theological idi-
om. Surprisingly, however, this move is neither as difficult nor
as threatening as it may first appear.

We need simply return to a religious language which has
always been available to us, the language of Scripture. At first
blush we might be tempted to claim that this language is
already more than familiar, that it is not really new at all since
it is already the common parlance of the churches. But a
moment's reflection should show us that this is not so.

Scriptural language has been for us a reserved language: reserved for particular times, special places, unique situations. We use the language of Scripture in church, in the liturgy, in prayer, in the sacraments. But for the rest of our lives—our working lives, our love-making lives, our lives of anger and despair, our lives of wasting time and simply having fun—we use or advert to scriptural language hardly at all. It is for this reason that while scriptural language has a familiar ring to our religious ear, it is quite possible that we have never used it seriously nor understood it properly, with the seriousness and commitment that it demands.

## God Is Love: The Nature of Reality

If it were possible to encapsulate the very heart of the Christian message or to lay bare the simple, solid bedrock of our faith in one single linguistic phrase, what would it be? Our answer cannot possibly be slow in coming, for Scripture has blazoned this revelation like a light to our darkness: "God is love" (1 Jn 4:8). This, I claim, is the most straightforward and most literal description of the God we worship. It bears such magnificent strength in its obviousness that any other description appears but a cheap deception. Surely we have heard this phrase quoted so often as to be tedious. Probably we have used it ourselves in moments that seemed suitable. It has a well-used and almost homely quality about it that possibly conceals its real intent.

## The Failure of Metaphor

And what is that real intent of the phrase "God is love"? Can we possibly abdicate all claims to rationality by saying that it is not meant to be literal, that, somehow, it is mere metaphor? The very seriousness of the Gospel message and the ultimate tragedy of the death of Jesus militates against such an obtuse interpretation. That "God is love" is a straightforward, literal claim, and to somehow misunderstand this is to be not merely dull of mind but, worse, dull of heart. Let us then be literal and straightforward with this claim: "God is love" means that the nature of God is love and nothing else.

## The Cosmos in the Context of the God Who Is Love

Now we can ask with a new seriousness: If the nature of God is love, what would the nature of reality be like if it were created by a God who is wholly and solely love? How would we respond to and value a cosmos and every item within it if "God is love" were the ultimate explanatory category? What would it do to us if we could recognize that all reality is the creation and reflection of a God who is completely love? How would we appreciate the human self if our only certainty were that this self is related to the God who is love? If, as we like to quote with stumbling understanding, we are created in the image and likeness of God who is love, what does this say about what we could and should become?

Not only does this illumine our intuitive perception of our own best nature, it demands that we consider the entirety of the cosmos with a newborn vision. If electrons and atoms and galaxies are also what the God who is love has allowed them to come to be, then surely it is arrogant to assert that they are mere objects and appreciable only as instruments for a few human tourists in the cosmos. This God who is love could only be related to that which is lovable, and what is lovable has value in itself and can never be written off, not even by God.

If we are willing to view the cosmos in the context of the love of God, it is quite possible that we would at last hear the voice of Scripture speaking with the seriousness with which it was intended, quite possible that "God saw that it was good" would come to mean for us what it really says. To understand the entirety of reality in the context of God who is love is to view the universe with the blessed light of the sun where previously we had been searching with a flashlight. Equally important, however, this renewed estimation of the infinite elegance of the cosmos might serve to fire anew what we always knew but could little say—the staggering size and beauty and loveliness and sheer elegance of this God whom we worship, this God who is love.

## No Foreigners in a Strange Land

And perhaps most important of all, this scripturally inspired estimation of the universe with its chaotic variety of items as somehow also the image of God who is love will do much to resolve our human existential alienation previously referred to: we humans are not the freaks of the universe, we are not foreigners in a strange land not our home. No longer are we the exception to a near-infinite expanse of cosmic reality other than ourselves. As if we had previously read with closed eyes and minds, the thought "All of creation is groaning in travail till Christ be born" suddenly arises out of its sheer poetry to assert with a straightforward clarity: we and the universe are one in the love of God. Not just ourselves, but the whole cosmos is Christed. If ever we thought that there were mystery in the cosmos, that mystery has now been compounded to infinity in the ineffable richness of the God who is love.

## To Love Is To Be in Relationship

Let us pursue this scripturally inspired lead that God is love to see what insights might come to fresh light. To begin, we need only ask what we ourselves mean when we say that we are in love. First, to be in love is to exist within a particular type of relationship. To exist within a relationship is not to be isolated or independent; it is to hold one's existence in interrelationship and interconnection with the existence of another. What would you and I be like if we never experienced the relationship of love, if we loved no one and no one ever loved us? Near despair, at least.

This is simply to point out that we are social beings and our social relationships are not mere accidents which could be done without; social relationships are the stuff out of which our self is created and has its being. To say that God is love, then, leads inevitably to the claim that God is essentially a social being. God also exists within interrelationships which are the contents of God's experience. If God is love, God is not isolated and independent but rather that One who is irretrievably bound to all in the relationship of love.

## To Love Is To Receive

Secondly, the relationship of love does not just point to something that the subject is doing out of good-heartedness or generosity or good-will. Since love is a relationship it is double-termed, that is, it takes two to love and not merely one. To be in love points, on the one hand, to my giving of the relationship, but on the other hand it points equally to the receiving of the relationship. No matter how we stretch the language, love which just goes out and never comes back to the lover is not finally love. All unrequited love soon dissipates.

To say that God is love is to say that the being of God is extended in loving relationships, but it is also to say that the being of God is constituted out of its reception of loving relationships. Only because God is love is God infallibly social; and because God is social he is infinitely receptive of the loving relationships of all the creatures.

## To Love Is To Be Involved

Finally, it is interesting to notice how many of our re-ceived definitions of love were designed to protect the infinite perfection of God. Commonly offered were definitions in this vein: love is the complete giving of self with no thought of return. It was suggested that disinterested love was the ideal type of love. Have we abdicated all claims on the real world when we say that disinterested love is even a possible meaning of the word "love"? To love means to be interested in, to share in, to be involved in the life and well-being of the other; more, it means that we are so involved because the relationship is important to us.

We love because we *want* to love, and we want to love because the richness and intensity of the relationship itself qualifies the very heart of our being and creates a feeling of selfhood unequaled by anything else we do. We are enriched and enlarged by our loving, and to deny this enrichment is to deny the very meaning of the relationship of love. We demean the God who is love by saying that God loves disinterestedly. God is interested in the quality of our experience because God receives from the richness of that quality.

It has always been claimed that God can love the saint more than the sinner, and the reason for this is simply that the saint can enrich God more in love than can the sinner. There is no mystery here unless we so create it by denying the very meaning of our loving relationships for ourselves. Love is a creative interrelationship of mutual giving and receiving, and if God is love, then God is so interrelated.

### The Scriptural God Is a Related God

Perhaps this analysis of love will give a renewed seriousness to our entire scriptural heritage. As was mentioned earlier, Scripture carries the patrimony of our religious language and we seek to speak that language meaningfully. No matter how much theology would wish to isolate God in supreme independence, the only God we know is the related God. Every possible claim that we can make of God as described for us by our Scripture is a claim about a God who is in relationship. God created the world; God called the prophets; God made a covenant with his people; God sent his Son; God saved the world—the only reliable language we have serves to emphasize that the only God we know is the God in relationships.

Again, if we are to trust those driven voices from the past, each and every relationship is of awesome importance to God. The whole theology of redemption through the Son is an everlasting testament to the value of these relationships to God. It is the essential relatedness of a social God which gives eternal value to every mustard seed, every lily, every lost sheep, including ourselves. We have not yet begun to unravel the mystery of our spiritual worth to this God of infinite love.

## As a Human Being, Who Am I?

If we hold our existence as the image of the loving God, perhaps we have here a distinctive way of ascertaining the meaning of our own selfhood. Those definitions of the *human* proffered by our various disciplines are remarkable mostly for their abstractness, and precisely because they are abstract they mean so little to us. To construe a human being as matter/ form, body/soul, matter/spirit, or rational animal speaks little, if at all, to those existential realities which are the substances of our most earthly lives—falling in love, crying out in pain, grieving at death, forgiving a hurt, responding in anger. In each of these cases we never call upon an abstraction to explain what is going on. Our language then becomes irre- trievably personal and subjective: *I* love, *I* hurt, *I* forgive, *I* am angry.

What is being pointed at here is that when we try to get some purchase on our personhood, some way of surfacing our identity into the public sphere, it is not at all natural for us to rely on abstractions or to call upon sophisticated categories. Magnet-like we are moved directly to quite ordinary speech which is totally personal. In those rare moments when we are forced to cry out in the face of a recalcitrant world: "I am a human being!" what exactly do we mean?

As a human being, who am I? Where do I begin to de- scribe myself? I can only describe myself out of my own self- experience, and so I begin. I am a striving being. I am a purposing being. I am an intending being. I am a willing being. I am a valuing being. I aim and strive and purpose and value because this is the only leverage of the self's existence in the world. We find ourselves in a vortex of relationships and the self's very existence is to achieve some not-yet-realized harmony, to bring about a state of affairs which is still in the making, to move toward a goal which would be worthwhile to possess.

## Being Is Relationship

Briefly, I am a relating being, and this vast network of relationships, like a murky tidal-pool, provides the stuff out of which and through which I experience myself as part of a world. To say that I intend, I aim, I value, I love, is simply to point out how my self is being formed out of the ever-present flow of events which constitute a universe patient of my responses and malleable to my strivings. I know myself as existing only within this active interchange of action and reaction, possibility and response, the not-yet and the coming-to-be, the complex pattern of which is my *self* now.

## Involved in Feelings

But we do not share in this relational flow of events as idle spectators. To say I strive, I intend, I purpose, I value, is to say in each case that I want something and I hold it dear. This is not neutral language at all but the intimately subjective language meant to embody how I *feel* about my world. Too long have we been misguided by the lusterless dogma that our humanness is characterized primarily by some cool and distanced rationality, as if we are truly human solely when we are thinking clearly, unencumbered by emotion.

The occasions of such clear thought in each of us are so few as to be humbling. Before, during, and after every thought we have we are already enmeshed in a pervasive flow of feeling so all-embracing that even our very rationality is but a modified form of feeling. We know that we exist, you and I, because we know that we feel. If it were possible to unravel our inner selves, in the same impossible way that we may try to unpeel the onion-skin only to find more onion-skin, we would discover that our whole selfhood is but the centering point of this ever-present, multi-toned flow of feeling of a world which not only allows us to be but constitutes our very being.

## The Primacy of Experience

Following this analysis we see that the first meaning of "to be" for us is in fact "to be experiencing." The first and final claim about our existence which must always be necessarily true is that we are experiencing beings. When we speak about our identity we are not describing first of all some abstract rationality or some disembodied principle; we are, rather, simply indicating that ongoing and multivalent interchange of experiential feeling which is charged with emotion and passion and desire. The self's feelings are the ways in which the self values its world and takes it in as part of its experience.

These value-laden feelings are the lodestone of reality; and the self is but the throbbing experiential heart which is both the cause and effect of this incessant and life-giving flow of feeling. It is for this reason that all of our personal speech—any sentence which begins with "I"—is in fact our attempt to place in the public domain how interiorly we feel about the universe and its various facts. "I want," "I intend," "I demand," "I value," "I love," are all alike, are ways of feeling about the events which surround us like air and are equally irrefusable.

## The Importance of Feelings

We must strive to bracket some of our received presuppositions here. Because of our Greek and Western minds, reinforced by the objective scientific enterprise, we tilt spontaneously toward the commonsensical bias that the key to reality is rationality. We manage to hold this strange claim while at the very same time denying rationality to any and all the objects within the universe except the human. This, upon serious reflection, gives us humans at best a tenuous hold on reality both for the reason that we do not now know what type and level of rationality might possibly exist in those hyperactive intergalactic expanses of outer space, and for the reason that our unique rationality sets us off as freaks and exceptions from the vast preponderance of reality which we call objective and non-rational.

Serious scientific and philosophical thinkers like Alfred North Whitehead and Charles Hartshorne have proposed the view that the entire network of cosmic reality is composed of experiential feeling. One beneficial result of such a view is that all of reality is somehow like unto ourselves; we and the universe are of the same stuff and essentially are about the same things, the quality and intensity of experience.

### The Emotional Quality of Engagement

Our personal verbs, then, denote our feeling-response to the influx of reality. What this amounts to, in opposition to our rational bias, is that the groundroot stuff of our lives is emotional. Liking, disliking; wanting, rejecting; loving, hating; being satisfied, being dissatisfied—what are these but our ways, not merely of responding to, but of incorporating within ourselves the plethora of felt data which comes to us in the guise of the world "out there." The only world "out there" that we know is the world that we experience *within* ourselves. Contrary to the coolest heads of our day, we never manage to think objectively and dispassionately or with calm detachment. We think about things because we are involved with them, they mean something to us, we are interested in or concerned about them; it is precisely this involvement, interest and concern which is clear and irrefutable evidence that we are in no way neutral but, rather, personally *engaged.*

The full meaning of this personal engagement lies not in some rational abstraction, but in the quality and intensity of the emotional feelings engendered. It should strike us that we are the victims of some tawdry paradise if the most we could do would be to stand over against reality in a posture of objectivity and neutrality and uninvolvement. Dare we say out loud something that has probably been lurking deep within us, even before we ever went to school to learn differently—that the world is alive around us and we are passionately involved with it, and the only relationships we care about are those fraught with passion and emotion and intensity?

What would it be, indeed, to be alive without passion? It is the passion of our feeling and the passionate involvement with those relationships creative of our feeling which gives the quality and tone to our lives. Our sincerest of strivings and most heartfelt of struggles is always the fierce desire for some intensity, depth and fullness of feeling. Are we afraid to admit that it is the vehement passion of our wanting, of our loving, of our thinking even, which generates the quality and value and intensity of the only thing we can truly call our own—our own experiencing? A life characterized by dispassionate objectivity, emotional uninvolvement and neutral value would, as our language rightly says, be *impersonal*—depersonalized and stripped of any human quality. That this should be set out as the intellectual ideal is sad tribute, perhaps, not to the fact that we were misguided, but that we were too faint of heart to commit ourselves to a reality which is as constant as gravity but whose passionate interchange might be a consuming fire.

## Our Body Is Our Home

Such a line of thought leads to the inexorable conclusion that the home of the self is within the body and the home of the body is within the world. Deep within we have always known this, but a dualistic worldview has dominated by its insistence that our real home is with the spirit in some other realm. We are, indeed, inspirited matter, but as the Scriptures so rightly insist, this is a living unity and not some recalcitrant union of two separate principles.

The best and highest of our thinking, no matter how abstract or how spiritual, is made possible by the functionings of this marvelously coordinated body, and this same thinking is triggered by the relationships of this body to a real world. The only life we know is life in this flesh, with these needs, these passions, these possibilities. No matter how fondly we may speak of the disembodied spiritual life in heaven, do we really know what we are talking about, and if we did, would we really want it?

## Our Body Is Our World

The habitat of the body is the world. It is not just the case, however, that the body is *in* the world; rather, the body *is* the world for the self. Because we are accustomed to think in terms of a world of objects, we have objective language about the body: its size, weight, shape, position. But if we are more careful and more honest, we must admit that there is no conceivable way to define that line of demarcation where the body stops and the world begins. Where would we divide our body from the world? Do we think we can separate our bodies from the world at the soles of our feet? What about the air which we take in to sustain life, the food that enters and becomes a part of us, the gravity which holds us to the surface of the earth, the rays of the sun which keep the earth and these bodies warm enough to survive? The massive and complex relationships of a cosmos extending beyond our ken all contrive to work together to make it possible for this matter, our body, to be enlivened. Our bodies are simply matter informed by this mysterious and gracious interchange, and as such these bodies *are* the world for us.

## Incarnation: God's World Is the Flesh

Once again, the message of the incarnation should be a quiet but firm testimony to the rightness of this view. It is not so much that the Word entered into the world; it is rather that the Word *became flesh*. However much we may wish to protect the dignity and abstract purity of the Godhead, this much at least we are permitted to say: in the incarnation, Jesus in his flesh took the world as part of himself. His body did not serve as some removable overcoat for a masquerading divinity on tour throughout the world. The world quite literally became the body of God. Ever afterward we have no right to dismiss this world as some second-rate practice field for the real life in heaven. The incarnation states that there is no practice and nothing is second-rate; life in this world is the life of the Godhead.

The thrust of this argument is to make us aware, possibly for the first time, of the inherent and undeniable value of life in our concrete daily living, life in these bodies, life in this world. Our embodied lives are the context and the stuff of our spiritual journey. And as mentioned earlier, the point of the journey is not the destination but the quality of the traveling. The journey of these embodied selves is the passionate struggle to seek out the deepest qualities of life itself, to be challenged by commitment and seek after ideals which constantly lure us away from our standing pat or from our lack of daring. It is the struggle to taste of life so fully that we begin to have an inkling of that fullness of life which is the Godhead. We have been told that not the lukewarm but the passionate will find their God.

Any spirituality which would denigrate our bodies as "prison houses" or dismiss our appetites as "lower" or distance us from our passions as untrustworthy and ill-befitting a higher kingdom is a spirituality which has refused to be serious about the incarnation and has misunderstood the resurrection. We live in these bodies, in this flesh, and this is where we work out our salvation. Spirituality is not for some privileged elite. Spirituality, if we hear Jesus rightly, is for everyone, for each of us in all circumstances and in every condition of our life.

The concern of spirituality is with the fullness of life, and the only life we know is fleshly and earthly and sensual. This is the stuff of spirituality and is available to every human person without exception. The primary problem for spirituality is the concern for wholeness, integrity, and unity, and such qualities can only be derived from the experienced relationships of our involvement with life and engagement with the world. We achieve wholeness by utilizing to the fullest the stuff of our experience, rather than by denying or diminishing it.

Jesus the Incarnate Word had many good words aimed at cultivating the beauties of life in this world. If we are somehow shocked by Jesus' obvious this-worldly love, we have the pale consolation of knowing that the antagonists of his own day were similarly shocked. He was accused of drinking wine and enjoying dinners; he was faulted for being rather casual with fasting and penance. His words expressed during the agony in the garden are perhaps the most tender and passionate testimony of how dearly he loved this life and how unwilling he was to leave this world. The resurrection is striking witness that his world-loyalty was not misplaced.

### A Creation of Love

Let us return for a moment to a question asked earlier: If God is love, then what would the creation of a God of love be like? The one unique item of creation which we know with intuitive intimacy is our own self. If after all our humanness consists in our emotional engagement with felt relationships, then perhaps it will become apparent why "love" has always perdured as one of the dominant words in our language, both secular and religious. For our loving is our taking in of proffered relationships, feeling them in the value-intensity which they carry from the giver, allowing them to constitute at least part of our selfhood.

We are familiar with the truism that "to love is to become the other," but were we bold enough to see its literal truth? To love is to receive and take in the feelings of the other, to feel them as one's own feelings, to be shaped in one's very being by this passionate impress of the other. While we live amid a seemingly random and confusing variety of relationships, we inevitably single out that mode and quality of relationship which is for us most creative and most transforming—and we name this relationship love. With intuitive wisdom we realize that love is the most life-enhancing quality of the self's experience, the root of its engagement and the heart of its passion.

In answer to our opening question about the nature of

creation, God could only create things which are lovely and lovable, only things which are good, as the Scriptures insist. If the spiritual journey has been described as the movement from darkness to light, perhaps this is because we live with eyes dimmed by objectivity and hearts grown lukewarm in their neutrality so that we can no longer taste and see, as Jesus instructs, the intrinsic loveliness of every item of the created order, beginning with ourselves, moving through our bodies, and reaching out to embrace all the cosmos.

### Eyes to See

How often does the voice of the Gospel repeat, like a patient schoolteacher, "For those who have eyes, let them see." What is there for us to see except the world which lies before our eyes? If we look at mere objects, then we miss the creative beauty which is the gracious rain for our parched souls. It is by no accident that Jesus pointed out the sparrows and the mustard seed and the lilies of the field almost as if we had never seen them before. To our shame, we have never seen them, and hence not valued them, as he has.

The centrality of love as promulgated in our Christian message cannot be dismissed as mere poetry. It is the most profound attempt to describe the very essence of the Godhead and, consequently, the essence of whatever God has created. Perhaps it is because we love so badly and so poorly that we readily search out a cheap substitute which would not demand so much passion from our souls. We would much prefer to purchase our eternal guarantee through law, through obedience, through the fulfilling of obligations. But to all of this cheap grace Jesus says no. He points down the road and bids us to go and find our neighbor—for what reason other than to embrace in love? Our loving must be the consuming passion of our lives. And when we do it, then only will we know why we do it. Then only will we know that nothing else is worth doing. But, if we believe Jesus, we will be well on the path to becoming godly, since God is love.

## God Is Love: Person to Person

Throughout this chapter we have been laying down the broad outlines of a worldview which differs remarkably from our traditional dualistic substance worldview. The fundamental evidence for this alternative vision resides in a serious appropriation of our biblical heritage. However, our own intuitive grasp of the meaning and value of our own self-experience also carries some evidential weight. Our vision must serve to illumine who we concretely are rather than delineate some idealized state beyond our present experience. It is with this in mind that I wish to develop one final concept in the light of the preceding exposition.

We have shown previously that a dualistic worldview portrays the Supreme Being as infinite and immutable. One of the implications of this view is that the very unchangeability of God demands that nothing outside of God can affect God or cause a change in God. But it should be obvious that this divine unaffectability—the fact that God cannot be affected by anything whatsoever—is a compliment gone awry. It is suggested that this view of immutability is misguided because the bedrock of our faith is the Gospel claim that God is love. Let us look at this issue more closely.

## The Language of Persons

The deepest wisdom in our long tradition has always insisted that God is finally ineffable—that is, the perfection of the being of God is somehow utterly beyond our speaking and our knowing. Nonetheless, God is so very important to our very being that the prophets and the mystics and the saints have always been driven to speak about the One who could not be described. Fully aware that their language was crippled and broken, an instrument too rough and crude to perform so fine a task, they nevertheless seized upon the only portion of the language which could in any way suitably express the ineffability of their God. What they chose was the language of *persons.*

With a sageness surprising in its correctness these early

spiritual heroes seized upon the ineradicable intuition: whatever God is like, God is most like a person. Thus with no apologetic explanation whatsoever, these mystics who inspired our Scriptures describe God and God's relationships with the world in a language which derives every drop of its meaning from human personal interchange. Are we so unreflective as to miss completely the plain fact that our sincerest religious language, our language of prayer, is incxorably the language of persons speaking to another person? And so when we peruse our Scripture and our tradition it is no amazement to us that we discover this lengthening list of personal verbs: God intends, God plans, God wants, God decides, God pleads, God forgives, God loves. These activities are proper only to persons such as ourselves. But if we are serious about this language, and in our prayer we are indeed serious, then we are led to some revealing implications.

## Personal Language Is Relational

The first implication of the language of persons is that all of these personal activities denote a relationship outside of and beyond the subject. If God does "intend," then there is a state of affairs which is not yet actualized and God is somehow involved in its actualization. If God "wants," then there is a state of affairs, for example, my salvation and your salvation, which is not yet actual and God has something at stake in seeing it actualized. If God "decides," then there are real choices and God is selecting among alternatives. And, obviously, if God "loves," this means that part of his present experience is modified by this relationship to someone other than himself. If God "creates," this means that God now exists in relationship to a universe whereas previously God existed in isolation. In brief, since personal activities are the way in which we relate to a world not ourselves and thus make it a coherent part of our own experience, these personal activities on the part of God denote those interrelational activities whereby God constitutes his present experience through relationships with persons and things outside of himself.

### God Is Affected

A second implication which is but a necessary outflow of the first is that all of these relationships demand a change in God. If God "wills" that something take place, it means that it makes a difference to God whether or not this is the case. If God is literally immutable, then no change can take place within God and it makes no difference what occurs outside of God. But our religious language denies this; in fact, it claims repeatedly that everything makes a difference to God. Let us not overlook too lightly the religious language of God calling and pleading and demanding the righteousness of his creatures. It is unmistakable that God is involved in all that is going on precisely because every bit of it makes a difference to God. Because God is very literally affected by everything that is, God is passionately involved in bringing about the perfection of all that is.

### What Does God Have at Stake in the Universe?

Finally, none of this personal language could possibly have any meaning or make any clear sense unless God experiences. Since experience is created out of the network of relationships to reality, and since God is that One infallibly related to everything that is, then it follows that God has the widest, the richest, the deepest experience of all. Traditional theology has always had a difficult and devious time trying to explain why an infinitely perfect and self-sufficient God would create a world outside of himself. I would suggest that the theory that God created the world for his own glory is a sort of not-so-crude version of a cosmic cheering section, and the theory that the infinity of God's love "overflowed" gets lost in a metaphor impossible on its own terms.

Therefore the question is: What does God have at stake in the universe? Why would the universe, and we ourselves, make any difference to God? The answer that Scripture propounds and which our religious intuition affirms is that God has at stake the quality of his own experience. Too long has theology neutralized God, deeming him so independent and self-sufficient that nothing could disturb this infinite tranquility. If the God of Scripture is anything, he surely is not the tranquil one. Prophet after saint after mystic drive home the point that the God of our worship is the God passionately involved in the affairs of his creatures. And the sole justifying reason for this involvement is the quality of that very passion. What God has at stake in the universe is the quality of his own experience. Dare we be so obtuse as to think that the incarnation and the redemption made no difference to God?

### The Experience of God: Love

But if God is God, what is the quality of experience that would make a difference? What, briefly put, is God doing? The answer should be to us a source of salvific joy: God is the infinite and perfect lover. Whatever God is about, God is about the relationship of loving. And since the love-relation is determined in equal part by the lover and the beloved, you and I have an everlasting and immeasurable impact on the love of God. The very passion of the involvement of God in human affairs testified by the prophets bespeaks the thirst of God for an intensity of experience not dependent on his will alone.

Need we note that the language of Scripture is *cooperation:* God calls, we respond; God asks, we answer; God commands, we choose to obey; God pleads, we are moved; God loves, we love in return. This is not the language of coercion and force; it is the language of concern, respect, desire and love. In our wildest dreams could we venture to express how important we are to God? Just as you and I create the quality of each other's experience through our gracious relationships of love, so also the depth of our being is created out of the quality of God's love, and this loveliness of ours can now be returned as gracious gift to the eternally loving One.

What we call our spiritual lives is simply an awareness of the importance of ourselves, an awareness that the qualitative intensity of our experiencing, which is the only thing we can achieve for ourselves, is at the same time the very thing we achieve for God. Perhaps the infinity of God is meant to point to God's infinite and inexhaustible capacity for experience. The power of God's loving will never be exhausted, and God's reception of our loving will never reach satiety. Rightly we stand in awe, mostly in awe at the majesty of our own selves.

### Genesis: The Clue to the Universe Is Personal

The religious import of this view is that we can look back at those opening scenes of Genesis and discern the most important of revelations: the clue to the universe—not just to us but to everything that is—is *personal.* The origin and source, the ground and end, of all that is, is personal. The origin and end of our supremely valuable human lives is personal. The marvelous fact is that we, inspirited flesh that we are, are not merely in accord with the nature of God; we are also in accord with the nature of the very universe. Whatever God creates will reflect what is of supreme value in God, namely, the personal.

It is for this reason that the entire cosmos, as Paul insists, is the building up of the body of Christ, the infinite wealth of God's experience. We are like the origin and source and end of all in the very depths of our being so that our sincerest aspirations and most integral strivings are in accord with that One who holds all together.

In our prayer we do not genuflect to the Unmoved Mover, nor do we invoke the Uncaused Cause. No, our prayer is a personal plea addressed always and only to another Person. And we will hold in faith till death the conviction that drives our lives—this Other, the Thou of our prayers, feels our pain, sympathizes with our suffering, grieves at our loss, enjoys our pleasure. No theology can ever deprive us of that. This is our faith: God is love.

### Selected Readings

A simple but readable presentation of this way of shaping our notion of God can be found in *Modeling God: Religious*

*Education for Tomorrow,* by Gloria Durka and Joanmarie Smith (New York: Paulist Press, 1976).

Norman Pittenger has written several popular books centering on the notion that God is love. He is especially good at working out the implications of this central theme for the entire Christian life. See, for example, *The Lure of Divine Love* (New York: The Pilgrim Press, 1979).

In Sam Keen's *To a Dancing God,* Chapter Five, "The Importance of Being Carnal," is a theological expression of the importance of the body for our religious life and experience.

Since our language about God is meant to be symbolic, it will function best when it draws the responses of our total being into the wealth of graciousness which is the supporting environment of our lives. A captivating account of the awesome power of transcendent symbols is given by Theodore Roszak in *Where the Wasteland Ends,* Chapter Ten, "Uncaging Skylarks: The Meaning of Transcendent Symbols."

John Cobb, Jr. offers a popular but compelling account of the theological and religious need for a more relational and experiential view of God than is usually available in the Scholastic tradition in *God and the World* (Philadelphia: Westminster Press, 1969).

*Scripture Reading*
The Gospel of John Chapter 17

# 4

# What Is God For?
# Life in Abundance

Our traditional view of God has caused some difficulty in trying to explain what God was doing within himself before the creation of the world. I do not wish this to appear facetious. But the problem arises because the only self-activity with which you and I are intimately familiar is the self-experience engendered out of the relationships flowing from outside ourselves. Our experience is an engagement with a throbbing world.

If, by impossible hypothesis, we could conceive of ourselves totally separated from the world and thoroughly shut off from our own bodies, what could our concrete experience possibly be? What we would have here would be a vacuum, and no experience would be possible. We are trying to pose the same question of God in isolation from a cosmos. A partial answer is already suggested in the assuring fact that the only God of whom we know is the Creator-God who exists with a cosmos. In this section I wish to explore some of the notions introduced in the previous chapter to test their worthiness, as religious notions. Subsequently I will apply these same concepts to our spiritual life.

We have spoken of the scriptural intuition which does not blush to speak about the experience of God, and we have tried to lay out the requirements of experience in the context of relationships. However, in spite of our central claim that God is love, and that love is only understandable as a form of

94

experience, it is still required that we offer some justification of why this should be so. This is the project at hand.

## The Final End: What Is Love For?

To come to an understanding of why the category of experience should be the comprehensive description for the illumination of the basic nature, not merely of ourselves, but also of God, we can approach experience with the question of the final end. The final end is that purpose or goal which organizes and makes sense out of all the sub-acts and items which contribute to achieving that end which is the one that the series aims to achieve.

Of any specific activity, for example, we can ask the question: What is that activity for? If a reason for the activity can be offered, then the activity is instrumental for the achieving of some further goal, and is not final in itself. If at some point we arrive at the answer: "This activity is not for anything else at all; it is simply for itself," then we have located a final end.

## Three Models: Experience, Love, Life

Quite simply, the final end explains what a whole cluster of activities is all about. Thus, if we propose experience as a primary category, we can ask the question: What is experience *for?* The same question, otherwise put, is: *Why experience?* What we seek here is to perceive why it should be the case that we are experiencing beings rather than non-experiencing beings. By the same token we seek to discover why it is more proper to say that God experiences than to say that God does not experience.

## Why Experience?

Before suggesting a way to approach an answer, let us lay out a cluster of models which all function exactly the same way. Each of these pertains to something which is intimate and essential to our being, and so the question is worth asking. We have already stressed the importance of love as a defining quality of our life. We can, however, ask the same question: What is love *for? Why love?* Why should it be the case that loving is better than non-loving? Even if God is love, why should this be the case?

Another model for this question concerns life. Our claim is that we are living beings, that life is important. What, then, is life *for? Why live?* Why should there be life rather than non-life?

## What Is Love For?

If each of us were to examine our interior life in order to discover the motivations which inspire our supreme values, what kind of answer would we give to this strange-sounding question: *What is love for?* The very strangeness of the question is a healthy hint that our basic intuition is correct—to this question there is no answer. Our very attempt to provide an answer causes nothing but problems.

We could claim, for example, that we love because by loving we are doing the will of God. Or we could say that by our loving we are getting to heaven, or, perhaps, by our loving we are saving our souls. Or it would be possible to think that our loving is of service to our neighbors. Such answers, as plausible as they may sound and perhaps correct answers in terms of our catechism, are sorely misguided and eventually destructive in their consequences. Why should this be so?

Notice that in any question of the form "What is something for?" the reason offered actually provides the instrumentality for achieving something else. For example, to the question "What is food for?" the answer might be, "To sustain the life of the body." Food then is in the service of something beyond itself, namely, bodily life, and food serves as the instrument for achieving an end beyond food itself.

Following this way of analyzing such questions, to give an answer to "What is love for?" would indicate that love is subservient to something else, or that the activity of loving is in the service of some end higher than loving.

## Love Is for Nothing

We should not be needlessly shocked or surprised at the straightforward obviousness of the only answer that can possibly do full justice to all that we mean by love. *What is love for?* The only possible answer is: love is *for nothing.* What could this possibly mean, since surely we love for definite and sincere reasons. Quite simply, this reality that we call love, this experiential quality and relational interchange, this giving and receiving of engaged selves—however we choose to describe love, the act of loving is done for nothing outside of itself. We love simply for the sake of loving, for nothing else and for no other reason.

Why do we love another person? Simply for the sake of loving that person. We do not love another because God commanded it; we do not love another in order to get to heaven. If either of these were the motive for our loving, then we would be using our love to achieve something else and love would not be the final end of our activity. To use love to achieve something other than love is surely the sourest of perversions. To use love to achieve something other than love is not merely to demean; it is to pervert the deepest meaning of love. Our entire integrity rests on the plain fact that we love for the sake of loving, and for nothing else.

The act of loving and the relationship of loving is its very own reason. We do not love others, for example, in order to get grace. To take this view would be to import a reason outside of the relationship of loving to justify why we are loving; and if this were the case, then we would not really be loving the other but rather using the other as a stepping-stone to our own grace. To love another person for the sake of some reward is to prostitute not merely the meaning of love, but the other person as well.

## Love Is for the Sake of Loving

To state this point positively, the act of loving is its very own reason. There is neither on earth nor in heaven a reason outside of the relationship of loving to justify or explain the activity of loving. Loving makes sense completely in and of itself. The very quality of the relationship of loving, the intensity of the personal interchange and the generation of a heightened self and a magnified other—these are the qualities which constitute love, explain love and serve as the reasons for loving. In this quite straightforward sense, love is its own reason. Perhaps this case is best made only to those who have lost themselves in love, who have been consumed by its passion and fulfilled by its intensity. If asked why they love they would give no reasons; they would simply point to themselves and say, "Look at me."

In evidence of this view, we need but reflect for a moment on the love-relationships of Jesus as alluded to in the Gospels. His pain and hurt at the death of Lazarus was not because Lazarus had gone to hell; it was rather the expression of the agony of the loss of a dear and precious friend. His love for Mary Magdalene was not designed to be instrumental for her salvation; rather, it was his love for her unique person which allowed her beauty and goodness to emerge. His tender cry to Peter "Do you really love me?" was a plea for the only relationship which fueled his passionate life. His insistent injunction, "Love one another as I have loved you," is never even remotely linked to a reward. To love one another as Jesus has loved us is to take on the life, and the death of Jesus. The only reward we need know is the loving and godly passion of our existence.

## To Love Is To Receive

Earlier on we alluded to the prevalent notion that love is somehow the complete giving of self with no thought of reward. This is both dangerous and self-defeating. But it was felt that love was somehow selfishly tainted if the lover were to receive some increment from this self-gift. If love were some sort of external and objective action like pouring a glass of water, putting a dollar in the hand of a beggar, or striking the oppressor, then possibly the agent could be selfless in this activity, though I doubt it. But more to the point, the very concept of loving demands on the one hand a deeply personal self-giving, self-surrender and self-forgetfulness in the interest of the other. On the other hand, if it be love and not some cheap surrogate, sacred or profane, then it of necessity requires a passivity, a receiving of and being influenced by the other. To define love in terms of what I do for or to the other is blatantly egotistical and we should struggle mightily against such profanation.

Love is to be defined also in terms of what happens to me, the lover—how I am affected at my deepest core and changed irrevocably. Why are we so fearful of pronouncing this bold truth: we love because it is the best thing we can do; we love because, to be our true selves, we can do no other. Let us forego the crippling delusion that we can love dispassionately and objectively; let us surrender the misleading half-truth that true love is selfless.

Our teeth as well as our sensibilities should be set on edge at such woeful abuse of language. To love is to be self-involved; to love is to be passionately related; to love is to be self-transformed; to love is to achieve a depth of satisfaction unparalleled by any other human activity. To put this in its most common terms, we love because we like it; we love because we enjoy it; we love because we personally get something out of it.

This is not to reduce our loving to a justified selfishness; it is, rather, simply to draw attention to something we have already experienced. Our own experience will bear witness to the fact that our most tender, compassionate and self-giving love, in the very face of its awesome demands and call to sacrifice and selflessness, is at the same time the most ennobling and enriching of our experience.

We find ourselves enlarged and strengthened, made stronger and more secure, challenged and affirmed by the very selfless quality of our outgoing relationship to the other. We touch here upon the very mystery of our own and of God's existence: our very giving is also a receiving, and our very loving is also a noble self-enhancement. Because the love relationship is necessarily self-involving, we are immeasurably enriched by our self-gift.

When we touch another physically, we also are touched. When we kiss another, we also are kissed. When we say "I love you" to another, we feel the power of our own deep experience coming to expression. When we merely gaze upon the one we love, our eyes are filled with a beauty which comes to us as gift. We find that we are so much a part of the one we love that it becomes impossible to sort out our feelings as given or received.

There need be no scandal at this seemingly contrary notion that our loving makes us feel good or gives us pleasure or satisfies us. Are we so alien to our own human condition that we earnestly believe that the quality of our humanity is best sustained by the surrender of pleasure, of joy, of intensity, of satisfaction? It takes no master of depth-psychology to trumpet this truth which is already in the pulse of our life's blood: we act only in behalf of those motives which give us some satisfaction. There is no "selfless" motive. We are inexorably self-involved in everything we do.

To put this point in the context of love, the question becomes: How deeply are we willing to involve the self, to what degree will we allow the totality of our being to be taken into a relationship, how far will we let ourselves be enlarged by the living reception of another? Let us be humble enough to face this simple but gracious truth: we in our loving are probably changed more and to a greater degree than is the one we love.

## To Love Is To Live Abundantly

If we wish to think otherwise, the echoes of the Gospels should haunt us and deny us rest. The promise of abundant life is linked inseparably with the injunction to love. To love is to be alive; to love humanly is to be alive in the most humane fashion. These are not two things, but one. Hence we love, finally, because it is fulfilling, it is growthful, it is energizing, it is creative, it is enriching. In his life and in his death Jesus has disclosed what all eyes should see: we are redeemed by the healing properties of love. And this surely constitutes our redemption in the most spiritual sense of the word: in our relationship to others in love, we move from an old self to be renewed; in our relationship to God in love, we shuck off the mean impediments of selfishness to become godly, for God is love.

## What Is Experience For?

Following this same model we can ask: What is experience *for?* Only the selfsame answer will do: experience is *for nothing.* Again, we cannot use our experiencing to achieve something else, something outside of experiencing. Our experience is for the sake of the experience itself. We do not undergo experiences for the sake of rewards, for the sake of heaven, for the sake of obedience. Experience cannot be utilized for an ulterior end. We are experiencing beings because experience contains its own explanation and its own justification. For what we mean by our experience is the attempt to organize our manifold feelings into some harmonious whole, to subsume our relationships into some structure of completeness, to achieve some level of intensity by our incorporation of the connections of the universe into our own being.

Our first meaning of experience, then, is our *self*-experience as we quite literally create the self out of the feeling-datum bestowed by our bodies, by other selves, by the physical world, by God. The end of experience, therefore, is simply the felt and passionate qualities of whatever is contained in our experiencing. And how do we in our interiority define our deepest quest? No philosophy need instruct us that what we seek is the intensity of our self-experience: experience in its fullness, in its richness, in its passionate intensity, and in its gracious gift of self-satisfaction.

A quick look at our very ordinary choices will highlight

this matter much more concretely. Our enjoyment of food is our savoring of the peculiar pleasure of tasting and eating; rarely do we enjoy eating with explicit thoughts of other effects of food on the body. We enjoy the sunshine on our skin for this special good feeling. We enjoy being in the company of our good friends because their presence before us brings a special quality to all of our feelings. The most casual of our concrete choices are aimed at making us feel whole and satisfied.

With this in mind, we pay new heed to the repeated urging of Jesus: "*Consider* the birds of the air; *consider* the mustard seed; *consider* the lilies of the field." Even my prosaic and unimaginative dictionary instructs me that "to consider" means to regard or treat with attention and solicitude. Do we not have here an insight into the wellsprings of the depths of Jesus' experience—a tender and passionate solicitude for the ordinary, the commonplace, the earthly? The qualities of his experience were shaped by this familiar but loving relationship to the multifariousness of the world itself.

It need take but a moment's reflection to realize that what we previously described as love is but a qualitative mode of experiencing. Experience is the more general category, and love but one of the specific modes. In our human ways of speaking and feeling we have fastened with instinctive rightness on the primacy of loving as the unparalleled model and matchless paradigm of what the ideal fullness of experience should be like. But notice the incomparable effect if we but pay heed: the fullness of our experience in loving is not something that must be deferred to another life or another realm. What we do here is no fugitive version of what we will do in heaven. We do it here, perhaps imperfectly and incompletely and lamely, or we will never do it at all.

The love of God is not a reward that is held like some prize for those lucky ones who have justified their lives by a host of actions that can have little to do with love—laws and obligations, rules and regulations. The loving of God everlastingly begins with the loving of God here and now. This is a fearsome truth, and perhaps we would have our security of reward measured by some more objective means. It is with heartrending reluctance that we give up the idea that salvation is something which comes to us from the outside. "Change your heart" are the opening words of the good news of Jesus; turn within and take your experience and your destiny into your own hands. Of all things in this life, the loving of God and of neighbor is not something that can be done for us by another. We learn to love or we die. We experience in the mode of loving simply because there is nothing else of such fantastic worth that we can do.

## What Is Life For?

Our third model, not surprisingly, follows along exactly the same lines. What is *life for?* Why live? Obvious by now should be the inadequacy of positing something outside of or beyond life to give meaning to life. Life quite literally is *for nothing.* In the words of what appears to be a cliché: life is for the living. We do not live for an afterlife; we do not exist here for the sake of a hereafter; we do not live naturally because we wish to be supernatural. We expend our lives here and now for the very qualities of that life, which at any given moment is the comprehensive fullness of our experiencing.

To focus in this fashion on the present satisfaction of our experience is not to deny the reality of our future life with God. The Gospel term of our life with God is not "immortality" nor is it "afterlife"; our Gospel term is, significantly, "resurrection." Since our only clue to resurrection is the evidence of Jesus himself, we must take our hints from here.

What is striking in the resurrection scenes of the Gospel is precisely the accent on the flesh-and-blood presence of the risen Christ. He journeys with his friends, allows his body to be probed for proof of its fleshly presence, breaks bread with his disciples and even has breakfast with them. Have we ever noticed how many of the resurrection stories are also eating scenes which serve to highlight the physical reality of the risen Jesus? The meaning of the resurrection does not seem to indicate a transformation into a completely spiritual type of

existence; it emphasizes rather the full blossoming of our present embodied spirits into a deeper and richer presence. Thus it
is that the qualities we have fashioned of our own selves are
the very qualities that are deepened and enriched. In this
sense, it is the self which we fashion now that is the only self
available for life with God. We also will be recognized by the
wounds and scars from this life.

### The Reward for Life

The only conceivable reward for our life is the satisfaction
of a life well lived. How do we go about justifying our lives?
We justify them in terms of the things we wholeheartedly
strive after, those things we commit ourselves to without reser-
vation, those things we take as supremely valuable. And we
justify ourselves in terms of these because it is such values
which give passion to our striving, intensity to our commitment, satisfaction, if not to our achievement, then to the
rightness of the struggle itself. If we feel passionately and
intensely about such things, then indeed we know there is
meaning in our life, there is value to what we do. If we wish to
justify our lives, we need not, as the worldly powers endlessly
insist, point to an accumulation of achievements like dollars in
a bank. Each one of us must but point to oneself and say: I have
lived with passion, I have lived with intensity, I have lived
with restless satisfaction; I have served the cause of life.

If the end of life is the enhancement of life itself, then the
bold of heart are inspired to risk their security and safety and
timidity to strike out in the only cause worthwhile, the cause of
life itself. Life in its heights, in its depths, in its breadth, of
which Paul speaks in lyrical flight, life in its richness and
fullness—this is the seeking after the abundance which is the
only reward the faithful need ever know. We dare never
forget the painful fact that the Gospels are addressed to fallen
and fractured human beings. The weight of our sin is that we
manage to sully the most lovely things we touch. We have
defiled life and defaced love. But the Gospel whispers urgently
to those few who are restless with the disease of brokenness,

those who will offer their imperfect and unfinished selves as balm to the wounds of disruption, as life to those who can see only death. The insistent news of goodness is: the healing is in the living; salvation lies in love.

## Resurrection: Witness to Life

The resurrection of Jesus as Christ is surely the most sublime symbol of life, and this alone explains why we are intuitively and irrevocably committed to the promise of the Gospels. The resurrection proclaims in the plainest and yet in the most striking of symbols: the end of life is the fullness of life. The sinful ones are those who are satisfied with the diminution of life, life narrowed and constricted, life starved or tortured, life demeaned to mere survival by lack of vision. The sinful ones are those who sit and wait, those who refuse to believe that life could be better for all if we would make it so, those too dull of heart to see that a life bereft of love can only lead to death. Let the dead bury their own dead, the Gospel tells us; life can only serve life.

The Gospel is history's most gracious and sustained plea of protest against the forces of death. No wonder that we esteem it as the Word of God. The end of life is the fullness of life, for me, for you, for all of us together sharing common blood in the body of Christ.

## To Pledge One's Heart

It is not by mean chance that the size of our lives can be measured by the size of our commitments. We are committed to those things in which we believe unwaveringly and with passion. The word "belief" has perhaps fallen on hard times, but I use it in its most original sense, that of the Latin *credo* and the Germanic *belieben*—to pledge one's heart, to give one's loyalty, to give the heart over to. We give our hearts only to what we love—not merely to possess, but in the very possession to be transformed into the image of what we seek with all our heart. It should be no secret to those who read the Gospel that those who dare commit themselves and give their hearts to the cause of life are the blessed ones who taste the abundance of life. For them, indeed, the burden is light.

By what strange obduracy do we refuse to recognize that the blessed ones of the Beatitudes are not expending their efforts on some deferred value; no, they are made happy here, happy now. They experience the abundance of life, we are assured, because they are willing to spend themselves to the death in the cause of life. So it is that our commitments are simply the concrete expression of our love, and our love is the willingness to share in life.

### God Is for Nothing

Since we are setting out the path of our spiritual journey, let us pursue this line of questioning one step further. Admittedly this next question is not ordinarily asked in such blunt terms; it should be asked, however, since a false answer will have tragic results, spiritually devastating. A new question then: *What is God for?* We might phrase the question less crudely in an alternate form: What is the function of God in our lives? The first question—What is God for?—is wrongly asked if it misguides us into thinking that there could conceivably be an answer.

But beyond a doubt there are many who do attempt to give an answer, if not conceptually, then at least in the practice of their lives. Perhaps out of a misplaced sense of piety we think that we should have an answer at the ready to justify our almost casual use of the divinity. But notice the insidious turn involved here. If the response is: God is for salvation, or: God is for the supernatural life, or: God is for heaven, or: God is for grace—in each case there is invoked a laudable desire and a praiseworthy ideal.

If I do indeed look upon God as somehow instrumental in achieving my salvation, then implicitly or explicitly I may attempt to *use* God to achieve my salvation. If I think that God is for the securing of sanctifying grace, then I may attempt to use God so that grace will be secured for me. If heresy exists, perhaps it is here. If I attempt to *use* God for the achieving of anything, no matter how spiritual or lofty, then I am making of God an instrument for the attainment of something else. I am making of God a means—God who is always and forever the final end, but never the means nor the instrument to achieve anything further. Expressed this bluntly, the crassness of this approach should be evident. To make of God an instrument, even for the most sublime of motives, is to abuse God and demean ourselves.

What must be seriously taken to heart in our religious quest is the fundamental claim of our faith: God is for us the final and ultimate end, always and only the end, and hence cannot be used as an instrument to anything else, not even our own good or our own salvation. We achieve a life of union with God only by loving God, and to love God means to commit ourselves to him and to his interest with wholeness and sincerity of heart. We do not *receive* salvation for this; rather, our living in love of God *is* the whole of our salvation, for then we have freely chosen to become what God has called us to be—in love with God and all else in him.

## The Love of God Can Only Be Enjoyed

Late in the fourth century St. Augustine already saw how viciously the invocation of the divinity could be used for the basest of motives. In Latin, Augustine made the distinction between *uti* and *frui.* From *uti* we derive the English form to *utilize;* and from *frui* we can hear the root of the English *fruition.* Augustine was firm in his conviction that we cannot *uti* God; we can only *enjoy* God. This is but a formulaic way of asserting that God cannot be used for anything; the God who is love can only be related to in love. Everything that we perceive of God, everything of God that touches our life, every influence of God that triggers our spiritual quest is but the relationship of love. And the only thing that we can humanly do in the face of such love is to respond in love.

In our loving of God we are sanctified, we are purified, we are challenged, we are made whole; we are shown naked in

our frailty and ugly in our sin, but we are taken from death to
life. No single one of these things is an end which comes to us
after we have loved; none of them is superadded as a sort of
extra bonus to a loving relationship. Each of these things and
all of them together are the fullest meaning of what it means
to be loving.

We love God *for the sake of loving God*, because this is
the best and finest thing we can do. In our loving we find
ourselves enriched and ennobled, affirmed and healed. It
should not be our own welfare that primarily motivates our
loving; rather, it is the very loveliness of God which attracts us
and lures us to give ourselves to a relationship whose mysterious depths will transform the very heart of our being.

Perhaps this is simply a matter of being honest with our
experiential awareness of what a real concrete love affair in
our lives really means. We cannot use our loving relationship
with another for anything; the quality of the love relationship
itself is the breadth and depth of love. Never can we love *for*
anything. We love, rather, because the relationship of loving is
the most creative, the most self-engendering, the most life-
giving of possible relationships. We love because we can do
nothing better. We dare not use for selfish purposes the God
who can only be related to, only enjoyed, only loved. Yet out of
this unique relationship comes the strength and power and
beauty of our lives.

When we bracket our scholarly definitions of God and
have the humble strength to look at what we know is true from
our own experience, then we are amazed that ever we could
have been so blind: God is that One to whom we relate
because we can do no other. The mystics and saints who are
the true poets of our spiritual quest are unanimous in their
gentle plea: God is Beauty, God is Loveliness, God is sheer
Grace, God is Good. Seek these with all your heart and you will
find God.

Beauty and loveliness and goodness are not things which
can be bought and sold, utilized for aggrandizement, or possessed like a precious museum piece. It is perhaps fortunate
that forever are we denied the right to *possess* beauty or

loveliness or goodness; it is the good grace of our lives that, with the love of God, we may yet *become* beautiful, and lovely, and good. God is not *for* these things, and hence loving God does not give us the right to possess these things. Rather God *is* Beauty and Love and Goodness, and thus in loving God we become godly by enfleshing this same beauty and love and goodness in our fragile earthen vessels. Are we large enough to hold with steadfast resolve and mature wisdom that *there is no reward for loving God?* We love God because we can do no other.

## What Do We Owe God?

We owe an everlasting debt of gratitude to our churches for carrying from generation to generation our religious tradition over the long haul of the centuries. We have an equal obligation, however, to criticize in the sense of critically evaluating the contents of this tradition in order to separate the authentic from the inauthentic. Admittedly this is serious business and cannot be undertaken casually. Yet all who read the Gospel with purity of heart are sure to find there the touchstone by which to judge whatever comes afterward. I offer this preamble because the following point seems to fly in the face of much traditional religious teaching, especially as witnessed in sermons and homilies and spiritual exhortations.

How often are we morosely reminded of our debts and obligations to God? How often are we threatened by the Commandments and judged by the law? How often is our religion laid upon us as a heavy burden and our relationship to God demanded out of the motive of guilt? Is there any way to enkindle our hearts anew to the very truest meaning of the word "grace"?

If, on the one hand, we see the religious logic of the assertion that God is for nothing, then, on the other hand, the same logic will allow us to ask this question from the opposite side, so to speak. The question is this: *What do we owe God?* Immediately our Church-sponsored answers flood our minds like a catechism free-for-all: we owed God obedience, obligation, observance of commandments, sacrifice, self-denial, abnegation of will, loyalty to Church authority. The list is nigh endless.

Let us put aside these answers and ask again: *What do we owe God?* Perhaps it takes heroic faith and the trust of the saints to say with undoubting confidence: *We owe God absolutely nothing.* In the depths of our souls there is a terrible fear of such an easy answer; we would rather that there be clean-cut obligations so that we may pay our debts and resolve our duty.

## We Owe the God of Love Nothing

We owe God nothing. By what crooked logic could this be true? The truth of this lies in God himself, for we say that God is love. The very meaning of the word "love" is that it is something that is done freely, graciously, without obligation attached. The love of God is the gracious gift of God to all the creatures. Even in our own imperfect lives we need no school text to tell us that when we love we do so freely, we do so willingly, we do so out of our own goodness. By the same token we see the contradiction in thinking that love is something done out of obligation, that love can be required by law, that love can be demanded.

That God is love and all of his relationships to us are loving entails the sobering and liberating conclusion that all of God's relationships to us are freely-given, gifted and gracious. Let us not use the language of gift and grace irresponsibly: gift means simply gift, that is, freely given. If gifted and free, then there is no obligation attached. If someone gives us a free gift out of friendship, then, despite popular opinion, we do not owe anything in return. The gift is ours to enjoy, and our enjoyment of the gift is all that the giver truly desires.

## God Is Love and Nothing Else

It has become almost standard to refer to the Gospels as revolutionary, but if that term is ever rightfully used it should be used to describe the revelation of Jesus: God is love, *and nothing else.* What Jesus knew out of the depths of his experience of the one he called Father was that the relationships of God are purely, simply, and everlastingly gracious. They are always gifted. And because of the giftedness of the love of God, there can be no such thing as a debt or an obligation to satisfy some duty. What God has done God has done freely. What we do in return is up to our choice and our response.

What possible return can be made to the gift of love? The only fitting response which shows that love has been received is the response of love. But our response of love is on our part free, gracious, unowed. We love because we want to love. We do not love because it is demanded or required by law. We owe God absolutely nothing, as Jesus knew from his own intimacy with the Father. It is the religious person, however, the person on the quest of the spirit, who begins with the good sense of Jesus, which is the good wisdom of sheer and overwhelming amazement at the unqualified giftedness of the love of God that floods like rainfall the lives of the just and unjust alike. The God of Jesus is gracious and all of his relationships are gracious.

If we choose to respond to this unconditional graciousness, we so choose to respond out of our own hard strength and our own good will. Should we not know without being reminded that the only response to graciousness is graciousness? To suggest that our relationship to God is a debt that somehow must be paid off is to insult God with the cheap language of buying and selling.

### Giftedness

If we but pay heed to our spiritual heroes we will find that they have already charted the path of spiritual discovery and their own traveling has left the footprints of their odyssey. The challenge to us is not so much to follow them as to do what they did and become what they became. And their charge to us is not a command, not even a demand, but simply the announcement of a message of good news: If you want to become who you really wish to be, if you wish to live fully, if you desire life abundantly, then the single and only thing you can do is to respond in graciousness to the graciousness that surrounds your life like air and holds you firm like gravity.

The spiritual person is the one who is deeply aware of the giftedness of the universe, the giftedness of one's life, the giftedness of those others who allow me to become, the giftedness of the God who has lured me into being. The spiritual person is that one who strives with unswerving passion to respond to the giftedness and the graciousness of a reality which is the never-ending and infinitely mysterious sacrament of the loveliness of God.

## Giftedness and Celebration

Perhaps it is the timely season for taking with renewed seriousness the theology of grace which is the theme song of Paul's theology. Paul in his conversion was overwhelmed by the giftedness of the relationship to God through Jesus Christ which brought him from death to life; he was awed by the universe which was a vital part of the working out of the plan to bring all things together in the body of Christ. The spiritual person is the one who is animated by the giftedness of the universe, fascinated by the giftedness of life, especially one's own life, and hence quickened by the holy urgency to respond to that giftedness.

## Response to Gift?

What can one do in the face of a sheer gift? When something in our lives is wholly and unreservedly a gift to us—whether it be the gift of life itself, or the gift of health, or the everyday gifts that friends bestow, or the ever-surprising gift of love—what can we possibly do in the face of such amazing grace? If, after our dull fashion, we immediately come to think of what we can do in return, of what would be an equitable exchange, then we have sorely misunderstood the nature of the gift and choose to free ourselves by calculating a debt. If in any way we attempt to pay back, then we have violated the graciousness of both the giver and the gift. Need we be such poor receivers? Quite simply, there is very little we can do in the face of a gift, except perhaps for two things that finally collapse into one thing which is no small thing at all.

### Thank and Enjoy

First and most obvious, in the face of a gift we might simply bring ourselves to say "Thank you." Our most unpretentious and yet sincere response to a gift is a simple thank you. But the test of that very sincerity is inescapably linked: if we do indeed appreciate the gift sufficiently to express our thanks, then we might also have the good grace to enjoy the gift. If a loved one presents us with a gift expressing thoughtfulness and concern, how can we express our thanks? Our thanks ring true only when we use the gift, when we enjoy it. The enjoyed use of the gift is to receive it exactly as it was intended, as a gracious enhancement to our lives.

What can we conceivably do in the face of the graciousness of the gracious gift of life? When we but consider the infinite calculus of random chance whereby you and I were born into this world rather than a hundred million other selves, we are driven to the edges of wonder—why me? And there is no explanation for the singularity of the choice which allowed me to be except sheer artful chance. In the face of such unowed giftedness all that we can finally do is to say "thank you," and the proof of that easy thanks is that we enjoy this precious gift. If we seize upon our lives by living them as richly and intensely and fully as our energy allows, then in this rightful use of the gift we are enjoying it to the full. No other thanks could be required.

### Celebration

Just as we have various rituals that enable us to say thank you in a gracious context, so also we have rituals that bring to enlivened expression our response to the gracious gift of life and the gracious gift of love. Religiously we enshrine the giftedness of life and of love in our liturgical rituals, and of late we have returned to the only proper name for such ceremony: *celebration.*

How can we possibly give vent to the wholeness of our response to the gift of life? We have the good religious sense to realize that the unique quality of the gift of life is of such uncommon character that we can only give flesh to our appreciation by immersing ourselves into a symbol which highlights this gift in purest and rarest form. For this reason our appreciation of life is ritualized in a celebration of life itself.

In those human affairs which give flavor to our lives we celebrate a host of trivial and grand occasions—birthdays, engagements, weddings, graduations—and when this list of occasions runs out we celebrate simply for the sake of celebrating. To be noticed here is that *one* unique feature which marks off celebration from all other human interchanges: the celebration is non-functional. There can be no ulterior purpose for a celebration, and the celebration cannot produce an end beyond itself. We do not fulfill obligations or gain merit or preserve good order by our celebrations. We celebrate for the sheer, non-instrumental joy of celebrating.

### Sacramental Celebration

Surely one of the loveliest possessions of our Church tradition is the sacramental liturgy. Each sacrament is not a ritualized exercise separated off from the ordinariness of our daily lives; rather, each is the heightening of a human occasion which in its very commonness points to unfathomable mystery. At baptism we gather to celebrate the fragile giftedness of the initiation of new life, surprising and unowed. At the Eucharist this vowed community gathers together to celebrate the life shared together in common pledge like the tender strands of one single body, so that the sharing of the bread is both the celebrating and the creating of that enhanced life we call the body of Christ. In the sacrament of reconciliation this community of sinners gathers, not to celebrate weakness and failure, but to celebrate the awesome and gifted fact that the failure, even deliberate in sin, need not dismember one from the community of life. These are mentioned as indications that the most gracious and grateful of human activities is the act of celebration in which we take cognizance of the fragile and beautiful preciousness of life itself.

The indentifying character of those who inform themselves by the food of the Gospels should be their dedication to the celebration of the mighty acts of their gracious God. To celebrate life, then, means to enter into it fully and unreservedly—not to avoid it, not to deny it, not to set limits around it or restrict it, not to demean it by taking it as a second-rate version of a better life to come. To enter into life fully, however, means also to share in its mysterious variety—life in its richness, in its passion, in its tragedy and in its suffering. To take these things upon oneself is, possibly, the beginning of redemption.

### Falling and Letting Go

It is not surprising that our language of love embodies this same note of celebration. It is intriguing to notice how our language creates expressions to describe love which would strike us as strange were they not so commonplace. Why is it that we speak of "falling in love"? Why should the image of "falling" be invoked here? Persons "fall" in love, which is to say, they do not plan it, nor control it, nor chart it out beforehand. The metaphor of falling underscores the essential element of unpredictability, of uncontrollability, and, equally, of non-manipulability. Since the bestowal and receiving of love is always in its essence a gracious gift, there is that quality about it which is unexpected and uncontrolled; since it just happens, before our attention can register we discover ourselves falling in a fashion unwilled but not undesired.

What is required of us in this relationship of love is not the intentional choice to fall in love, but, rather, once falling, the wholehearted choice to let go. For those of us who like to think that our life can be manageable and predictable by the firm hand of our willful choice, this *letting-go* quality of love is surely the most difficult lessen to learn. Sadly, unless we do let go we will never really fall in love.

I am reminded of an incident in my own life a few years back when I finally had the opportunity to fulfill a youthful ambition—that of becoming a skydiver. Actually, skydiving is too pretentious a word for what I in fact did, which was to reluctantly climb out of the plane to hang onto the wing strut out of sheer fear, and finally to let go because there was absolutely no face-saving alternative. But once having let go, the gentle sail earthward was silent and peaceful and charged with the thrill of life.

The point of this personal tale is simply that the letting-go quality of our loving also points to the riskiness of which we are afraid. Like floating down in the parachute where there is nothing to do but enjoy the sweetness of the sensation, so also being in love comes to us naturally and is fullsome joy; what comes hard to us is letting go. But if one does not let go, one will not float down.

## Something Like Dying

If one is afraid to let go of oneself, if one fears that loss of control will forfeit identity, if one prefers the security of the known to the risk of the unknown, then the probabilities of falling in love are severely diminished. Poets have long hinted that falling in love is somewhat akin to dying. We do lose part of our old ways and even of our old selves as we become something new with the assumption of this relationship. We have no way of knowing beforehand whether or not the exchange is worth the price. The irrevocable lesson of life is that to grow one must leave behind the earlier stages. Only by letting go of the settledness and the security of the predictable do we move into that strange territory of surprises and new possibilities. When at last we do let go, we find that what we are moving into can be joyful and enriching, but most of all it is growthful.

## Follow Me

Have we ever taken seriously the invitation of Jesus: "Come, follow me"? When guardedly we ask "Where are we going?" we receive only the reply which is in fact a challenge: "Come and see." No promises here, no rewards, and surely no security. The holy lesson is that if we do not move on in life we may well rot where we are. As much as we may prefer to sit and rest for a while, the "follow me" is the ceaseless challenge to take our lives into our own hands, to move on, to move ahead, to dare to leave home for the sake of the kingdom. For only by leaving the familiar brokenness of our past do we allow the opportunities for healing to spring up as if from a dead seed.

Perhaps this view of the giftedness of life can shed new light on the crucifixion of Jesus. The message of the dying of Jesus who embodied and proclaimed the fullness of life is perhaps that the only thing worth dying for is the cause of life itself. If we know through intuition and Gospel that the only thing worth living for is life itself, then we must finally admit that we know also that the only thing worth dying for is life. Anything less than life is not worth the supreme energy of our most heroic efforts, nor is anything less than life worth the sacrifice of our dying.

## The Inspiration of Life: Resurrection

We have been rightly reminded that the theology of the Gospels is not a theology of death, but rather a theology of resurrection. It is the living symbol of the resurrection that should inspire us with the death-defying energy to submerge ourselves in the vicissitudes of life in the service of that alone which will outlast death. The spiritual person who has allowed the resurrection to take hold of those forces which drive us always toward transcendence will believe in and be committed to the struggle for life, life in its abundance and life in its fullness, because this is the very cause of God.

If we take seriously the enfleshment of God in the incarna-

tion then we lay claim to the most ennobling mystery of all:
this flesh and this earth is the sanctuary of God. Whitehead,
that philosopher with the soul of a mystic, has said, "The world
lives by its incarnation of God in itself" (*Religion in the Making*, p. 149). Not only do we walk in that habitat in which God
makes his home, but we enshrine in our own selves the living
sacrament of that sacred presence. Every bit of our breathing
and eating, not just the eucharistic meal, is our feeding off of
the life of God and, living sacraments, we carry this sacred
presence like food to the world.

### The Reality of Struggle and Uncertainty

We dare not, however, be overly romantic concerning an
issue which is so vital to the meaning of our very being. We
need little reminding of our world of starvation, war, oppression and nuclear threat. With the honest realism of the Gospels
we accept that life is a messy affair. However much we lay out
our patterns of order and systems of structure whereby some
semblance of coherence can hold the chaos of our experiencing into some manageable whole, our everyday experiencing is
garbled and confused by the random disorder and startling
unpredictability which is the primordial character of a creative
and restless reality.

Though we may chart a course across the galaxies we have
never been able to chart the course of our human destiny,
either individually or collectively. Not only do we not yet
know who we may become, as Paul suggests, but we do not
even know a sure direction. But if we hear Jesus aright we
would have it no other way. His own living demonstrated that
life is not a charted map, predictable and error-free. Like him,
we can but take our lives as a personal adventure in which we
must strike out to discover what the world can be and what we
can become within it. We do not know where we are going; we
do not know what fierce impediments will rise up to strike at
us; we do not know what joys lie hidden.

Thus we may not chart our spiritual odyssey by imitating
the life or the style of the giants of the past. God has no desire

of spiritual mimics. Our only sincere imitation can be our venturesomeness, our willingness to take the name "Christian" upon ourselves even though we do not even know what this will be since it has never before been done uniquely in us.

The point here is that uncertainty and unknowing, even a certain lack of direction, are the hallmarks of the Christian life. Just as there can be no rule book or road map for falling in love, so also there can be no sure pattern or structure for the Christian life. Too long have we been schooled to trust the direction of others, to entrust our lives to the guidance of a Church with centuries of experience, to heed the counsel of sages wiser than ourselves. While we dare not surrender the wisdom of the ages we also dare not surrender our lives.

To be a Christian means to join that vast and glorious horde of saints who have struggled to find their God. If they were fortunate enough to find such love we pray our thanks and take stout courage that God is no mere fiction. But then we must strike out to find God for ourselves with this assurance only, that God will not be where he was before.

## The Passion of Jesus

When we recall the stories of the passion of Jesus Christ we ordinarily assume that the word "passion" refers to the sufferings endured by Jesus, and this is surely correct. Should we not wonder, however, that so much of our theological understanding of Jesus should be focused on what represented but a few short hours in his earthly life—those hours between one Thursday evening and the following Friday afternoon? In no way do I wish to deny the importance of those hours of suffering, but I think we can consider the passion of Jesus in larger terms. Should we not be enthralled by the passion of Jesus for life? Should we not be captivated by the passion of Jesus for other people? Should we not be given pause by his passionate concern for the cause of the poor and the helpless? It was, in fact, this passionate involvement of Jesus in the lives he touched that set him off from others. Caught up in the loveliness and beauty of God, Jesus saw that loveliness lurking within the lowliest of creatures and that beauty shining through every face.

The stature of Jesus' death is in direct relation to the size of his life which was driven by the greatest of passions. It was not just that he was acutely aware of the flowers and the seeds, the fields and the vineyards. The way the sun rises and the way the rain falls, how the mustard seed grows and how the fig ripens—each of these revealed for him the workings of a loving Father who does all things graciously. Can we have any doubt that Jesus loved this earth more than we ever dared say? We dare not forget that his final benediction was not a farewell, but a promise: "I am with you all days." Perhaps it is time to strip ourselves of the arrogance which would hold that only we human beings are the members of the body of Christ. This earth with its marvels of life, this infinitely elegant cosmos spinning out galaxies beyond our counting—this is the passionate body of God.

### Weakness or Strength?

Let us conclude this chapter with one final affirmation. As mentioned earlier, it is unfortunate that so much of our formal religion insists on beginning the religious enterprise with human condemnation: we are fallen, we are sinful, we are damned, we are ungrateful and wicked. Somehow, this ill-tempered premise seems to say, the more we can convince ourselves of our worthlessness and degradation the more fit we are for the loving grace of God. By some wayward logic, true love can only begin with degradation. The human-God relationship rests most comfortably on the premise of human weakness. The silent assumption behind this premise is that we human beings experience ourselves primarily as persons of desperate and unsatisfied need: the need for salvation, for redemption, for spiritual strength, for heaven. Once we are willing to admit our helplessness before these needs, then God can step in and graciously fill them. This is a twisted irony that has probably done more hurt than we will ever know. This obtuse reasoning would have us believe that the most crucial and central and enhancing of all the relationships in our existence, namely our relationship to God, must be based on weakness.

## Love: A Relationship of Strength

If we but look at that informing and creative relationship of our lives, the relationship of love, we will see that when we love another sincerely and are loved truly in return we are intuitively aware that we do not love out of weakness. We love always and only out of our strength. We discover that the larger and stronger we are within ourselves the more able we are to love. Our very act of loving gives us an intimation of our own strength, and the love which is returned convinces us of our beauty. The size of the love is completely conditioned by the size of the persons involved. At that moment of revelation when we are struck as if by lightning by the inexplicable fact that we are loved, we feel then, as if for the first time, a sense of our own goodness, our beauty, and our size. For to be loved means that one is desirable, worthwhile, of precious value. It is precisely this intimation of our self-value that impels us to respond out of that which is deepest and richest within ourselves; we find ourselves growing to match the size mirrored in the loved one's eyes.

It is therefore a perverse turn to hold that the one necessary and essential relationship of our lives, that between the self and God, should have to be a relationship based on weakness and worthlessness. By what misguided sense could we seriously believe that God's greatest love is bestowed on those creatures who are most worthless? Let us finally affirm with the boldness of our faith: God loves us because we are lovable; God loves us because there is something within us that is beautiful, and rich, and lovely.

To say that God loves me personally means that I am inherently lovable, I have dignity, I have value, and I have great beauty. And the greater the size of my goodness and my beauty, the more can this God love me. We are not directed to grow less as the Baptist did; we are invited to become ever more. It is out of the great passion of our love that we relate to God, not out of the size of our guilt. Because we wish to respond ever more perfectly to the love of God we will strive to do away with our selfishness, our obstinacy, or hard-heartedness. Because God loves us we give up our sin, and not the other way around.

### Conclusion: What Do We Give to God?

Linked closely to this notion of weakness was the theological assumption: There is nothing that we can do for God, nothing that we can give to God. God is infinite and complete and hence the relationship must always be one-sided. God will do for us, and we can only receive. To this let it be said that whatever else such a relationship may be, it surely cannot be the relationship of love. For, as described above, the self-giving out of strength is an ineradicable condition of our loving.

Out of our sense of self-value, then, we might ask without impertinence: *What do we give to God?* In much of our tradition, the answer has been: *nothing,* absolutely nothing. If this were true, then indeed we would be worthless and valueless. But if we continue to be seriously literal with our claim that God is love, then the question makes new sense. The Gospels have suggested an answer which we have been too timid to take literally: *we give to God the gift of Fatherhood.*

We tend to think that parenthood is a single-termed word and stands by itself; we also tend to think that the relationship of parenthood is one-directional, from parent to child. A moment's reflection should show how wrong this is. Do we ever stop to consider that the word "parent" makes no sense unless there exists a child? In a very real sense, the parent creates the child. But in a sense equally real, the child creates the parent. If there were no child, there could be no parent. In the subsequent living relationships between parent and child, the relations from child to parent are as much constitutive as are those of parent to child.

## Sons and Daughters of God

With this in mind, we are everlastingly grateful for the Fatherhood of God, for without God we would indeed be nothing. But, on the other hand, it is we the children who allow God to be Father. We the children must in fact be the sons and daughters who show forth the image of the Father in the way we speak and act, the way we relate and love. How often do the parables of Jesus enjoin upon us the only lesson we ever need to learn: *If the Father is like this, what should the sons and daughters be like?* As we take on the image and likeness of the Father, we become godly. We do give to God the gift of Fatherhood. Herein lies our terrible strength. We qualify the experience of God. We make a difference to that everlasting Lover who will never, never let us rest in peace.

### Selected Readings

Joseph Haroutunian has written a somewhat neglected but impressive book in which he seriously deals with interpersonal relationships as the key to the spiritual life: *God with Us: A Theology of Transpersonal Life* (Philadelphia: The Westminster Press, 1965). See especially Part Three, "Love in the Common Life."

In *Apology for Wonder*, Sam Keen makes a strong and appealing case for the recognition of the graciousness existing within our own lives which can be the catalyst for our sense of worship. See Chapter Ten, "Wonder, Grace and Gratitude."

John W. Dixon argues from much the same direction as does this present work and comes to much the same conclusion in his fine book, *The Physiology of Faith* (San Francisco: Harper and Row, 1979). In relation to this present chapter, see especially Part Six, "Care and the Kingdom."

The remarkable book *Person/Planet,* by Theodore Roszak, makes an urgent plea for the inalienable dignity of the human person which is inexorably linked with the splendor of the earth itself. See especially Chapter One, "The Rights of the Person" (Garden City, New York: Anchor Press and Double-day, 1978).

The thinkers to whom I am most indebted for the concept of God developed here are Alfred North Whitehead and Charles Hartshorne. Both are difficult, but unusually reward-ing. See, for example, Hartshorne's *Man's Vision of God* (Ham-den: Archon Books, 1964), especially Chapter III, "The Two Strands in Historical Theology."

*Scripture Reading*

The Gospel of John Chapter 14

# 5

# The Context of Prayer: Faith

The one activity which most sustains our spiritual life while at the same time embodying the very quality of our faith is surely the activity of prayer. It is quite probable that the quality of our prayer is a direct expression of the quality of our spiritual life. Could it be that if we knew how to pray we could relinquish our nervous concerns for the systems and methods of the spiritual life? In the first part of this chapter I will set out the context of prayer. Instead of giving a definition of prayer—impossible in the same sense that giving a definition of love is impossible—I prefer to concentrate on what we are attempting to accomplish within ourselves when we try to pray. Once this context is made clear, I wish to examine some of the presuppositions which underlie our traditional model of prayer and which are implications of a substance worldview. Finally I will suggest a different model of prayer that might perhaps be in closer harmony with our deepest religious striving.

## A Misleading Model of Prayer

In many of our treatises on the spiritual life, the concept of prayer is handled straightforwardly; there is presented a logical definition of prayer and the method for praying properly is laid out. While I respect the seriousness with which prayer is considered I find weaknesses in such an approach.

Perhaps our first question should be: Why are we concerned about praying at all? Why is it that we are somehow persuaded that if we are to be spiritual-minded, prayer must be of utmost importance in our lives? Why is it that we assume that there can be no such thing as a spirituality without prayer? What are we really trying to do when we pray?

I pose these questions because in the deepest recesses of our own hearts most of us will be forced to admit that we pray poorly. It is not that we have not tried to pray nor that we have not been persistent over long periods in our efforts. On the contrary, we have tried, repeatedly and sincerely, but somehow the quality and intensity of our efforts have not guaranteed worthwhile results. At heart, we admit that whatever praying is, we do it poorly and thus we must do it badly. As all of us know from our own disillusioned experience, it is easy to give up on praying.

## Goal-Oriented Activities

Perhaps much of the problem concerning prayer can be located in the type of model which implicitly supports our notions of what sort of activity praying should be. Without recognizing it, when we consider prayer as an activity we resort to the same sort of model which makes sense out of other activities in our everyday lives—activities like writing a term-paper, building a cabinet and repairing a car. What is being pointed at here is that so many of our daily activities are goal-oriented; a whole cluster of sub-acts are worked together to produce some visible effect—the finished term paper, the well-made cabinet, the repaired car. The success of the activities can be easily judged by the quality of the product. The criterion of success or failure is easily invoked to judge whether or not our activities have been worthwhile. If by chance we discover that the end-product is consistently poor or worthless, with little regret we will abandon those activities in favor of others of more promise of being productive.

## Prayer as Goal-Oriented

Perhaps unconsciously, it can be with this particular model in mind that we approach the activity of prayer. Without real reflection, we come to prayer with the low-level assumption that praying should in some fashion be effective. If there are no results, in some sense discernible, then we find it difficult to explain why we should continue to engage in prayer. If there are no appreciable effects, then we will almost spontaneously surrender these efforts in favor of other activities more obviously justifiable by their products and hence surely more satisfactory to us.

Can there conceivably be anything more wrenching to our souls than the admission that we are spiritual failures? Do we dare ever whisper within the sacred space of our silent selves that we are, yes, tired of trying to pray, bored with the effort? I would suggest that such a reaction is neither selfish nor self-serving. And yet the wearisome repetition of our repeated prayings neither comforts us nor assures us but rather drags us into a lassitude of self-doubt. Without making a conscious decision about the matter we find that we are praying less, and eventually not at all. Can anything be spiritually sadder than the very commonness of this experience? Each of us has been there, often.

Important to notice, however, is that this experience of fruitlessness and this frustration of attempting to do something which only too patently does not work is quite possibly nothing but the melancholy yet predictable result of a misguided understanding of the very nature of prayer. Can we rechannel our thought processes about a matter religiously so vital to us sufficiently to forego any desire for effectiveness in some straightforward, measurable sense? If, however, we dispense with any notion of results, have we not sacrificed the very purpose of our prayer? This quandary simply brings us full-circle to our opening question: Why do we pray at all? If my suggestion is correct that the fundamental model for prayer is misconstrued if imaged after the model of productive activity, then it could be religiously rewarding if a more humanly meaningful model could be considered.

## An Alternative Model of Prayer: "I Love You"

The direction toward an alternative understanding of prayer can be charted if we consider the close alliance of two parallel questions. It might be fruitful to reflect on the fact that the question "Why do we pray?" has its closest analogy in human affairs in the question, "Why does the lover say 'I love you'?" Let us concentrate on the latter question for the moment.

Why *does* the lover say, "I love you"? Consider that in the intensity of this precious relationship the lover has uttered sincerely and passionately "I love you" a thousand times already. He is not proclaiming a new fact heretofore unrevealed to the beloved, nor is he telling her something she has not already known and known well. He is not even describing his present activities, since the activities of loving need no words to explain them. And yet the lover will say, time and time again, and the beloved will never tire of hearing, "I love you." Why should this be so?

Every single one of us who has had the good fortune and the sweet grace of being deeply in love with another knows in the rush of our pulse and the surge of our body exactly why we proclaim, not just occasionally but repeatedly, "I love you." The plain and unvarnished answer is so very simple: I say "I love you" because I can do no other. From the depths of my being I am driven to express the richness and graciousness of what is going on within me, and the only words I possess to point to the lovely intensity within me is the plain and simple, "I love you."

Notice here that the expression of love comes out of a felt and experienced relationship with the beloved, an awareness of self as being transformed and heightened by the gifted presence of the beloved. At this point, the phrase "I love you" is not the describing of the occasion; it is, rather, *the very relating in love.* The saying of "I love you" is *the doing* of the relationship of loving. I say "I love you" because I am actually in love and my saying is, at least in part, the activity of loving itself.

## Why Does the Lover Say "I Love You"?

Crucial to understanding what is going on in this context is the realization that the phrase "I love you" is not uttered in order to produce any results. The expressing of love linguistically is not designed to have any evident effect. This is, however, not to be construed as claiming that nothing happens when love is verbally expressed. To invoke this rather jaundiced terminology of cause and effect, *the effect* of loving is the love relationship itself.

As explained earlier, love is a relationship which is self-enclosed, in the sense that there is no further end to loving than the very relationship of loving. With this in mind, to say "I love you" is the doing of something which is already present, something which is already occurring.

To repeat our opening question: Why does the lover say "I love you" and why do you and I say to those special ones who grace our lives, "I love you"? The answer is that you and I say "I love you" because we *do* indeed love; we express our love because we *do* love. It is not insignificant that the saying of love arises from intimacies and secrecies so deep within ourselves that we have no apt language; thus it is that we do not describe our love, but enter into the relating which is the loving itself. Thus the strange paradox that *the saying* of love is *the doing* of love. No effect beyond this is possible; to seek an effect beyond this is to prostitute the saying into some other sort of doing.

If we can accept this model of the relationship of loving, then perhaps it will become clear that we say "I love you" as an expression of our very being; the saying of the phrase is our struggle to say out who we are. It is the depths of my selfhood struggling to become ever more itself. We are attempting to give some articulation to the reality of the self whose identity is being discovered in this relationship of loving. The end of saying "I love you" is, therefore, *the lover,* and the very saying is the being-in-love. I love because I am then best myself, and my speaking it out to the beloved is part of how I become my own best self. Obviously the straightforward language of cause and effect is crippled here: *the cause* of my saying "I love you" is *my-being-in-love,* as *the effect* of the saying is *my-being-in-love.*

Perhaps each of us is only too familiar with that situation, whether in our own lives or that of others, in which the lover has gradually discontinued speaking out "I love you." No one need clarify for us what is happening; we know with a sure instinct that the love-relationship is shriveling and heading for death because the experienced love is no longer pressing urgently for expression. If the person were then to reinvoke the saying "I love you" in the desperate hope of rekindling this love, it assuredly would fail. The saying "I love you" cannot cause the effect of love; it is, on the contrary, the effect of loving, and hence its saying is caused by the loving which is already lively and creative.

In sum, you and I will say "I love you" not because it is something we are supposed to do, nor something that is expected of us, nor something that is an obligation required of us, nor something that fulfills our stuffy norms of propriety. No, we only rightly say "I love you" when in fact we are in love, and because we are indeed truly in love we feel very good about saying it and we would have it no other way.

### Prayer on the Model of Love

We have pursued this particular exposition concerning the relationship of love because I think we can make a convincing and meaningful case for comprehending the concepts of prayer and praying on this same model of this relational context of loving. On the one hand, we must leave behind our almost undismissable notion that we pray in order to achieve something. To regard our prayer as an instrumentality in the cause of something else is to wholly misconstrue the true nature of our religious endeavor.

We do not pray because we are really trying to get something else, no matter what this something else might be: holiness, grace, heaven, union with God, consolation. Prayer is not the means for achieving a separate good nor is it rightly viewed as some sort of spiritual activity which has, if not material, then at least spiritual effects. Even though such a view is perhaps so deeply ingrained within us as to appear quite natural, it is at root but a rather clumsy application of a cause-effect notion to our activity of praying. Prayer is in no wise a productive activity in the sense of causing changes, even changes within ourselves.

But if this is true, then we are driven back to our original question: Why do we pray, and what are we trying to do with our prayer? To return for a moment to the analogy of love, it should be noticed that the phrase "I love you" can be used in a thousand different ways. It can be said in the cause of seduction, or for deception, or to give assurance; it can function as a rhyme in our songs or an apt sentiment in a poem, and it can also be used of coats and hats and new cars. But no matter how diverse and numerous the appearances of this phrase and no matter what its application, it is only properly and rightly used in one single context and in no other. "I love you" is only properly spoken in the context of love; all the other uses are parasitic and eventually self-defeating.

It is only the context of love between lovers which wholly and without remainder gives the meaning to the phrase. Only the lovers know when it is spoken rightly, and they will know out of the context of their concrete loving. Outside of the context of loving, the phrase "I love you" is trivial and cheap, non-productive and sterile. And if by some peculiar chance some stranger were to ask, "What do you mean by this saying, 'I love you'?"—what possible answer could we then give? Would it be of avail to point out the words in the dictionary? Surely we would throw up our hands in sad despair and say, "If you have not done it, you cannot know it."

## The Context of Prayer: The Life of Faith

In a similar vein, prayer takes its meaning and has its full significance only within a specified context; outside of this unique context praying is at best a going through the motions and at worst a ritualized form of magic. Our concept of prayer is too important to us to allow such easy violence to its very meaning. What, then, is the context out of which prayer comes and through which it has its meaning? We know this truth but perhaps it is our very self-doubt which denies it to us: *the context of prayer is the life of faith.* This sounds too obvious to be consequential; it should not be at all noteworthy that people with faith are the ones who pray. The argument here is not with the fact that there is a relationship between faith and prayer; our argument is with our implicit assumption concerning the direction in which this relationship goes.

### A Wrong Direction

We need only hearken back to the religious exhortation and spiritual direction we have heard repeated to the point of weariness: if your faith is weak, pray harder; if you have doubts of faith, pray; if you are losing your faith, you must pray more; if you are indecisive about a matter of faith, pray. The subtle fallacy which works such mischief here is the direction which is postulated—the movement is always from prayer to faith. Both the point and the result of our praying, it is assumed, is an increase, or strengthening, or confirmation of our faith. Here we have but another fugitive version of the cause-effect principle disguised in the most religious of terms.

The misguided assumption is that prayer is that type of activity which can produce an effect; prayer stands in the relation of cause to this desired result. And since faith is a matter of such weighty religious import, we dare not cry out in protest against this irresponsible maneuvering of our deepest, dearest desire—the desire to pray well. What has gone so painfully awry here? What has gone amiss is our sense of direction.

In this particular case of the relationship between faith and prayer, we have completely reversed the direction. And the direction is this: *because we live lives of faith, we pray.* The false and spiritually misleading direction is this: *we pray because we want to have faith.* It is quite possible that much of our personal despair over our lives of prayer is simply a reflection of this deep-lying and unwholesome confusion about the right relationship of faith to prayer.

## Prayer Comes from Faith

Our prayer, accordingly, plays precisely the same role as our saying "I love you." It is because we are already faithful persons, already living our lives to the best of our skill informed by the faith of the Gospels, that we must bring to articulation both who we are in our faith and what the concerns of this faith are for us. What makes sense of our praying, thus, is the lives we are leading, and nothing else. In the form of prayer our speaking out of faith is part of what is meant by being faithful, and not productive of it.

Prayer, therefore, like the saying of love, is the articulation of the deepest reality of the self, and it has its origin and source in our perception and appreciation of our own interrelationship with reality which, because of faith, is also our relationship with transcendence. It is in this context of our lives faithfully lived in relationship to transcendence that our praying is also the putting of ourselves into this relationship.

At those times when we have prayed well, we have prayed out of the very depths of our being. We sense immediately that prayer is not something that is done lightly or casually. Just as we say "I love you" when we feel the love, so also we pray when we feel touched by some momentous experience; always it is the quality of our experiencing which impels us to the expression of prayer. In those moments we pray, because it is the best thing we can do. Our own reaction to these stirring qualities of our experience is the impulse to speak out, or to cry out, and in this very act of expression we are trying to bring ourselves together: we are trying to integrate these various and possibly discordant experiences into some semblance of unity so that we may be integral and not fragmented. The form of our speaking out is to place multifariousness into the context of faith. But our speaking out does not create faith; on the contrary, our faith—in this case our holding of ourselves in a context larger than ourselves which is our relation to the Transcendent One in whom we live and move and have our being—causes us to seek our integration in that very relationship to transcendence.

In the messy and confused interchange of our lives, it is our effort to search out meaning for our existence, our drive to engage in activities that are meaningful, our relentless struggle to achieve something of value within ourselves and for others—it is qualities such as these which inspire our praying and urge us to entrust ourselves to powers beyond our obvious vision. It is this entrusting to meanings and values which lie yet beyond us which I term our relationship to transcendence; and the act of so relating to transcendence all of us call praying to our God.

## The Prayer of Faith: Relationship to Transcendence

We notice that we pray best when we are most profoundly touched. From the depths of our pain, we cry out in prayer; from the depths of our suffering, we plead in prayer; from the depths of our loneliness and frustration and anger, we express our anguish in prayer. It is not just the negative aspects of experience, however, which occasion our praying. From the depths of our joy, we shout in prayer; from the depths of our wonder, we sigh in the awe of prayer; from the depths of our experience of surprise and giftedness, we pray in gratitude; from the depths of our being loved, we pray in great awe. Always it is the touching profundity of our experience that impels us to speak out, to say who we are by the light of this experience so that the saying is likewise the becoming. So it is that we hold ourselves together, assemble our bewildering fragments into some sort of graspable unity, by seeing our scattered pieces in the context of a meaningful whole. It is by setting ourselves in this context that we place ourselves in the embrace of the Transcendent.

It is precisely this relationship to the Transcendent which we call our God that provides that our speaking out is prayer and not mere crying in the dark. Living in faith means holding our lives in a context larger than ourselves. To live by faith means seeing that the meanings and values of our lives, although for the most part finite and corruptible and imperfect, are not mere random and fragmented pieces to be extinguished at our death; they are, rather, worth our life's energy and even our blood because they derive their ultimate value, not merely because they are part of ourselves, but because they are equally part of that One who holds all things together and treasures each item with individual love. In this way it is faith which makes our lives livable.

## Who Will Hear Our Cry?

By far the great majority of events which constitute the stuff of our lives are not directly attributable to an obvious cause or evident agency. Merely to say with resignation "So it goes" is philosophically cheap and an abnegation of all value. In those precious moments, for example, of love, when we are overwhelmed by the gracious quality of our life and the giftedness of our own good experience, to whom or what do we express our thanks? We do not send love-notes to the cosmos. And yet we must somehow give voice to our gratitude. In the face of injustice and suffering, especially in one's own life, and in the face of senseless and needless pain, to whom or what do we complain? Who or what will hear our cry for surcease and release (surely not the agents who inflict pain and injustice)? Where is the understanding that will finally make sense of these scattered pieces? Whose sympathy can work our brokenness and suffering into a redemptive wholeness?

Is my death the relinquishment of all intensity and the destruction of all that was in me of value? Or is my death a movement into the wholeness of life that is enriched by the good that I have become? These questions arise out of our own lostness and our own struggle for worth, and what we seek desperately is some justification of the best that is within us. Why struggle? Why endure? Why persevere in the good at all? Whose affirmation will give us the driving power to sacrifice selfishness to the greater good? Is there a basis that I should trust that not all is lost, all is not wasted and in vain?

Perhaps the most profound of religious questions is the one that each of us must face alone in the interior space of our own souls: Do I count? Do I make a difference at all—not just now at this moment, or in this life, but everlastingly? Thus it is that what we call our lives of faith (and not mere abstract faith) is the concrete living of our lives in a context which makes it possible to affirm that our most intense struggles and our most precious values are so inherently worthwhile that, despite the finitude of the cosmos and the finitude of our tiny selves, they will have everlasting value in the fullness of life which we call God. And because the inherent value of our lives is of infinite value to that Total Other, our inner souls will demand that we struggle to become the best and the finest, thus turning us away from easy pleasures and cheap satisfactions because the cause of life is so great that it will eventually demand of us a death, the loss of all chances.

Our praying at its best is a grappling with these issues which have the largeness of life. Notice that the praying comes out of the life-struggle itself, and our very praying is the actual placing of ourselves in trust to powers beyond ourselves. The lived conviction from which we will never be swayed is that the One whom we call God is that One to whom everything counts, to whom everything makes a difference. This Holy One who is love is concerned about and involved in the greatest and least among us since these are the content of his love.

## Unique and Personal Love

Our undying religious claim is that God loves each of us personally, with a unique and tender care, and with this one profound and incomprehensible assertion we lay purchase on the infinite value of every moment of our lives; we are the content of God's love, and therefore, foregoing traditional theological reluctance, we shape the quality of God's feelings. Only on condition that this unfathomable conviction is the life-force of our existence and the wellspring of our own unique hold on life will we ever be quickened to engage in prayer. Our indefatigable living out of this conviction constitutes our life of faith, and the concrete life of faith is the day-to-day embodiment of this conviction in specific acts of trust, perseverance, patience, praise, and love. It is only a life lived as defined by these qualities which provides the context for the life of prayer.

The conclusion here is that prayer flows out of faith, so that the deeper and more committed is our faith life, the more sense will our prayer make. It is precisely because we are caught in the struggle to live faithfully that we cry out, we complain, we question, we challenge, we doubt and we submit. All of these doings and various others represent our concrete grappling with meaning and wholeness set in the context of a Transcendence which, although inescapably mysterious and little understood, is finally trusted. Notice that our prayer is not the petition that an unresolved situation be resolved, not the request that some effect beyond our power be produced. Our praying is rather the resolving of ourselves; it is placing ourselves in the context which gives meaning to our experience where we do not yet see meaning. Thus the praying itself is the meaning-making activity which makes tolerable what seems random, and bearable what seems senseless.

## The Effect of Prayer: The Pray-er

If we are willing to abandon the almost adolescent desire "to get something out of" prayer in the sense of using prayer as an instrumentality to further our own good, then perhaps we can concentrate on our own faithfulness. It may well be the case, as difficult as this is to admit, that we do not pray well because we do not live faithfully. We can be random and disjointed in our commitments, casual and thoughtless in our promises. We can be halfhearted in our striving and mindless of our duties. In our sacramental liturgies, especially in our Eucharist, we have vowed ourselves to the God who is love, and from this point on the problem lies not with God but with ourselves. If, however, we endeavor to inform our lives by the leading of those vows (as, for example, concretely portrayed in the Gospels), then our prayer arises as an expression of our faith in those powers which transcend us.

As our living is never abstract and theoretical, neither can our prayer be such. For this reason the shape of our prayer will be an expression of faith in this life, in this universe, in the one God who holds all together. As the saying of "I love you" is a vowing to entrust myself to the presence of the other, so in like fashion our praying, as the expression of our being, is the entrusting of ourselves to the creative and supporting, though mysterious, relationships which flow from the universe and from God. This actual abiding and trusting in these relationships is the effect of prayer. This, then, is the lovely paradox of our God-informed lives: the only real effect of prayer is that we be prayerful. And being prayerful here means simply that we live our lives by faith.

Do we have the largeness to endure the insecurity of knowing that the effect of prayer is never a particular effect; the effect of prayer is, rather, the quality of the *pray-er*. The one who prays is the one who holds oneself in trust to God and to the universe; and the point of our trust is not that all things should be good nor all things right, but, surely, that all things should be bearable. Just as in the relationship of love there is no effect except the lover, so also in the relationship of prayer there is no effect except the pray-er. Both the lover and the pray-er can be identified by the obvious quality of their lives— why is it that "renewed" and "reborn" come so quickly to our lips?

Even those of us who are too timid to embrace whole-heartedly life in its passionate and bewildering intensity can see in the lover and the pray-er convictions and attitudes and values which give to them a claim to confidence and joy beyond our knowing. That is their faith. What flows from prayer is not the resolution of conflict, the removal of doubt, or the cessation of pain; what flows from prayer is the self in trust, the self in right relationship, the self with the confidence of a lover. There is no promise that prayer will solve anything; there is only the promise that prayer will allow us to cope with everything.

If we can but suspend our persistent yearning to use prayer as the instrument for spiritual or material betterment and refuse to regard the worth of our prayer in terms of its effectiveness in making us feel better, to be comforted, to be enlightened or even to be made fast in faith, then we might be in the proper position to discern the truth of prayer which in the depths of our hearts we always knew without being told. And the fearless truth is this: *our praying is an act of love.* The faith-context for our prayer which we have been insisting upon is finally nothing else than the context of love.

## Our Praying Is Our Loving

The soul and substance of our Gospel is that the Transcendent One who is the source and end of all our being is the gracious God who is love, all love and only love. It is not by dint of whim or fancy that thus far we have scrutinized the notion of prayer by placing it within the context of the analogy of the love-relationship. Perhaps because we have so casually separated our lives into sacred and secular spheres, we have in fact come to believe not just that there are two realms, but, worse, that there are irreconcilable divisions of our activities— those which are spiritual and those which are mundane. Can we be so insensible to our own inner reality to even entertain the lusterless thought that to be our best self we must divide our very being?

Too easily overlooked because of its stolid obviousness is the plain fact that all of those specialized and reserved activities which have acquired for themselves a distinctive religious terminology and thus give the somber impression that they exist in and for a separate realm are in reality nothing but quite commonplace and ordinary activities. It is just ordinary activitites which most serve to define the human configuration of our everyday striving for worthwhile selfhood. I refer here to such taken-for-granted human activities as hoping, trusting, striving, believing, having faith in, and loving. It is worth noting that our will and ability to do these sorts of things well is the determinant which defines our humanity and makes possible our most valued human experience. Our most intimate, interior personality is not only shaped by, it is the creation of, those things we believe in, hope for, trust in, and strive after. Precisely because these are the essential identifying characteristics of our human endeavor are they also the significant activities which are seized upon to make sense out of and give meaning to our spiritual quest.

We quite readily, for example, have faith and make love in the ordinary commerce of our everyday lives, and we do these things meaningfully and satisfyingly without the importation of religious terminology or spiritual explanation. The ordinary man-on-the-street can quite readily give a down-to-earth explanation of what it means to love his wife without invoking God, or grace, or supernatural life. As ordinary and commonplace as these activities may be, however, they are so essential to the integral process of self-creation that they are rightly sorted off as those very things which give the quality and the tone, the significance and the passion, to the demanding enterprise of experiencing our humanity in the most humane of contexts.

## The Faith of Love

With this background it should be a source of amazement to our dull sensibilities that we, ordinary people all, and some of us only randomly and occasionally religious in any explicit or formal sense, do manage to exercise great faith and make firm acts of faith with full commitment and integrity as one of the indispensable wellsprings of what is the very finest in our human interchange with other persons. I refer here to the commonplace but never ordinary relationship of being in love.

Every relationship of being-in-love to which we find ourselves drawn with such ease and willingness is the root-ground for our most personal and fundamental acts of faith, hope, and trust. Each time that we stand before another and say with whatever integrity we can summon, "I love you," we perform the most fundamental and existential act of faith ever within our power. For to be in love is to have faith in this other person—faith in the other's integrity, sincerity, commitment, loyalty and will. This is no idle or trivial claim. For when we are in love we quite literally place our hearts and souls into the hands of the beloved; we entrust our well-being and welfare to this relationship which is yet in the process of being created; we live in the firm hope that the passionate goodness so far experienced from the gifted relationship will continue only to increase and multiply.

To be in love is to commit our own destiny to the beloved who will have an irresistible control over who we will be. To be in love is to move into the land of the unknown and the realm of not-yet; it betokens the coming-to-be of this self, not isolated and independent, but only as informed and qualified by the presence of this other. And the inherent value of our own self-experience is committed and entrusted to a power and a decision which is not our own. This surely is faith, and trust, and hope in their most radical and essential form, and it is the very bone and marrow of what is most prized in our lives.

## The Faithfulness of Love

So it is that what is best and most valuable and most intense is that lived quality of our lives from which we sense our true humanity, that which is the creative source of our blossoming and growth into the fullness of persons, that which constitutes us as selves rather than objects, is the very human and accessible act of faith. To be-in-love then is to exist in faith; and this being-in-love as a concrete actuality over the long-haul of the years of our lives is then our passionate struggle to live faithfully—faithful to our commitment to another and to self, faithful to this relationship with its unexpected demands, faithful in gratitude for giftedness, faithful in our own loveliness.

It is with astute wisdom that our wedding ritual should include the words "for better for worse, for richer for poorer, in sickness and in health." For all is not sweetness and light, and these are some of the unknown qualities which can yet rise up out of and because of this relationship; in the possible moments of anguish and suffering occasioned by the unpre-

dictability of human constancy we repeatedly face but one
selfsame question: Will I be faithful? For to be faithful is to
continue in love.

## Love-Faith

If this analysis in some way rings true to the touchstone of
our own experience of loving and being loved, then we will
have an intuitive grasp of this simple yet primordial truth:
faith and love are but the two sides of the self held in commitment, two aspects of existing within a relationship which is
both gratuitous and gracious, the twofold activity of the mirrored self created by the presence of lovely others. Precisely
because this experience of love-faith sits as the unfathomable
life-root of our experience as person, it has been seized upon as
the indispensable paradigm for our comprehension, not merely intellectual but also existential, of our relationship to the
supreme value of our lives, the Transcendent One who is the
God of love.

As was developed earlier, our acceptance into our lives of
the assertion that God is love commits us to but one single
relationship—the relationship of faith-love. What we call our
faith is but the concrete living of our lives in faithfulness to the
love which has already come to us in the gracious and sacramental presence of all the universe. Within this context it can
be understood how prayer is the activity of the faithful person.
Just as the lover feels compelled to say, "I love you," so the
faithful person feels constrained to pray.

## Why We Say "I Love You"

Just as we do not say "I love you" in order to fall in love, so
also we do not pray in order that we may have faith. The
saying of love and the speaking out of prayer arise out of love-
faith and are in themselves a way of being both loving and
faithful. In much the same way that what we call the "acts of
love," such as holding, touching, kissing, and sexual intercourse, can be separated from the relationship of loving only

with the danger of profanation and prostitution, so also the expression of faith which we call prayer cannot be separated from the concrete, soul-engendering relationship which is love-faith. Because I love this other I kiss and touch and hold; likewise, because I have faith in the God who is love I express my passionate commitment in prayer because this is the only thing, as it is also the best thing, that I can do.

In similar fashion, our being-in-love is not meant to resolve our problems, remove our doubts, substitute for our inadequacies or transform our imperfections. It is, rather to provide the meaningful context within which we are enabled to struggle to resolve our very own selves. From the loving relationship we receive both the motivation and the energizing power to work against our own weakness toward that ideal good which the beloved has already seen within us. In parallel fashion, our prayer cannot be intended to answer our inadequacy, or supply for our lostness, or remedy our pain, or remove the injustice which weighs upon us. Rather, within the context of faith, our prayer is the making of meaning out of these disorderly and disruptive qualities of our experience; prayer gathers these inequities and inequalities into a totally new context and provides meaning by placing our own selves (rather than the discrepant items) within the relationship of the God who finally holds all things together unto good.

Just as each saying of "I love you" both places us before the beloved and simultaneously discloses something new and remarkable about us, so also each speaking of prayer is both placing ourselves before the God of love and coincidentally discovering an uncommon wealth in our very weakness. This is simply another way of observing the non-instrumentality of both love and prayer. Neither relationship is designed to produce effects external to the relationship; this is not to say, however, that love and prayer are inconsequential because they are non-productive.

What can be called the effects of loving and praying are the enhancement of the experienced qualities which constitute the very essence of the lover and the pray-er. To love is to become more lovely, as to pray is to become more faithful. The effect lies in the enrichment of the relationship itself, and nowhere else. When we love and when we pray we grow larger and we grow fuller. It is this abundance and none other which lures us into loving and praying.

## What Do Lovers Do?

The intimate relationship between love and faith as they occur in our most ordinary of situations can serve to shed new light on our relationship with God. In the case of love, we might ask, "What do lovers *do?*" The point of this question is to focus our attention on the manifold activities which do in fact take place between lovers. For example, lovers will hold hands, embrace, kiss, and have sexual intercourse. All of these activities belong in a most intimate way to the relationship between the lovers. But can any one of these activities be singled out as the uniquely special activity of loving? Is any one of these absolutely essential to the relationship of loving?

Not only is the answer to this question in the negative, but it serves to point out that all of these activities only gain their meaning *within* the relationship of loving and do not constitute the relationship itself. Again we ask: What do lovers do that is distinctly and uniquely the act of loving? The answer is that lovers do not do anything special in terms of overt or external activities.

What lovers *do* is to make themselves *present* to and for the other. It is for this reason that all of the activities in which lovers engage, some of them special to this unique relationship and others common to a variety of relationships, are but instrumental activities through which the intimate and recessed self of the lover becomes present to and before the beloved. Being-in-love is this mutual interchange of radical presence within the other and the reception of the other within oneself.

If we look upon love as this "presence within," then, not surprisingly the finest language of poets and mystics becomes astonishingly clear—beholding the world through the eyes of the other, thinking with the thoughts of the other, feeling with the feelings of the other. Cool-minded skeptics would have it that all such images are objectively impossible and serve as mere flights of fancy. Lovers know differently. Love is in fact this mutuality of shared selves which is constituted by this uniquely interpersonal interchange in which two do become one and the self of the lover is now inescapably enhanced by the qualitative presence of the beloved. To hold otherwise is to belittle and trivialize our most precious and creative experience, our everyday and concrete being-in-love.

Such loving is the ordinary stuff of our most commonplace lives. We have the uncommon good sense to realize that such loving, after the fashion of the yeast mentioned in the Gospels, works subtly like an infection of the spirit to transform our ordinariness into spectacular and vibrant abundance. When we are in love we have every good reason for living.

## What Do Faithful People Do?

In our love-faith relationship with God who is love the same essential features constitute the very essence of the relationship. In our religiously faithful lives we perform a host of activities which we instinctively regard as the crucial focal-point of our faithfulness: we engage in liturgy and celebrate sacraments, we share in formal prayer and remove ourselves to the silence of private prayer. Does any single one of these activities, or all of them together, serve to constitute what we mean by our relationship with God? Once again, the answer must be negative. And yet the wisdom of our spiritual predecessors has sensed rightly that it is in these activities of conscious self-dedication that we place our very selves into the presence of the transcendent One and feel the weight of that Other press upon our lives.

It is for this reason that a real function of our prayer is to unveil ourselves, to speak out of our depths, to overcome our timidity and say out who we are before our God. This deliberate showing forth of our truest selves, in a mixture of faith and doubt, confidence and fear, struggle and weakness, is the placing of ourselves before the presence of God, while the love which draws us forth outside of ourselves is the presence of God within us.

Recalling that one of our most traditional of theological tenets proclaimed that God is everywhere, we need only realize that the presence of God inexorably and infallibly surrounds our lives like air just as God's love is as sure as gravity. It is we, thoughtless at times and selfish at times, who must bring ourselves into the presence of that One who is never absent. Can we be attuned, not to the poetic, but to the literal quality of Paul's proclamation: "I live now, not I, but it is Christ who lives in me" (Gal 2:20)? This is the unambiguous promise of the Gospels—the faithful ones will become godly, by coming to the presence of the God who is as close as our own heart.

### Why We Pray

It is through our praying, therefore, that we seek to put ourselves in tune with the One who is never absent, the One who is present to our waking and our sleeping, to our good will and bad. The effort of our praying is not so much that God become aware of us, but, rather, that we can steep ourselves in that holy presence which lurks behind all human faces and even appears in the shape of bread.

All of our sacramental activity is but our ritualized praying in which we seek to discern and to trust the relationships which create us, that we in turn might create ourselves in the image of that creative power which we call the God of love. To hold faith in a power which transcends us and is ever shrouded in mystery is surely not evident or obvious, and rarely could it be easy. Perhaps it is that we pray poorly and we pray badly because we love poorly and we love badly. The only context for my loving is this neighbor who stands before my face; if here I can say "I love you," then I will discover prayer.

### Selected Readings

Wilfred Cantwell Smith, more than any other current thinker, has concentrated on the understanding of the notion of faith. The range of materials he covers is formidable, and yet the wealth of insight afforded is immensely rewarding. A good introduction into the work of Smith can be found in *The Meaning and End of Religion,* especially Chapter Seven, "Faith," and Chapter Six, "The Cumulative Tradition" (San Francisco: Harper and Row, 1978). For a more extended treatment, see *Faith and Belief* (Princeton, N.J.: Princeton University Press, 1979).

William McNamara, O.C.D. has written a popular work on prayer and contemplation which contains a good deal of useful material, *The Human Adventure: Contemplation for Everyman.* Especially relevant to the issues of this present section is Chapter Five, "The Heart of Religion" (Garden City, New York: Image Books and Doubleday, 1976).

Paul Holmer has worked out most carefully the relationship between faith and faithfulness in *The Grammar of Faith.* See especially Chapter Seven, "Theology and Concepts."

*Scripture Reading*

The Letter to the Ephesians Chapter 3: 14–21

The Gospel of Luke Chapter 18: 9–14

# 6

# The Power of God:
# Coercive and Suasive Power

The preceding discussion of prayer represents the attempt to be both serious and literal with that decisive and unrelinquishable revelation of the Gospel: God is love. By using as our model of the spiritual life the paradigm of the relationship of love, it is hoped that our own existential awareness of the qualitative value of our loving will bring an understanding to our faith life that this verbal presentation, halting and imperfect as it is, can never hope to do. If we look upon our prayer as a mode of relationship rather than as an objective type of activity, perhaps we can discern a singular resonance between the strivings of our love and the strivings of our faith. This will make of our praying a wholly interpersonal interchange with no purpose beyond the passionate intensity of the interrelationship, which is the love of God.

Such an approach is not without its problems. Can any of us deny that, whatever else we may have done with our prayer, we have attempted to use it to achieve for ourselves goods, spiritual or material, which we deemed a pressing need for our own best welfare? What I refer to here is the traditional and cherished notion of *the prayer of petition.* If we wish to hold to the claim that prayer is a non-instrumental activity and hence cannot be utilized for further ends, then we have the telling challenge to explain and make sense out of our prayer of petition which is surely one of the most common practices of believers. As a necessary preliminary to a discussion of the prayer of petition, this chapter will be an investigation of what we mean by *the power of God.*

## Prayer and the Power of God

We have stressed beforehand that the only religiously coherent way to understand the reality of the God who is love is to affirm that the only relationships possible for a loving God are the relationships of love. This is not to take away any prerogatives from God or to set limitations on the power of God. But if, as we assert, God is wholly and solely love, then what exactly would be meant by the power of God and in what fashion would this power be exercised? Because of the very far-reaching religious implications of this question for our spiritual lives, a careful investigation of the concept of power is crucial to our religious understanding.

As has been pointed out, the religious significance of the revelation that God is love is to remove God irrevocably from the status of an idol. The God of love is the God of gifted and gracious relationships whose essential character is to hold all things in love. Of all the relationships which we manage to engender within our human enterprise, the relationship of love is that unique one which cannot be utilized for further ends—love is for the sake of loving, and for nothing else. This ineradicable feature of the nature of love entails the non-instrumentality of our relationship to God.

God is for love, and for nothing else. In response to our earlier question "What is God for?" we saw that the only religiously plausible answer had to be: God is for nothing. God can only be related to in love; God can never be used for ends and purposes beyond the relationality of love itself. To attempt to use God for the achievement of any good, no matter how noble or spiritual, is the attempt to use God, and if God could be used God would be an idol. If there is one claim that has always stood at the heart of our faith it is the tenacious assertion that our living God is not an idol.

Is it possible, however, that what we staunchly proclaim

with our lips we subtly deny in our actions? I refer here to our most frequent and possibly our most satisfying use of prayer—the prayer of petition. Let us be scrupulously honest and straightforwardly admit that we do ask God *for* things. I submit at this point that the specific nature of the things requested is irrelevant—whether salvation, grace, eternal life, or a raise in salary. In each case we work with the silent assumption that our right relationship with God can be productive of good effects in and for our lives, and this we find not only religiously consoling but also personally rewarding.

I am not suggesting that what I describe here is done out of malice, ill-intent, or even dim-wittedness. The notion of prayer as petition is something that has ridden through our long tradition with sublime consistency and seemingly with a Gospel blessing. How has it come about that the non-instrumentality of the God of love is so readily and unquestioningly joined to the instrumental use of God in the cause of petitions? It is this strange paradox which we will search out, and the heart of this paradox lies in our concept of power.

## Being and Power

The substance worldview which provides the underlying presuppositions for most of Western theology is based on the existence of objective being. Any reality which could be said to exist in any definite sense had to be describable within some category of being. With this starting point philosophers proceeded to investigate the variety of beings contained within reality and then to differentiate these beings into categories. Regardless of the classifications arrived at, the common thread running through all distinctions of being was the concept of power.

One of the foundational minds of Western philosophy, Plato, said succinctly: "Being is power." If we but consider such unexceptional and taken-for-granted distinctions as living/non-living, animal/mineral, rational/non-rational, and material/spiritual, we see that in each case the root of the distinction lies in an analysis of what type of power the being possesses. For example, the distinction of living and non-living as applied to the concrete reality of a dog and a rock is simply a specification that different activitites are possible for the dog than for the rock. In the same fashion, the distinction between rational and non-rational is simply a differentiation based on the appreciation that a rational being can perform operations which lie outside of the power of the non-rational being.

## The God of Power

This is an obvious and straightforward way of categorizing reality, but the implications are far-reaching. Notice how these categorical distinctions come into play when applied to God. Here we have the divisions of finite being/infinite being, caused being/uncaused being, conditioned being/unconditioned being, and ordinary being/supreme being. (Remarkable but not unexpected is the easy use of the categorical description "supreme being" as a proper name, as "Supreme Being.") All of these distinctions are readily understandable as simple distinctions of power. The momentous weight of this salient point must be fully appreciated, for it lays down the bedrock presupposition of the traditional understanding of God.

The inevitable implication of this style of categorization is the patent but sometimes unanalyzed entailment: the Supreme Being is that being with supreme power; the Infinite Being is that being with infinite power; the Uncaused Cause is that being with absolute causal power; the Unconditioned Being is that being whose power is conditioned by no other. It is suggested here that our traditional Western allegiance to the God of absolute and supreme power is no accident; it is the direct and inescapable result of seeing the inherent value of being as a matter of the degree of power. Philosophically, the highest conceivable compliment to the divinity was the attribution of infinite and unconditioned power.

## Power and the God of Love

What is much more difficult to comprehend is how those who stood rooted in the Gospel tradition could so comfortably hold in balance the God of unfathomable love and the God of infinite power. In reality, it was an uneasy alliance and never for one moment was there a safe balance. The philosophical definition of God as the being of infinite power was the attribution which not only dominated, but dictated to, all subsequent theological exploration of the nature and workings of the deity. The concept of God as love continued to have homiletic force and preserved a depth of spiritual value. But the God of power served as the ultimate explanatory principle which defined the relationships of the universe.

Most of the terms which were predicated of God even in religious usage, such as the majesty of God, the sovereignty of God, and the absoluteness of God, carried their special weight because they were understood within the context of the infinite power of God. This attribution of supreme power to the Supreme Being is a direct result of our perceived relationships to power in our objective world: power is the ability to produce effects. The effective use of power is one of the overarching instrumentalities in our unflagging attempts to manipulate a universe of objects, to subdue the chaos of randomness and potent forces into a semblance of utilizable order, not merely to improve our fitful human lot but also to avert disaster and destruction.

## Tensions Between Love and Power

Perhaps it was in terms of some strange comfort that we seemingly held together in some improbable tension the two divergent poles: our prayers were addressed to the God of love, but our theology was formulated in terms of the God of power. This very improbability was invoked for religious purposes: on the one hand, God loved us with infinite and infallible love; on the other hand, failure to respond to the love and will of God would result in God's damnation of the sinful soul. Stated in its most vulgar terms (for that is what it is) we have here perhaps the classic theological example of the carrot and the stick. While our most noble and most supreme ideals were

set forth in terms of the love of God, the final and coercive
motivation was not inspired by the selfless response to love but
rather in the selfish fear of punishment or hell. The God of
supreme love was also the God of infinite power, and what
God's love failed to accomplish, his power could more than
make up for. This crude reduction of the consummate value of
our full-hearted response to the fullness of life to our half-
hearted and self-interested avoidance of evil, not for the sake
of God, but for self-love and self-protection, is not merely
religiously false; it is also spiritually destructive.

Such a dispiriting result is inevitable, however, if God is
construed primarily in terms of power. If we but analyze how
much of our popular form of religious practice was based upon
establishing a sustaining relationship with that being who had
unqualified power to produce within us and within our lives
good effects as well as bad, bring about our salvation as well as
our damnation, procure our blessing as well as provide an
indefectible curse, perhaps we will be compelled to admit that
our deepest motivation for a relationship to God was the
manipulation of power. Dare we whisper this in the inner-
sanctum of our souls: *God was useful.*

The disconcerting outcome of this unspoken premise is
that our relationship of love to the God of love, the only salvific
relationship available, was reduced to a form of ungracious
self-indulgence. In its crudest form we were proclaiming that
it was indeed worthwhile to love God, for this was a matter of
very high reward and beneficent favors, as well as of punish-
ments and untoward mischief. God was worth loving because
God could do many things for us and to us. I state this matter
in its starkest forms because of the serious religious implications it entails; it is more than worthwhile to be not merely
clear but fully convinced of this matter, because our very souls
are at stake.

The religious problem can be reduced to a topic previously discussed: Do we dare make an instrument out of God? Do
we worship God because God is then somehow subservient to
our purposes? Do we pray to God because we are interested in
the effects of power? To state the case almost paradoxically: Is

the infinitely creative force of our lives the force of power or the power of love? The position taken here is that we must choose between the two; we cannot have both. The ultimate reasons for the unavoidability of this choice have already been presented in the previous chapter; however, they will be systematically developed here.

## The Problem: Two Types of Power

Perhaps it is the very notion of power which confuses us, for at the surface level there does not appear to be anything inherently wrong with the use of power or with the manipulation of power for the production of good effects. This sort of relationship to power constitutes the bread-and-butter of our daily living in an objective world. But for the very reason that the utilization of power is such a commonplace of our everyday lives, we perhaps unwittingly lump together a variety of notions derived from our experience of power which are in fact quite distinct. It is suggested here that this blurring of distinctions is the root-cause for the misconception of the type of power we mistakenly attribute to the God of love. I will analyze a basic distinction in the types of power under the heading of *efficient causality* and *final causality* with the subsequent correlations of *coercive power* and *suasive power*.

## Efficient Causality

In a substance worldview we see ourselves as existing within a world of objects. The objectivity of the items within this universe of beings will be determined by the power exhibited. Within this world of objects our common understanding of power is simply that power is the ability to produce a result; it is the ability to bring about a change in something else or the ability to bring about a difference—in brief, power is the capability of a cause to produce an effect. It is in a world of objective beings, whether atoms, rocks, mountains, or suns, moons and stars, that the notion of power is construed, basically, as the ability to have an effect on objects. What power will be required to move an electron, or a rock, or a moon? This type of power which can bring about an effect in an object has traditionally been termed "efficient causality," and it refers to the power inherent in one object which can be brought to bear to produce a change in another object.

Beginning with the classical exposition of Newton, the entire rise of modern science has been founded upon and made possible by the precisely calculated notion of efficient causality. However, to refer to the power which an object has to affect another object is to compute the degree of force. Whether we advertise the horsepower of new cars or estimate the detonative capacity of a ton of dynamite, we are simply prescribing the amount of force that will be exerted against counter-forces. For this reason, what is termed efficient causality is at bottom a matter of force, where the distinctive characteristic of force is that it is necessarily force over or force against.

## Brute Force

Our common parlance quite easily and rightly adds the word "brute" to the word "force," and we are not at all puzzled by what we mean by brute force. Brute force is power exerted over or against another, and such exertion of force needs no consent from the recipient. Brute force is effective precisely because it is the power of force exerted against lesser powers. Because it is power *over*, the agreement or cooperation of the lesser power is in no way required.

Herein perhaps lies the base meaning of the appellation "brute"—it can work effectively in direct opposition to choice, freedom, and consent. In a context of free-choosers like ourselves, efficient causality and brute force obviate completely the need for choice or the consent of the free-subject. We are familiar with and not at all threatened by the brute power of a locomotive engine; we are equally familiar with but a bit more threatened by the brute force of a nuclear bomb. Such items are simple indications of the way in which the world of objects can be manipulated to serve human purposes. But, unfortunately, we are also familiar with the brute power of a well-equipped attacking army and the brute force carried with the tear-gas and billy-clubs of a police line breaking up a demonstration.

That the efficient power of brute force is such an unremarkable commonplace of our lives is perhaps a desperate commentary on how far we have abdicated all claims to the real world of our personal lives. Parents strike their children, and the reasons they can do this is because they are stronger and thus have power over weakness. What are genteelly called authoritarian governments operate by the powers of repression—the power to kill, imprison, torture—in each case a greater bureaucratic power working against individual weakness. All governments, whether civil or ecclesiastical, claim to function by law, but the motivating weight of the law is the power to inflict punishment, whether exile or excommunication. The point of these examples is that they are neither extraordinary nor remarkable but are rather the taken-for-granted stuff of complex social intercourse. However, in each case the power is a force set against weakness and a power that will effect the result regardless of the choice or will or cooperation of the personal subject. It is for this reason that this model of power can be termed *coercive.*

### Coercive Power

Coercive power at the level of human interchange is the imposition of one person's will upon another by the exertion of force. That coercive power both at the social and the individual level is such an unquestioned cliché in our unavoidable dealings with the recalcitrant—whether the unruly child, the protester hurling obscenities, or the revolutionary cadre throwing fire-bombs—serves as a damning indictment that our social and personal heresy has vanquished religious orthodoxy to the level of romantic idealism.

When the club or the tear-gas is aimed at our own heads we are stirred to cry out with instinctive creedal faith: "I am a person; I am not an object." So right. Persons are not objects and hence persons can never be used, instrumentalized, or made subservient to other purposes. Why then do we so readily abandon this intuitive good faith when, for the best of good ends, we are willing to use force, violence, and repression to induce cooperation from the will of others?

Is it possible to see the straight line drawn across a substance worldview which leads to the perception of all reality as mere objects and ends with the forceful manipulation of persons as objects in the pursuit of worthy goals as a laudatory and righteous enterprise? Unhappily, we are too deeply habituated to the practical functioning of coercive power in our social universe to dare entertain the seemingly blasphemous thought that herein might reside our primordial sin. If coercive power is such a violation of the inherent dignity of human personhood, might it not also be a violation of the essence of the universe itself? With our twentieth century scientific minds and our twenty first century technology we find it unimaginable to tame a universe into our home without the widespread application of efficient and coercive power. We are so used to it; it seems so right.

## Personal Coercive Power

Through the almost unconscious weight of our Western worldview which has reached its peak in the highly efficient manipulative powers of scientific technology, we have somehow naturalized ourselves into the acceptance of systematic coercive power as the conquest of enlightened intellect over the chaotic forces of unruly matter. It comes to us with undeniable hallmarks of necessity and naturalness. That coercive power should also stand as the trademark of human social relations is accepted as the necessary, even if unpleasant, consequence of human recalcitrance to the good and fallenness from grace.

The resulting models of authority, both religious and secular, have enshrined coerciveness as a cultural given under the rationalization that a certain amount of coercion was a fair price for the social good. Both princes and Popes were spoken of as having "power over" their subjects, and in each case it was a power that could be enforced. The freedom of the children of God which was our inalienable Gospel heritage was understood as freedom to obey rather than freedom to create our own lives.

The argument is not that coercive power has not done some good at various times and places and for certain people; the argument is, rather, that coercive power is at all times and places, even with the noblest of intentions, a violation of human freedom and a ravishment of the person. It is both to treat persons as objects and to justify the end by the means—the effective demolishing of the natural basis for any urgent claim to the inherent sacredness of every human person.

### God and Efficient Power

Because our basic model for God has been that of Supreme Being, the essential characteristic which defined the divinity was supreme or absolute power. I have no doubt that a deep and compelling religious intuition underlies this need to view God in terms of power, and hence this is not the burden of my objection. Where objection can be made is in regard to the type of power attributed to God.

Since our generalized and unreflective use of the concept of power is derived from that model of power which is most influential in our lives, namely, efficient power, this selfsame model will be applied to God with little question as to its appropriateness. We find it near impossible to eradicate our catechism-level assertion that God is that Being who can do anything at all (except a contradiction); everything is within the power of God. When this claim is fleshed out into concrete examples, every incident pointed to is a clear-cut case of efficient causality. God, therefore, is that being worth respecting, honoring, and obeying, simply because of the awesome and unpredictable power which could on the one hand create us and on the other hand destroy us.

However much security and comfort such a model of divine power may afford us, we are well advised to reappraise it in the light of our spiritual quest. Is efficient power really the model for our fundamental relationship to God? Is our basic relationship to God a relationship of power to weakness? Are we committed to the service of God motivated by fear of the power of God? Do we see the inherent worthwhileness of the God-relationship in the fact that God has the power to supply for our weakness, that God can do for us those things which we cannot do for ourselves? To state this in its most vulgar form: Are we interested in God because of what God can do for us?

## God: Worthy of Worship

Such questions are neither silly nor inconsequential since the types of answers offered will necessarily characterize the essential nature of our spiritual odyssey. We should not be afraid to forge answers for ourselves, however, since our religious instincts are often better than certain theological conclusions. All we need do is to make the simple turn into our own souls and ask: *Who is our God?*

Let us part company for the moment with the philosophers and theologians who speak easily about God and associate our sensibilities with those who speak to God out of the depths of their own experience, those in the Gospels, for example, and the great mystic-saints. All without exception would cry: God is that one worthy of worship; God alone is worthy of worship. Rooted in their Gospel heritage they point to Jesus as one who intimately knew God; if anyone had ever rightly worshiped God it was Jesus. As to what worship would mean in the concrete actuality of our lives, Jesus has stated the case as clearly as it could ever be stated: "Love God with your whole heart, your whole mind, your whole soul, and with all your strength" (Mt 22:37).

God is that One of such fantastic importance that that incredible and almost unachievable totality of response—the wholeness of heart, mind, soul, and strength—is the only necessary and sufficient quality of worship. But we dare not miss the import of the opening word, which is "love"—*love* God with the totality of your being. The inestimable value of God is that God alone is supremely lovable, and hence to God alone can the wholeness of our life and striving be committed in love.

## Is Power Worthy of Worship?

If God alone, however, is to be worshiped, what is it about God that is worshipful? Because of our own inadequacy, is it really power that we want to worship? Because of our own inability to achieve good ends, is it supreme efficient power that we worship? Out of our undeniable sense of finiteness and weakness, is it power that we choose to worship? Are we indeed so alienated from our own personhood that we could conceivably commit our hearts to supreme power? Are we in fact so secularized that we imagine power to be the most sublime of qualities in the universe?

Is it possible that our interest in the God of power is predicated upon our own desire to manipulate that power? Are we possibly interested in devoting ourselves to God because of those things which God can do for us? Do we worship God because of the effects he can bring about or the favors he can procure? Do we worship God because this will bring about our salvation? Need it always be the case that we worship God with an ulterior motive in mind? Are we so crass that our very desire to worship is contaminated by the desire to use God for our own purposes? If the notion of efficient power continues to be a defining characteristic of God, then the above-mentioned abuses will almost inexorably follow. To relate to a being with supreme power while forsaking any interest in that power is perhaps too much to ask.

## Final Causality: Suasive Power

We have already alluded, however, to the fact that the presupposition which originates the logic of attributing supreme efficient power to God is the perception of a world whose basic realities are objects. It is beyond reasonable question that efficient power is the manner in which objects are manipulated and utilized in the objective world. But to allow the logic of objects to dictate the relationships between interpersonal subjects is to sever ourselves from human rationality altogether. The only right place to start is within ourselves and to analyze what we mean by responding to or exerting power.

Our intuitive awareness as well as our religious affirmation is that we are uniquely individual persons, human selves with power of self-decision and self-direction. Only a moment's reflection on those singular occasions in our own lives when we felt most growthful and creative, when we felt that we had enlarged the boundaries of our selfhood and experienced a deeper sense of self-worth, will reveal that these were those rare and special times when we took charge of our lives, made a decision out of our own strength and moved toward a goal which we found both attractive and compelling. We acted out of our own strength from no other compulsion except our inner desire to achieve an envisioned good. It is these self-decisions which are the source-point of human growth and movement and our creative decision blossoms best only when freed from all external constraint. In sum, we are persons and not objects, and we are most true to our essential selfhood when we respond from the wealth of our own power of choice, rather than when power is imposed upon us.

On the other hand, we feel most abused and demeaned when the will of another is imposed upon our own, when threat or force of whatever sort—psychological, emotional, physical—supplies the coercion which causes our will to submit. In these cases we do not choose straightforwardly the proffered good; we choose, rather, the avoidance of evil to ourselves.

## Response to Ideals and Values

If our own experience verifies this account of things, then perhaps we can see the logic of substituting a different model for our understanding of power. The root question is not: How do we move objects around the universe? How do we exert power to effect changes in objects? The question shifts, rather, to a personal one: How is power exercised between persons? How do persons exert influence on one another? How does a free person influence a free person to act freely?

On the one hand, we have experienced our power over others so that they have chosen something we deemed desirable, and likewise we have felt ourselves responding willingly to the power of others over us. On the other hand, in these situations there need not be the slightest hint of coercion or suggestion of compulsion. We have experienced a form of power which works efficaciously within the context of human freedom.

If we try to analyze exactly what steps we take in order to induce a free person to choose freely, we will discover that our first step is to propose reasons for the desired choice. We intend that the offered reasons serve as motivation to influence the other's choice. But why is it that these suggested reasons should function as motivation? Ordinarily those things which we select as reasons will contain a purpose, a goal, or a value, and this purpose or value suggested in the reason is proposed as a value worth striving for. The value, however, resides within the goal itself and is not extrinsic to it. It is the inherent worth of the end itself which exerts a power of attraction drawing the will to choose it.

### Persuasion

The only suitable activity of the agent in this case is that of *persuasion.* If we are to respect the freedom of others, the only legitimate power we can exert is our ability to influence, and we influence free choice primarily through persuasion. This persuasion is exercised by the presentation of a final cause, which is a value or a purpose which contains within itself the reasons for choosing it. Our activity of persuading is always our attempt to show forth the inherent beauty and intrinsic goodness of the end or goal in view. It is finally not our power but the power of the inherent attractiveness of the end which draws the free subject to choose. It is important to notice here that effects are produced, choices toward action are made, but the power involved in no way is coercive. The type of causality operating here is termed final causality, and the form of power embodied is called *suasive power.*

The contrast between coercive and suasive power is something about which we are experientially aware. These two modes of power have only one thing in common: desired goals are achieved and desired effects are produced. As to their manner of operation and the mode of force employed they are at completely opposite poles. The power of final causality is not coercion; it is rather a drawing power, that is, the inherent power of beauty, goodness, and value to attract us to choose. We are enticed by something that appears good, and precisely because it appears good we strive to achieve it.

In Whitehead's lovely phrase, we are "lured" by the good, the beautiful, the right. When we desire something, we are persuaded to choose by something attractive within the object itself; we are responding to the inherent worth which we perceive likewise as worth for the self. This luring power of the inherently valuable is called suasive power, since the power of persuasion which lures us to choose is intrinsic to the end itself and in no way external to it. It is a tribute to our humanity that we spontaneously respond to our power of choosing the good and the beautiful for the one and only reason that they are good and beautiful.

### Suasive Power and Freedom

This suasive power which lures can only make sense if there is such a thing as free choice. Absolutely essential to the concept of suasion is the freedom of the chooser; in fact, precisely because the chooser is truly free the only meaningful power which would not be a violation of that freedom is suasive. Choice can only be made as a free response to something inherently attractive and persuasive in its own right. Whereas coercive power works against the will of the chooser and must work against weakness, suasive power can only function in the presence of freedom and works optimally in the face of greatest strength.

If we but consider our own life-choices we will notice that our most creative choices were not made out of weakness—we were not giving in, nor were we avoiding something, nor were we fearful of some result; on the contrary, our finest choices were made out of great strength. These were the occasions when we were fully aware that we faced a matter of great consequence, that there were real alternatives, that the choice pursued would have a profound effect on our own lives; out of the sense of our own strength that the choice was fully in our hands we made a decision that would have weighty effects and we would take responsibility for the consequences.

This is both a position of strength and a condition for self-growth and creativity. Life-choices, such as the choice to get married, the choice to enter the religious life, the choice to serve in the ministry, and even the choice to live celibately, are rightly made only out of personal strength and freedom. We alone are responsible for the persons we become, and our becoming is informed by the attractive and suasive values that lure us to move toward their achievement.

### The Power of Suasive Power

The attractive and luring quality of suasive power should not deceive us into thinking romantically that simply because we are responding freely the path to achievement will be easy, or painless, or uncomplicated. It is worth noting, rather, how much we are willing to endure in the struggle to achieve something we truly esteem good. If one chooses to study for a graduate degree, for example, one finds that one also must put up with endless classes, tedious examinations, tiresome term papers and exhausting comprehensives. We are willing to put up with these trials because the goal appears valuable enough to make endurance possible. Or consider the married couple who desire to have a child: bringing a child into the world means also sustaining the child in the well-being of life, and toward this end sacrifices even to death are not uncommon.

Difficulty, pain, effort, suffering, endurance—these are all overshadowed and made tolerable by the inherent value of the final end, but in no way do they disappear. Why is it that we even strive for some good in the face of hardship and pain to ourselves? We so strive because the value of the goal is perceived, not as an achievement which merely accrues to ourselves, but rather as a condition of our own self-growth and self-worth. We know with an untaught wisdom that we are primarily involved in our own self-creation, and the form of our creation is shaped by those values we take into ourselves.

It is a striking feature of the person as chooser that one's self is perceived as a transcending being invariably moving beyond the present toward the future. What we perceive as ends or goals are always out beyond us, lying in the future, and it is for this reason that their only power is suasive rather than coercive. They are not yet a concrete reality in our lives and hence cannot exercise the efficient causality of physical objects. Rather we are lured to move beyond our present stage of experiencing toward a satisfaction which yet lies ahead; we are lured into a richness of experiencing still in the making, informed by an ideal not yet realized.

## The Power of Ideals

Final causality is the category which best explains how we make our free choices. The descriptive words which we spontaneously invoke to describe how we respond to ideals are indicative: we say that we are attracted by an ideal, find it desirable, feel lured by the ideal, by its value. None of these terms implies force or coercion; moreover, none of them can be coherently meaningful if coercion is entailed.

Our own personal experience can supply the only worthwhile litmus test here: In what occasions have we felt ourselves most growthful, most enriched, most fulfilled? It is those occasions in which we have responded out of our strength to the beauty which is available for the enhancement of our lives. Once again, the only concrete example that can be personally persuasive is the relationship of love. The very meaning of love demands that there be no force, no power over, no coercion. Why do we fall in love? Because we are attracted by the beauty of the other and the desire to hold this other in a relationship that will qualify our experience with the intensity of this beauty. The loveliness of the relationship itself lures us into the involvement of our response. and the relationship itself has the power to entice, to attract, to draw us out of ourselves and into a relationship whose very satisfaction includes possibilities for the future.

We love best only when we love both out of freedom and out of strength; we love well only when the loveliness of the beloved is more suasive than our own selfishness. We cannot be forced to become better, but we can be persuaded. We cannot be coerced into loving, but we can be lured. The graciousness of the universe and its God is such that those values most creative of our very being, enshrined in the ideals which inspire us and the ends which lure us, are in fact available for our choosing. The quality of our lives is defined by the worth of the striving in which we are willing, not merely to involve, but to lose ourselves.

As part of the conversion story of St. Francis is the tale of his opening the book of the Gospels three times and there finding the passage which enjoined him to set out on a journey without shoes, without purse, without a coat, and to offer to all whom he encountered the peace of God. With characteristic spontaneity, Francis responded with deep conviction: "This is what I want to do; this I wish to do with all my heart." The rest of the story of the life of Francis is but the beautiful and tragic history of the making of a saint as he responded with the goodness of all his strength to an ideal of Christlikeness which brought him finally to a tragic but sublime death.

What has attracted millions of us in the centuries since his death is the awesome but lovely power by which this gifted, spoiled, but sensitive young man responded with the wholeness of his heart to an ideal of beauty that gradually transformed him into the beauty of Christ. Such beauty of life is possible to all of us—this we know. What we lack is Francis' passionate conviction that such an ideal can be enfleshed in each and every one of us. As his life richly demonstrates, to respond to such an ideal embarks us upon a life of adventure

and risk and darkness. What sets it apart, however, as supremely worthwhile, is the intensity of its passion.


## The Lovely Power of Suasive Power: Love

Lest this view of the suasive power as the formative power
of our lives sound too ethereal or impractical with little hold on
reality, let us review some instances in which there can be
absolutely no doubt that suasive power is real power. It can
easily be objected at this point that suasive power is so romantic a view as to be useful only to poets or hermits, but the daily
newspapers give the lie to this easy dismissal. We are all too
familiar with numerous factual accounts describing the desperate attempts of parents to save the lives of their children—a
father who cannot swim unhesitatingly going into a raging
ocean to rescue his drowning child; a mother rushing into a
burning home in the attempt to save the child within. Surprisingly, the cool-headed bystanders will invariably do their best
to restrain these heedless and impulsive efforts which are
fraught with the risk of death. And this is precisely the crucial
point: a parent will risk his or her own life in order that the life
of the child be preserved, and in many cases the parent dies in
the attempt.

The point of these examples is that force and coercion are
totally meaningless in this context. The parents are compelled
to act the way they do because they are drawn by the inestimable value of the life of the child, a value so precious to them
and so overwhelming that the sacrifice of their own lives is not
too great an exchange for the realization of this good. This, I
suggest, is the awesome power of suasive power—a power so
persuasive that it can draw us to risk our very lives. Anyone
who has endured in the relationship of love knows the sacrifices and trials beyond imagining that are willingly suffered for
the sake of the relationship itself. Life is rarely sacrificed out of
a sense of obligation; it is frequently sacrificed, however, in the
pursuit of good. Humanly speaking, can there be a more impressive power than this?

## God and Suasive Power

It is surely no accident and no philosophical failure that the personalistic language of our Scriptures applies to God the most striking and the most intimate of suasive terms. We find there, with image heaped upon image, a God who in his intimate dealings with his special people refuses coercive force and relies instead on the intimacies of a relationship in which only suasion can have a voice. The scriptural image is always that of the God who calls, and the choice to answer that call with one's life is entirely the privilege of the chooser. There are images of God pleading with the people that they lead lives of righteousness and justice; there is a story of God being caught in an argument with Abraham, and it is God who changes his mind. In the prophet Hosea we have the sad and tender image of God begging for the return of the faithless wife. In those desert scenes where God moves out ahead as a cloud of dust by day and a pillar of fire by night, it is up to the free choice of the people as to whether or not they will pursue that ever-transcendent guide.

As Jesus calls his first disciples, each is distinctly and uniquely summoned. His injunction "Follow me" is but an invitation and the right of refusal is irrevocably their own. As in the case of the rich young man who chooses to remain in the security of his possessions, he was not left with a threat or a curse; rather Jesus simply looked upon him sadly.

All of these examples and numberless others indicate that our spiritual forerunners who struggled mightily with their God knew instinctively that this life-and-death struggle lay in their own hands. Their destiny was a matter of choice, and however they chose to establish the ends that would shape their lives, they would live with the consequences. Their God stood before them ever as a challenge: a challenge to enter the struggle with a wholeness of heart, to do battle with the powers of destruction and death even to the death, to be faithful always to the call of life. That Transcendent One who moved always out ahead of them was the challenge of a transcendent ideal of such supreme beauty and ineffable loveliness that only the life-struggle of passionate commitment to those values which serve to enhance the quality of life for one and for all could satisfy that rapturous enchantment with a suasive power of such intensity. Only free persons can answer a call to freedom, and only a power which is suasive can lure us to give up our slavery and strike out in the cause of life itself.

### God Is Love and Nothing Else

The major theme of this entire exposition has been that it is at the cost of our very souls that we forsake the one unique biblical claim which stands at the foundation of our identity and which alone can put us in relationship to the source and end of our very being: God is love. Here we must be intrepid enough to stand unflinchingly with the same convictional faith: God is love *and nothing else.* We dare not foul our good news with our own inadequacies and insecurities. We cannot afford to claim that God is love and then, as if love were somehow insufficient, add to that claim that God is many lesser things besides. No. God is love—period. God is not supreme coercive power. God is not threat. God is not reward and punishment. God is not the security of the righteous. God is not law and order. God is not on the side of any cause whatsoever. God is not the wreaker of vengeance. God is not the validation of moral opinions. God is love—and nothing else.

It is quite possible that the essential failure of faith on our part is a failure of nerve. We simply do not have the strength of nerve to be relentlessly thoroughgoing with the most precious of all faiths—the faith that God is love. While we readily proclaim in homily and prayer that our God is love, in the concrete practicalities of worldy affairs we are both unwilling and fearful to trust the lovely and tender quality of love itself. The proper way to run a world, we cannot help but think, is to have love supported by power. What love cannot do, power surely can accomplish. Thus it is that with possibly the noblest and yet with the most foolish of motives we could not surrender the all too human notion that God must have coercive power to enforce his love. This surely is not done with malicious intent. It has its origins, rather, in our pallid human faith which would like to believe that God can rely on the power of love, but we frail humans cannot.

We are so insecure in our strivings and so protective of our narrow interests that we do not have the verve to rely on the suasive power of their inherent beauty. We live within that strange and self-defeating irony where we would force others to be good, compel them to act rightly, coerce them into loving. It may be that God is love and nothing else, but we, fragile and fallen humans, while assured that we too in the image of our God are love, are unquestionably and remorselessly many other things besides. We are insecure and weak, we are selfish and narrow, we are arrogant and defensive; and because we find ourselves such a strange and unruly mix we discern no unredeemable contradiction in our use of force, coercion, even violence, in our pursuit of the deepest values of our existence.

Do we not feel in the depths of our hearts that our innermost being is cruelly divided and that we ourselves have caused the division? To project this schism of the self onto God is but a perverse reinforcement of the fracture caused by sin. Because coercion by power has become such an established part of our lives we unwittingly prostitute the good by submitting it to force. Is the God of love indeed so weak that he must also resort to coercion to achieve what is of supreme good for both God and ourselves? Could a God of coercion possibly remain unsullied by the means of coercion?

## God Will Not Be Coercive

We have here symptoms of a religious schizophrenia that can cripple our spiritual life at the very core. To postulate in any way the use of force or coercion on the part of God is to admit an absolute and irredeemable failure. It is to admit, on the one hand, that we who experience ourselves as centers of inherent value and worth cannot finally seek after the good, search out the beautiful and love the lovely; an irresistible efficient power must break us and force us into the mold of God's vision. Such a view holds that we cannot be trusted, and hence God's power must be able to override our weakness.

But if we have no control, then we have no choice and no merit. We do not seek the good; it is thrust upon us. We do not love the lovely; it is forced into us like a medicine. Are even the poorest and weakest among us willing to suffer such violence to our very selves? Sadder still, on the other hand, this is to admit that even for God love does not suffice. Not even God the supremely beautiful One can trust his own beauty to lure the creative choice of those who strive by destiny to have beauty within their lives. Not even God the supremely Good can trust his own infinite goodness to suffice for that bottomless yearning of his creatures to create their satisfaction by taking into themselves and becoming the image of all that is good.

Did not our spiritual ancestors already know that the weakness of grace was the mystery of the love of God? Were not our religious forebears imbued with the gentle vision that the vulnerability of God was the necessary consequence of his nature as love? Does not the symbol of the cross inscribe across our hearts in letters of blood that the one solitary thing that love cannot do in the face of coercion and violence is to become coercive and violent?

The story of the cross is not so much a tribute to the forebearance of God who in his infinite patience would not use his power to annihilate such evil. The cross is, rather, a timeless testimony to the absolute faithfulness of God to his very being, which is love. Because love is founded on freedom it can be ridiculed and rejected and betrayed. It is the cross which reveals what kind of a response is possible for God in the face of such betrayal. The only response is love, suasive, kindly and forgiving. Perhaps the only limitation upon God is the limitation of his own goodness which requires that his only power is the suasion of love. Beyond the suasive force of God's inherent and infinite lovableness there is no other power, nor need there be any.

### The Failure Is Ours

The problem is not with God, as Scripture testifies; it is with us. Because of our ruptured and fragmented lives we have poor vision and halting will. But it was for such as us, the sinners, that Jesus spoke of the tender patience of the loving Father. He asked that we who have eyes should look out and see. He asked that we who have hearts should learn how to trust. He asked that we who have souls should foreswear all else for the life of the spirit. We, poor ones, are afraid to trust our own goodness. We, with our cracked mirrors, have little confidence in our own beauty. We, insecure in the slender hold on our own self-worth, have little hope for survival except through violence.

It was Jesus who pointed out, in his body, that survival with violence is worse than death. The message with which Jesus died proclaimed to all the lost and confused and disinherited ones of the earth that the love of God suffices for all, and all the magnificent and terrifying powers of the earth are finally humbled before the sway of God's love. We have heard this message, but we do not believe it and we do not trust it. We trust force, and coercion and violence. We commit the supreme blasphemy when we imagine that God would have to stoop so low. God is love, and nothing else. Either we are persuaded by this beautiful power and thus respond with the unconditional wholeness of our heart, mind, soul and strength wherein we find our brokenness healed as we are recreated in the godly image of love, or else we settle for the coercive idolatry of power that will finally lead us into death because it is so ungodly. Whatever the case, let us finally forego the worshiping of the God of love as an idol of power.

### The Search For Commands

Unfortunately we are so easily trapped within our own narrow vision that even when we seriously approach the Gospels we carry a bias that can be a jaundice to our understanding. With surprising regularity much traditional spirituality has mined the Gospels to discover those commands which lay upon us like an eternal obligation. The scriptural commands were seen as the absolute and irrefusable demands that would serve as the final measuring-rods of our lives. The degree of compliance or non-compliance to the commands of God would on some final day be resolved by juridical judgment and our damnation would be but the consequence of our abject failure in the supreme duties of our life. Such a view makes our final destiny a matter of fulfilling commands laid upon us, and thus it is our own eternal well-being which should motivate our faithful compliance.

The inherent self-interest of this view is but selfishness thinly disguised under the noblest of motives. If, however, we achieve our salvation out of selfish motives, then we are selfishly saved. If this should sound like nonsense it is because this *is* nonsense. Too casually have we invoked the will of God to bolster a list of commands and demands that oftentimes bore little relation to love but a hearty resemblance to good order. What then can be said about the commands laid upon us by the good news of Jesus? Are we perhaps so insecure and half-hearted in our loving that we fear the risk of trusting our own best selves? Do we prefer to feed our passionate desire for intensity of life by means of the paltry token of obedience rather than the full-hearted but risky commitment to love wherever it be found?

## Commands: Invitation and Challenge

A second look at some of the commands that claim our ultimate loyalty may shed a new light on what our spiritual quest is about. Pre-eminent as a summary of our Gospel life is the bidding of Jesus, "A new command I give you, that you love one another as I have loved you" (Jn 13:34). The audience of his day was only too familiar with the commands and regulations of a bureaucratic religion. With repetitious consistency Jesus strives to reduce all obligations to a single one, and we cannot help but be curious about the singular irony of linking love and command. How indeed is it possible to establish something as the object of a command when its only and total reality consists in its free, gracious giftedness? To love out of obligation would possibly fulfill an obligation but it would not be love as we mean it.

Such a perverse quandary should surely serve as an intimation that Jesus has puzzled out a language in the context of his hearers which says something quite different. The very real impossibility of commanding love should constrain us to re-think the quizzical import of this utterance. Could it be that this is not a command at all (since that is impossible) but, instead, an invitation? What is the life of Jesus as we know it but an enfleshed invitation to do as he did in our own concrete but unique earthly dealings? Would we suffer in response if the impact of this declaration were but a plain and simple invitation: "I invite you to love one another"? Do we so doubt our own interior strength and assurance of will that we would prefer the obligation of a comand over the graciousness of an invitation?

### The Invitation of Jesus

Along these same lines, the calling of the disciples is instructive. James and John are pictured busy with the work of their father's boat. As Jesus passes by the seashore he simply says, "Follow me." We have also chosen to read this "Follow me" as a command, and dire consequences have been threatened to those who do not heed it. But the scene at the boat does not carry this tone at all. The two men, avoiding a direct answer, ask a further question "Where are we going?" to which Jesus simply replies, "Come and see." Since these two had no way of knowing who Jesus was or what authority he allegedly possessed, they were not in a position to think that they could be commanded by a total stranger. But their very question "Where are we going?" gives the scene away.

Quite rightly these two perceive the "Follow me" of Jesus as an invitation to go his way, and they do not feel themselves under any constraint to do something they have no inclination to do. What they hear from Jesus is "I invite you to follow me" and they realize full well that they have the right to answer yes or no to this unexpected invitation. The very indefiniteness of the "Come and see" strengthens the case. There is here no hard and fast obligation, no clear command, but simply a gentle invitation to follow this stranger wherever the journey should take them; seemingly the destination is of little import as compared to the journey itself.

From the scene portraying the Last Supper which Jesus shared with his special friends we have taken into our most solemn of rituals the seeming command, "Take and eat; take and drink." Have we been placed into the position where the very source of our life must be taken on command, for, if not commanded, there lingers the possibility that we might refuse to eat? As with the food we partake in every single meal, is it not the case that we are invited to share in what is offered? With the possible exception of small children who are usually told what to eat, do we not make our own choices as to how we will respond in the sharing of this particular food? Jesus leaves to us that most gracious of invitations "Take and eat" and we respond because this bread is something we truly wish to share and not because we are under an obligation.

## The Challenge of Jesus

Perhaps in a certain sense "invitation" is too slight a word to bear the burden of our spiritual destiny, but at least it conveys the sense that the response is a matter of choice and not of coercion. Would it matter to our souls if we loved, followed and ate only because we were threatened by a command and were too timid to do otherwise? Where is it written that the kingdom will be possessed by the timid and the fearful?

Let us consider for a moment, then, that these three cases are indeed invitations, but invitations which also contain a challenge. To accept such an invitation is to risk something; like the taking of a dare, we are not certain we have the will or strength to carry through. We respond to a challenge with a mixture of temerity and fear, for we are testing our strength against our own endurance. Are we large enough and bold enough to take the challenge and thus strive beyond our known capacities to discover a new affirmation of our size, or shall we stay close to our securities and discover nothing of our own powers?

Let us take these injunctions as challenges: I challenge you to follow me; I dare you to love one another; I challenge you to share my body. Since these things are neither commanded nor expected, it will only be the bold of heart who are willing to dare the risks involved. What will happen to us if we leave all to follow this strange invitation? We do not know, cannot know. All that we do know is that this stranger lures us with a secret power that we would like to share, and we will risk the comforts of home to discover who we may be. What will happen to us if we dare to share in this body? Again, we do not know; all we know is that we are hungry and unfulfilled and our sense of emptiness is worth risking for the passionate life promised in the sharing of this body.

*Is* there anything imaginable that is worth the risk of loving one another? We do not know. What we do know is what it is to be unloved, and any risk is worth the price of forsaking such alienation. Will we be better off if we share the bread, follow, and love? The strange one made no promises and gave no assurances. We will have no guarantee that we are right except our own satisfaction of having taken the challenge. "Taste and see" is his final invitation and challenge. But the choice is ours, always ours alone. And the issue is the size of our lives.

## God Will Never Coerce

What we have left, then, is the rarest and most precious of affirmations: the Holy One who is worthy of our worship is the God who will not coerce, who will never force. The God who is love will never work against our will. His only power is the supreme attractiveness of his beauty, goodness, and love. We will, unless we have by habit grown too dim-witted and dull-hearted, feel ourselves drawn and lured and enticed. Whatever response we manage to make will be from that integrity we have managed to muster from that peculiar mix of fact and ideal which is the only stuff of our lives. Whatever we do with ourselves is dependent upon the size of our visions. Only the God who is love has the largeness to permit us to become whoever we will become. This is the meaning of love.

## The Will of God: Love

This exposition of the concept of power can also serve to give us a more coherent and religiously satisfying understanding of the "will of God." The will of God who is love can rightly will but one thing—the love of his creatures. Our love for God will be a free response to the beauty and goodness which we perceive in ourselves, in others, in our universe—the only intimations available to us of the loveliness of that One who is the source and end of all that is. The primary commitment of our faith is a faith in ourselves and in our universe—the faith that the knowing and striving and loving of our faithful hearts is finally in harmony with the source and end of all.

Our deepest conviction is that we are not led astray by the most committed of our strivings or the most sincere of our lovings. This world and this neighbor must suffice, for that is all we will find of our God in this time and in this place. Our faithful living will be our tireless seeking out of the love of God within our own small selves and in the midst of this ordinary company of believers who walk with us in faith.

The strange mystery of our spiritual quest is that only those who taste and see will ever discover the deepest secret of Jesus. As we seek out our neighbor and our world, we discover not God, but the satisfaction of our lives. The abundant life is not the reward, but the living, of the life of love. We need but pay heed to all those gentle reminders of the Gospel: forgive, have mercy, make peace, be patient, search out justice, fear not. As we do these things with all our heart and strength we do not merit a reward that will come to us at some later time; rather their very doing is our sharing in the abundance of life which is the promised life of all those who become godly.

### Becoming Godly

Our spiritual quest is to become our own best selves, to achieve that identity which is the ideal in the mind and heart of God. But this does not mean that there is some perfect abstract version of the self in the mind of God against which we will be measured. God's ideal is rather his own beauty and love, and in order to seek this with all our heart we use the only means at our disposal—our selves, our neighbor, our world. We love our neighbor because that is all there can be for concrete loving; we serve our neighbor because there is none other. Thus it is that in our forgiving, our walking humbly and meekly, our feeding the hungry and touching the lonely, we discover that we have entered into the very life of God. Our only evidence will be the passion of our own lives, the intensity of our own being, as we share ourselves in the cause of life itself and refuse to be distracted by lesser, though attractive, causes. When we boldly accept the challenge into our lives and follow Jesus, others will see that we, like him, are becoming like God.

*Selected Readings*

One of the finest discussions of the power of God based on an analysis of the biblical heritage has been done by Lewis Ford in *The Lure of God: A Biblical Background for Process Theism* (Philadelphia: Fortress Press, 1978). Especially helpful is Chapter One, "Divine Persuasion in the Old Testament."

In *Stories of God,* John Shea's chapter, "The Story of Trust and Freedom," Chapter 4, is a valuable reminder of the human response and cooperation called for by God in the Old Testament.

Since an understanding of the power of God involves an awareness of the inestimable dignity of the human person, the ardent analysis of Theodore Roszak on behalf of the fragile dignity of the person is deeply rewarding. See especially Chapter Four, "The Third Tradition," in *Person/Planet.*

A short but lyrical expression of the relationship of God to ourselves and to the world can be found in Whitehead's *Religion in the Making,* Chapter IV, Section 4, "The Nature of God."

The consequences of our implicit worldview upon our beliefs about God are discussed with remarkable clarity by Paul Holmer. See Chapter Five, "Metaphysics and Theology," in *The Grammar of Faith.*

One of the most comprehensive expositions of this view of God as the relational and processive God of love is that of Daniel Day Williams, *The Spirit and Forms of Love* (New York: Harper and Row, 1968).

*Scripture Reading*

The Gospel of John Chapter 15

# 7

# Prayer in the Context of Worship: The Meaning of the Prayer of Petition

If we are willing to profess that God is love and nothing else then we must be ready to abandon the notion of efficient and coercive power. Both by tradition and by habit we have become accustomed to the inner security which assures us that no matter how desperate our human situation becomes because of our individual and collective choices, God at least has the effective power to make all things right in his own time and in his own way. Our commitment, however, to the suasive power of God as the only intelligible understanding of the God who is love finds its affirmation in the intuitive mode of our praying where we do not hesitate to confide, to plead, to cry, and to complain to that Holy One who understands and accepts us as we are.

But our uses of prayer are various and diverse. That we should speak out our petitions in our prayer is not at all unusual. To cry out in our need, to call out in our desire, to seek redress against injustice—if these could not be made known to our God in prayer, then surely he would not be the God of love. On the other hand, if the concept of efficient coercive power is not rightly applied to God, then what is left? Who has the power to help us in our need? If the suasive power of God's love cannot function as efficient causality in our world and within our lives, have we not lost something of our very notion of God? In this chapter we will attempt to harmonize the notions of suasive power and petitionary prayer into a coherent model. If this model is religiously satisfying and emboldens our spiritual quest, then we have been successful.

### Prayer of Petition

Why is it that when we think of the concept of prayer we ordinarily have in mind but one thing: the prayer of petition? The prayer of petition has risen to such a dominant place in our religious consciousness that rarely do we stop to reflect that it represents but one of several modes of prayer. To allow the prayer of petition to occupy this unique position is to distort the meaning of prayer. Our earliest and simplest catechisms taught us that there are at least four basic types of prayer; only when they are held together and in balance do they form the complement which is the full meaning of prayer.

Although there may be variations, the four basic types of prayer are usually listed as the prayer of adoration, the prayer of thanksgiving, the prayer of repentance, and the prayer of petition. Notable here is that petition is invariably listed in the last place, not in the first. That it has first place in our own minds is perhaps an indication of how we have neglected these complementary forms of prayer.

I mention this point for a practical reason. Though we may be deeply attracted by the concept of the suasive power of God, we also feel a distinct discomfort at the sacrifice of coercive power. If it be true that God does not have efficient causal power, then why do we bother to pray? We simply cannot deny the fact that within our own religious consciousness we have established a very close relationship between the concept of prayer and the concept of power. Since it is this peculiar entanglement that creates a number of difficulties, it is important that we take a serious look at exactly what is implied by our prayer of petition.

To offer a prayer of petition is fundamentally to ask for something, or ask God to do something. Out of our own need or want, or possibly out of our good will toward others, we are asking God to somehow intervene in world affairs. However, if we are in fact asking God to do something which has a discernible effect, then it cannot be denied that we are asking God to exercise power. Whether we want it to stop raining in time for our picnic, or want our home-town football team to win the big game, or want our country to be victorious in war, or even if we want the conversion of a loved one—in each case our desire is that God exert some sort of power. Of necessity, our request of God is that he exert some form of efficient causality in order to bring about some specified effect. Even though we know well that the ordinary activities of the universe are governed by a system of physical laws which describe cause and effect, we are asking that God interfere in that orderly series in order to produce an affect which would not normally occur. Bluntly put in this fashion, we are asking that God manipulate the affairs of the world, which is to say that events would not have occurred in a particular way unless God had intervened.

### Petition as Manipulation

Viewed in this light, we might see the danger in the very notion of manipulation. In a certain sense, the sophisticated technology made possible by modern science is but a way of manipulating the causal sequences of the physical universe in order to produce desired effects. But the manipulation here is simply the deliberate use of the orderly laws which already exist. This does not seem to be the same case when we petition God to interfere in the world. To use a trivial example which is nonetheless clear, what would it mean if we prayed to God that our favorite team win the big game? Are we asking that God physically interfere in the movements of the players—for example, causing an opponent to drop a pass? If not this, then what? The same approach would hold in the case of praying to God that our nation be victorious in war—we are assuming that physical events can be manipulated by God to produce other than their normal result. The case is put rather starkly here, but perhaps we manage to gloss it over because we ordinarily pray with good motives and the best of intentions.

## Manipulation of Persons

The case becomes even more problematic when the effect desired concerns the interior life of another person. Suppose, for example, that we have a dearly loved friend who is an agnostic and spiritually rootless. Out of our concern for the unhappiness and meaninglessness in the life of this loved one, we pray that he or she might be converted or find the true faith. Once again, the rightness of our motive is beyond question, but what exactly would we be asking God to do? Are we asking that God somehow touch the mental life of that person, somehow interfere with the natural mental functions to produce a new idea, or new understanding, or new purpose? If we are not asking for this, what exactly are we asking for? If it were possible for someone to interfere with our own interior functionings, whether of the mind or the will, then indeed we would call this manipulation. When we are deceived into thinking something or conned into wanting something which otherwise we would not have thought or wanted, then we feel that we have been manipulated and we resent this intensely. We know instinctively that such manipulation is an insult to our personhood, even when it is done to us with good intentions.

If God could somehow manipulate the interior life of another to bring about a religious conversion, then by the same logic God could also manipulate each one of us without our knowing. Could even God use such an immoral means to achieve even the best of ends? Beyond the issue of morality, however, any form of manipulation between persons simply stands as the total contradiction of love. To hold another in love is to be fully receptive of that other in his or her freedom and integrity. Though we may persuade, or lure, or cajole, we may never, never manipulate. For the God who is love to manipulate us for any reason at all would be for God to violate the very nature of that love. The only power available to the God of love is the suasive beauty of love itself. Perhaps it will be objected that this is not really what we mean by the prayer of petition, and hence in no way do we intend that God manipulate persons or things. On the one hand, however, if our prayer of petition in any way assumes the efficient power of God, then the above problem must be honestly faced. On the other hand, if some form of manipulation in ordinary affairs is not what we intend or ask for, then what exactly do we intend, and what exactly do we expect to receive from our prayer of petition? In order to work toward an answer which is both religiously satisfying and also does justice to the nature of God and our own deepest needs, let us first look at our prayer of petition in the much broader context of all the rest of our praying.

## Prayer in the Context of Worship

Prayer is not a religious topic which can be separated from the rest of our religious lives. Prayer is only understandable if it is seen as part of a larger context, and that larger context will define the meaning of the entire spectrum of our religious activities, including prayer. That larger category which defines the very meaning of our religious lives is the category of *worship*.

No matter what act we may perform in our spiritual journey toward God, it is primarily and fundamentally an act of worship. We briefly discussed the concept of worship previously as the total response of our being to the God of love in the attempt to bring our finite and fragmented selves into the integrity of God's all-encompassing experience. The form of this total response is succinctly phrased in the Gospel: "Love God with your whole heart, your whole mind, your whole soul, and all your strength" (Mt 22:37). Whatever other activity we undertake must somehow be an expression of worship, for worship is not only the primary religious activity; it is the only properly religious activity. It is for this reason that whatever else we may intend by our prayer, this prayer is first and last an act of worship.

## What Can We Do for God?

Previously we had posed the question "What do we owe to God?" and our answer was "Nothing." To the God who is love nothing is owed, because everything is gift. We may, however, turn the coin of this question to its opposite side to ask: "What can we *do* for God?" As part of our religious lives we perform various activities—prayer, liturgy, mortification, service to neighbor, and many others. By means of these activities do we actually do anything for God? Does God receive any measurable benefit from our activities? In exactly the same way that to the question "What do we owe God?" our answer was "Absolutely nothing," so also to the question "What can we do for God?" the answer must be "Absolutely nothing." As strange and humbling as this may first appear, it will make good sense if we ceaselessly focus on our essential faith that God is love.

From the God of love there is nothing but gifted and gracious relationships; the love of God is freely bestowed, not out of some weakness, but out of the supremely beautiful strength of God's nature as love. In this sense, God does not love out of need; God loves out of the integrity of his fullness. In similar though imperfect fashion, we also love out of our fullness and strength; those who love out of some need are using love for an ulterior purpose and already the relationship is being trivialized.

To actively love another is not straightforwardly to *do* anything for that other. The point is not that the lovers do anything for each other; the point is, rather, that their being in love enlarges and enriches both of them, and this is at the heart of the very meaning of being in love. All that one can do in the relationship of love is to offer the fullness of oneself to the beloved, and to accept in whatever degree possible the proffered fullness of the beloved. This is a matter of presence; it is not a matter of activity at all.

## Celebration

If it be true that we can do nothing for God, then what is the point of our worship? The answer appears to be so obvious that it is surprising that we could ever miss it. What can we do before the gifted and gracious relationships of the God who is love? We can only *celebrate*. Every act of worship is thus nothing else than an act of celebration.

What can we do, whether before persons or before God, in the face of the gracious gift of love? We can only celebrate that love, and we celebrate that love by responding to the loveliness that is offered to be part of our lives. We cannot use love for any ulterior purpose; we can only celebrate its gracious existence in our lives by responding in love.

How do we celebrate the God of unfailing gracious relationships? We celebrate by being grateful and by being gracious. Our own graciousness which we extend across those lines of intersection that create our human world becomes our living gratitude made real by our own graciousness. We celebrate the gracious gift of life by living that life as graciously and gracefully as possible.

There is nothing we can offer in return for our life—no debt to pay, no obligation owed; all that is left to us is to live that life with whatever passion and intensity we can achieve by entering fully into all its conditions in our search for abundance. Likewise there is no return to be made for love except the gracious loving itself. Life and love are sheer gift; all that we need do is enjoy to the fullest their passionate giftedness.


### Prayer Is Celebration

With this in mind we must always remember that every act of prayer is first of all an act of celebration. It is primarily our own gracious response to ever-present graciousness. In this sense, prayer, like love, is its own end. Prayer is not done for something else, nor is it the instrument for attaining spiritual or material goods. Prayer is for nothing, in any sense of an ulterior purpose. Like celebration, prayer has no end outside of itself. The specific form of celebration which constitutes prayer is the overt expression of my very being as self-with-God. That Transcendent Other who is the origin and end of all is not over-against me, nor beyond me, nor removed from me in any way. Of all the gracious and unowed relationships which flood from the universe to create my being, the primordial and determining relationship which holds all the others together into this valued self is the relationship which we call God.

This being-in-God is the unfathomable and mysterious gift which is my self, this concrete and earthly mixture of body and spirit, flesh and soul, satisfaction and endless desire. This multivalent riddle of passion and ideal is not simply my self before God, or my self with God, but wondrously my self-in-God, since the creative relationship which funds my being is simultaneously God's experience of myself.

Only the analogy of love can shed light on this awesome puzzle: God's relationship of love to me, while creative of me, is equally the presence of myself within God. As incredible as this truth may be, it is exemplified repeatedly in concrete fact in the ordinary and unspectacular lovings which are the leaven of our daily lives. In the most ordinary and the most sublime of senses, we exist within each other.

### Presence in God

The celebration of our prayer, then, will be the setting forth of ourselves within this context of the gracious presence of God. Like the saying of "I love you" our prayer is first and foremost the bringing to expression the relationship itself: a speaking out because of the presence of the Other and for the presence of the Other. The background of our prayer is our own religiously lived lives, and the meaning we bring to prayer is the acknowledged presence of the Gracious One in whom we live and toward whom we move. The celebration of prayer is thus our own felt existence before and with the God of love, so that the point of prayer is not to establish a relationship between ourselves and God but to bring to focus the relationship that is infallibly there.

It is for this reason that our prayer has the non-functional aspect of celebration and is not rightly utilized for some other instrumentality. For the very same reason, since prayer is primarily a way of relating, there is no straightforward or obvious method of praying, just as there can be no techniques of love. Our prayer, rather, will be a function of all the other relationships from and to the world and others, so that the quality, the intensity, the passion, and the commitment which tone our relationships within the world will be the quality of our prayer. When we bring our self before God in prayer, what self do we bring but that one which already concretely exists within a context of relationships as broad as the universe itself? Those very qualities which most enhance and give meaning to what we are doing within the world will be the tone of our relationship in prayer.

The sense of commitment and the sense of conviction which sustain our concrete struggle for meaningful and satisfactory experience represent the faithfulness which gives sincerity and integrity to our relating in prayer. We are who we are whether we pay heed to God or not, so that we do not change ourselves when we begin to pray. Rather, we bring this struggling and imperfect self to our prayer, and in the praying, as in the loving, we find that we are changed. The prayer, finally, is the *pray-er*.

It should be obvious now that the primary end of our praying, like the primary end of our loving, is not self-improvement, nor is our prayer, like our love, designed to procure goods for ourselves. Prayer, like love, is defined essentially not by what we get out of it but by what we put into it, and in both cases what we put into it is our very selves. However, since we do in fact bring our petitions to our prayer is it possible to understand this petitionary act meaningfully within the context of our religious lives? I do think there is a way, and I would like to develop it by presenting some analogous examples.

### Celebrating the God of Rain

Within the popular understanding of our own American history we have all heard the stories of the early encounters of the first Europeans with the native Americans, the Indians. There existed an obvious conflict of cultures, and most of the records preserved for us were written by the Europeans.

Among other things in the popular lore, there is the story of the rain-dance. The rain-dance of the Indians was commented upon by the settlers with both wonder and derision. It was considered naively superstitious that the rain-dance, however intricate and complex, could cause rain. The popular and unsophisticated acceptance of the rain-dance as a religious rite which functioned as the cause aimed at procuring the specific effect of rain is still common.

It is only within our own century that such scholars as anthropologists and sociologists of religion have brought a new methodology to their study of divergent cultures and peoples. The method is called "participatory" and simply entails that instead of studying the culture from the outside as an observer, one attempts to join the culture and participate in its life from the inside. This would be the difference in perception, for example, between the skeptic who observes a group of people receiving bread to eat in a rite called the Eucharist and the believer who receives the body of the Lord. What was discovered by this participatory study was startling to the presuppositions of the Western observer. What was discovered was this: no native Americans had ever in the history of this culture danced for rain. Never had they looked upon the rain-dance as the ritual cause for the production of rain.

The purpose of the rain-dance, rather, was simply to celebrate the God who makes rain. The ritual dancing was celebration pure and simple. Whether it rained after the dance or not, this was not the point, for their God was the rain-making God and all they could do was to celebrate this peculiar bounty. Their dance was an expression of their trust that the rainfall would always come because the God in whom they believed was the God of rain.

## Sacraments as Celebrations

The very same approach may be applied to the liturgy of the sacraments in our worship. A theology based on a dualistic worldivew saw the sacraments as the instruments of grace in the sense that the sacramental rite itself had a certain causal efficacy in the production of grace. More recently, the recognition of the sacraments as the celebration of the wondrous acts of God has become more prominent.

The sacraments do not cause grace in any direct sense; they are, rather, the celebration of what the gracious God has always done, is still doing, and will always do. No human activity can cause God to give grace; what we can do, however, is celebrate the graciousness of God who has graced us already from beginning to end. The Eucharist is perhaps the clearest example of this non-instrumental celebration of life. At the heart of the Eucharist is the very ordinary experience of sharing a meal together. On special occasions we speak of celebrating Thanksgiving or celebrating Christmas, and we usually celebrate with a special dinner. A celebration of dinner is non-instrumental in the sense that its total purpose is the sharing of bread and the sharing of life together.

You will notice how selective we are in inviting those who will share the celebration of a dinner. Never do we invite enemies to celebrate dinner with us; we invite only family and friends, usually close friends. Because the sharing of the food at the dinner is a symbol of the mutuality of our shared lives we are not at all indiscriminate about those we choose to share with. We select those to whom we are close, those whom we love, those to whom we are bonded in special ways. The very sharing of the meal is a concrete symbol of this bondedness while at the same time it works also to reinforce this same bondedness. The meal is a celebration of the togetherness which is the source of the quality of our lives, while at the same time it is the actual sharing in the quality of that togetherness. In this way a celebration, like making love, does the very thing it celebrates.

### Eucharist: The Gift of Life

In the ordinary commerce of our lives we have special friends and dearly loved ones. One of our fondest ways of expressing our love is to present a gift to the other; the gift is of some cost to ourselves and is offered freely as a sign of the love and esteem we hold toward the other. Anytime we offer a gift, however, like a ring or flowers, we offer something which is external to ourselves and external also to the relationship of love. But this external gift is the best we can do to express in a visible sign the quality of our love and the mutuality of our lives.

When we sit together at the table, however, to share the food, and I pass the bread to the loved one, I quite literally share the gift of life. Even though the bread is external to both of us, when I proffer it as a gift it is received and consumed by the other; thus what I have given is that which sustains life itself. This is the root symbolism of our eucharistic meal: we celebrate a dinner among friends and loved ones in which we share the bread that gives life. Our visible sign expresses the fact that together we share the same life, feed off the same food, hold life in common.

Our lives are not independent and isolated; they are inter-related and mutually supportive. Our lives in common feed off the one same food which is the body of Christ, so that each of us lives off exactly the same life. In the face of the awesome mystery of the giftedness of life, all that we can do is celebrate the giftedness of life itself by sharing the gift of life with others. In this way the eucharistic celebration brings about the very thing which is being celebrated—the sustaining power of gift-ed life.

Since the quality of our lives can be precisely determined by the quality of our relationships with others, the eucharistic sacrament celebrates that life-empowering quality of love which only exists in its sharing. And since it is the body of Christ around which we gather and which we share in the eating, we point to the God of life who has always given life, continues to give and to sustain life, and will never fail us in the gift of life. We do not cause life, we celebrate it; and our very celebrating is an enhancement of its gracious quality among us. The life we share is the very life of God; the life we take and the life we share comes from God and returns to God. This is why we so rightly call it the bread of life.

In this eucharistic celebration friendship and love are both expressed and deepened; in the Eucharist we become the gracious children of the gracious Father. At the heart of this exposition is the basic point that there is no direct causality at work in the activity of celebration. We do not celebrate human meals together nor do we celebrate the eucharistic meal in order to obtain ulterior ends. The enhanced vitality of the celebration is what the celebration is for, and either we share in the abundance of life which flows from the sharing of bread or we remain beggars. The sacramental rite of life is likewise a rite of love, and it is by God's good gift that by our participation in them we may become enlivened lovers. This is the very meaning of life, for God and for ourselves.

## Petitions Within the Eucharist

Viewed in this light, it may be the case that we come to the eucharistic celebration with our petitions, but our very petitions will have their meaning only in the context of our shared lives and the enhancement of the quality of those lives. Whatever happens occurs within ourselves by virtue of the very relationships we celebrate. Qualities such as health, happiness, and the welfare of friends are already qualities, even if imperfectly, of our shared lives which we bring to our celebration as part of ourselves. Any healing that takes place within us will also be at least a partial healing of all our relationships. By placing our petitions within the larger context of the life of God we find that we can live with our brokenness because we are already on the way to wholeness. In our celebration, we do not make petitions to God because he has power; we make petitions because God loves us.

## Petitions Within the Love Relationship

Let us place our prayer of petition in the context of another analogy, this time the analogy of a human love-relationship. I present here an entirely fictional case and I ask your patience as we piece together a good number of details. Let us imagine a husband and wife who are deeply in love. They have been married for twenty years and have four children and the usual cluster of problems—mortgage payments on the house, dentist bills, crabgrass in the lawn, a few problems with the local school, little money for some frills they would enjoy. On this particular morning the alarm clock does not go off as usual, and upon awakening the husband realizes that he will be late to work, so he begins to rush. Because of his undue hurry he cuts himself while shaving and burns his mouth on the too-hot coffee. When he gets to his car he sees that it has a flat tire, and while changing the tire he cuts a gash in his finger. Because he is now running quite late he speeds on the way to work, is pulled over by a policeman and is given a speeding ticket. As he finally reaches his office he is met by his angry boss who dresses him down because his lateness has caused the loss of an account. By this time his mood is so sullen that the rest of his day continues to go badly. At the end of the day as he crosses the lawn heading for the front door, the neighbor's dog bites him in the leg. As he opens the door, his wife is standing there and with a smile she asks, "Honey, how was your day?"

In your own imagination try to sympathize with the plight of the husband at this point. The pain, the anger, the frustration, the anxiety and the meaninglessness of his whole day, possibly his entire life, have worn him down to the point of exhaustion. In this condition he encounters the smiling question, "Honey, how was your day?" What is his response at that particular moment? I would suggest that at this point he proceeds to tell her exactly how his day was. Out of great anger and great pain he seeks to express himself; out of a sense of frustration and anxiety he relives his hurt. With detail after ugly detail he lays out the entire horrid story of his day, every single thing that happened, all his feelings of anger and frustration. After every misguided incident has been recounted along with his sense of frustration and hurt, what exactly is taking place? What is being asked for?

## What Does a Lover Do?

I would suggest that at this point the husband is not asking his wife to do anything. He is not asking her to fix the alarm clock, to cool off the coffee, to fix the flat tire or to fix the traffic ticket; he is not asking her to speak to his boss or to take care of the neighbor's dog. In this sense he is not asking for anything at all. In this emotional speaking out of his anger and frustration what is he seeking? He is asking only that his wife understand; he is asking that she accept him in his pain and have sympathy with his anger. What he asks is that his hurt be understood. When his entire story is finally spoken out, what does his wife say? Simply "Honey, it's all right." No more than this: "Honey, it's all right." This simple and ordinary phrase spoken by the one who loves him expresses acceptance and her understanding of her husband in his situation. And this acceptance by her, this understanding by her of his pain and his anger and his frustration, spoken so simply by "Honey, it's all right," does what? Her acceptance is the beginning of healing. These broken pieces are brought together and held tenderly by this one who loves him and, in her love, not merely understands, but feels his pain.

## Love as Healing Power

If at that moment the husband were to survey his life, the amount of work he must put in to support his family, the weight of his debts, the relentless claims on him by his children, the unjust treatment at work—where does he find the motivation and the energy to put up with this wearisome and corrosive tediousness of stupid, repetitive events which mean so little? Why is it that at that moment he simply does not walk straight down the street, leaving behind all these claims and all these hooks on his life which simply drag him down? Why is it that he knows, as we know, that the very next morning he will get up once again and return to the same routine and endure the same burdens? Where does he get this strength and this desire?

He derives this renewed motivation from her loving acceptance, her sincere understanding, which is the beginning of his healing. All this stupid mischance and injustice are bearable because he is sustained by one who loves him. He has not asked her to do anything at all, and in a certain sense she has not done anything at all. He has simply manifested to her the bruises in his heart, and she with her "Honey, it's all right" manifests that she accepts him and sustains him in her love, receives his brokenness and shows him that love does indeed make all things worthwhile.

## The Enabling Power of Prayer

If we use this fanciful incident as an analogy of what takes place in prayer, it may shed new light on the functional relationships which are most important. The weight of the example above points out what may be termed *the enabling function* of prayer. Notice that nothing in this situation has the relationship of cause and effect; there is no direct petition for certain effects on the part of the husband and there is no causing of specific effects on the part of the wife. It is the very relationship of understanding and acceptance which at that point is but the concrete form of her love that is the beginning of healing.

If we apply this model to our prayer life we will see that what we bring to our prayer is the concrete condition of our very selves, shaped by a multitude of conditions mostly beyond our control. We come in our pain and our frustration, in our anxiety and our confusion, in our outrage and our pity. What we speak out in prayer is our selves, our selves toned and qualified by these qualities which are the source of our lostness, our will to quit, our loss of any good meaning. Out of such intensity we speak and cry out to the God who is love, who infallibly not only understands but also sympathizes with our pain and our suffering. In the context of prayer what we feel from God is the vague and unuttered, "It's all right."

The function of God and the function of love is not to make all things right and all things good. No, God and love can do nothing to change the actual state of affairs. But what God and love can do is to make all things bearable. Even in the concrete affairs of our daily lives, situations which appear intolerable are not made bearable necessarily by their removal or dismissal, nor even by their correction. I would suggest, rather, that intolerable situations become bearable when they are placed within and shared by the strength of those who love us. No matter how bleak the outlook or how crass the injustice, we find that we can bear up and endure the struggle if we are supported by the sympathetic affirmation of the love and concern of those closest to us. We grow strong, not by virtue of adversity, but by virtue of those loves which give us the desire and strength to endure. We do not go to our loved ones with requests that they do what we ourselves should do; we go to our loved ones, rather, to be affirmed in our goodness and assured in our worth. With such assurance, we are willing to struggle mightily, because the cause is our own good selves.

It is in the context of the all-embracing God who receives and feels our pain and our passion, who takes in our broken-ness and understands our anger, that we offer our petitions as an expression of ourselves in prayer. God is that One whose response of acceptance is infallible, whose patience is unfail-ing, whose support is indefectible. Who will make sense of our shattered pieces? Because we pray out of our lived faith it is always the quality of our faithful lives that we bring to our prayer, and it is because of this lived response that we are already created and supported by the loving relationship to God. It is out of our praying itself that we feel accepted, supported, affirmed; our praying out of ourselves is thus the beginning of our healing. It is out of praying that we feel drawn to endure, lured to continue our struggle for good no matter how difficult, enticed to seek beyond the obviousness of cheap satisfaction, inspired to work against our ingrained self-ishness.

For whatever reason would we ever want to do these things of such difficulty and endurance that we would hesitate even to begin? We are so enabled by our prayer, because our praying, imperfect and possibly even selfish, is the manifesta-tion of our living trust in the gracious relationships which hold us in being. By setting our lives and their many-dimensioned complexity in the context of the loving God, all things are made bearable, and, more than bearable, worthwhile. We not only endure, we strive to become better, and in that very striving we feel that enhanced quality of a life suffused with meaning. In this sense, then, we have not asked God to do anything for us; we have but asked God to receive us, to understand us, to hold us in his love. Since nothing is incomprehensible to God, he understands us in whatever furious or ecstatic passion with which we stand before him.

### The Pray-er Is the Prayer

Because our petitions arise out of our own sense of need, because they reflect the inadequacy and weakness of our lives, they stand as a symptom of the fragile and precarious quality of those lives. We have an unspoken vision of life in its abundance, but in reality our taste of abundance is soured by our own imperfection and that of others. The expression of our needs is one way of speaking about the weakness within ourselves; our petitions point out the empty spots that we would have filled and hint at those dark spots which still confuse us. When we express our petitions in prayer it is not so much that we are looking for a distinct effect but rather that we are seeking the healing of our own lives.

It is thoughtless to assume that since no discernible effect has resulted from our praying then our prayer has been a failure. Like the saying of love, nothing has changed but the quality of the lover. Our own personal self is the effect of our prayer, a life enriched by the quality of its trust and a self enhanced by the quality of its love. Once again, the *pray-er* is the effect of prayer; we need seek no further nor look for anything other than this.

We are empowered by means of this expressed relationship to the God who is love to move against our own imperfection, to hold our weakness in the context of the God who affirms our strength, to envision ideals of abundance which are worth our strenuous energies and our unfailing commitment. Like the rain-dance of the native Americans, we celebrate the graciousness of a God who makes the sun rise on the just and the unjust alike, who makes the rain fall on the good and the bad equally. We celebrate the gracious God who always gives good gifts, the most precious and unfailing of which is God's presence within our lives and within our very selves. In our prayer we know that we are healed because we are loved by an infinite love; we will never be lost because we are precious to this One who desires us more than we can ever know.

### The First and Final Gift: The Presence of God

The approach to petition that we are suggesting here is that it is not the function of God to exercise some form of efficient causality to bring about specific effects within the ongoing universe. The effect of God's supreme suasive power is already the entirety of the universe with ourselves as part of it. God is related to every item of the cosmos and to each one of us by the power of suasive love. Whatever exists is already the outcome of God's suasive luring to goodness and order, and whatever is yet to become will do so in response to this same lure.

The primary effect of God, if we insist upon that language, is the primordial *presence* of God to the cosmos, to and within ourselves. Our very being is already made possible by this creative-love relationship to the Origin and End, the Alpha and the Omega, of all that is. The mystery of creation is that we have a choice about who and what we will become, the awesome mystery that we will not be coerced, not even to our own goodness. The supreme mystery is that the sheer power of suasive love has already accomplished so much that love has already brought us to a foretaste of abundance which will ever leave us restless.

### Communicate—Commune

Another factor associated with our idea of prayer as petition is our Western tendency to canonize the intellect. By cultural tradition we have a bias toward the rational analysis of reality, with the subsequent dismissal of the emotional and valuational aspects of our experience as of lesser importance.

Because of this cognitive bias, our understanding and definitions of prayer tend to reflect this primacy of rationality. Many of our received definitions of prayer, consequently, will utilize as the basic model of prayer the image of intelligent communication between persons. It is thus that the model of prayer becomes some form of "talking with God." Prayer has been described as a conversation with God, as a lifting of the mind to God, as communication with God. The burden of these images is that prayer is made possible by the linguistic activity of high rationality.

There is no doubt that the very seriousness with which prayer was understood effected that our so-called highest faculties be the specific activities of prayer. If, however, we reflect upon our analogy of loving we will see immediately how meaningless it would be to reduce the activities of loving to the workings of the intellect. The making of love surely must be much more than a form of linguistic communication. In exactly the same sense, the model of rational communication may be too narrow and restricting for the types of things that actually constitute our prayer. One of the ongoing insights of our current age is the re-emphasis of the pervasive importance of our feelings, emotions, values and attitudes which bring a tone and a quality to all of our human relationships, even our linguistic relationships, and without which we would be more computer-like than human.

If "communicate" is perhaps too heady a word to describe the complexities of our prayer relationships, it might be possible to invoke a word with the same basic root but without the emphasis on intellectual activity. Let us try the word "commune"—the same word from which we get "communion" and which denotes the activity of becoming one with, of coming into harmony with, of sharing intimacy in a oneness. In the everyday interchange of our lives we do a good deal of linguistic communicating for a variety of purposes; but in those rarer, more somber and serious moments, we also commune with another. We may compare, for example, a young, newly-married couple still inspired by the fire and passion of their first love. They do a lot of communicating with each other, a lot of speaking, a good deal of pointing out the endless variety of their newly-discovered world together. On the other hand, we may picture an elderly couple, already married for fifty years, for whom the weight of age has slowed their activities to a near standstill. They sit in their rockers by the hour, saying little if anything. Yet each knows exactly how the other feels, knows even what the other is thinking. Their linguistic communication is rare, but their ongoing communing is pervasive and almost total.

## Commune: Becoming One

What is being suggested here is that while rational communication is an important, probably necessary, part of our human lives, equally important and every bit as necessary are the multiple modes by which we commune with each other, with the universe, and with God. Just as any couple that is sincerely in love works out a complex variety of ways in which to express the intangible qualities of their relationship and which carry their meaning only within the context of that relationship, so also each of us has an almost inexhaustible creativity in surfacing our deeper feelings, attitudes and values. Sometimes, as in the case of love, to attempt to put this deeper experience into language does violence to the unique and almost sacred nature of our unspoken and unspeakable relationships. We find that our communing is multi-leveled and multivalent: we commune psychologically, emotionally, physically and cognitively. We commune in speech and in silence. We commune with presence as well as with absence. All of these things are a holding of ourselves within the texture of the universe, a way of letting go to the supportive relationships which sustain us like the air we breathe, physically and spiritually.

On some special occasion each of us may have had the good fortune to sit on the seashore to watch the sun set into the ocean. As that huge globe of fire slowly drops itself into the horizon, suffusing the atmosphere with a richness of color and warmth, it is quite possible that our only response can be a low moan of wonder. Words are useless. But there is that momentary intuition of the grandeur of the universe, the size and elegance of the cosmos which holds us in being. It is moments like these which give us our unspoken sense of the beauty of God, and for the most part we have no way of surfacing what we feel. I suggest this as a moment of our communing with nature and with God; I also suggest it as one of our finest moments of prayer.

## The Emotional Content of Prayer

So it is that the linguistic form of prayer is surely an important part of our experience, but there is much more to our prayer than this. Even our speaking can never be neutral and objective; everything we say is toned by our feelings and laden with emotional quality. More often than not it is the emotion which we want to express to God, and the language is but a crude package for what we feel. Let us be honest enough to admit that most often it is our anger, or our fear, or our pain, or our joy, which we wish to communicate to God—we have a desperate need that he understand how we feel. Let us be bold enough occasionally to abandon language altogether, to commune with God with our silence, with our posture, or simply with the pervasive feeling of anger or hurt that roils within like an ulcer. Let us trust our instincts here, as we must always do in our loving. Our moments of prayer have perhaps been more frequent and true than we ever dared think.

Most of all, let us trust our God who surely is beyond need of our words, our God who is present to us in our waking and in our sleeping, in our good times and our bad. It is precisely because our feelings are the content of God's experience that he sympathizes perfectly with them and treasures them everlastingly. As with our love and our faith, we commune with God not for the effects produced or for the goods achieved, but because we are lured by our own inner longings to gather the universe, others, and God within ourselves, as this is where we experience the fullness of our own being, a hint of our own abundance.

## The Language of Commitment

On the other hand, it cannot be denied that we are inexorably linguistic in nature and that language is our natural human habitat. That world which is distinctively human and personal is a world created and informed by our miracle of language. I refer here not to the simple ability to name things like "cat" and "dog," but the world which would not exist but for our linguistic activity—the world of promises and of vows, the world of commitments and of future purposes. These things exist because we have brought them into being so that we humans can deal with the universe as if it were really our home; we shape it to our needs and mold it to our purposes. It is our language which allows such wonders. The intricate intercourse of human interchange is handled mainly through our language, and even our emotions and values will find their way into words.

It is no surprise, therefore, that our notion of prayer should be so firmly rooted in language, appearing at times almost impossible without language. But our use of language in prayer, though completely natural and distinctively human, is not merely at the level of conversation or communication, which would be the verbal equivalent of reading the newspaper or the telephone directory. Our prayerful use of language is to use it for those uniquely human activities which cannot be duplicated outside of language. With language we make promises and speak vows, we commit ourselves and we specify values which exist only in the future. These are the activities which our language brings to prayer.

Notice, however, that such human acts have the totality of their meaning in the self-involvement of the speaker who performs these acts. When we promise or vow to God, we are not using language primarily to say something about the world or even about God; we are using it to do something to ourselves, to involve ourselves in a relationship which lays obligations upon us. When we make a commitment to God we are prescribing how our self will stand in relationships which are yet in the making. It is for this reason that the language of prayer is not primarily the language of communication (though it may, and usually does, include this).

### Prayer as Commitment

The language of prayer is, rather, fundamentally the language of vows and commitments. Since the context of our prayer is the ongoing life of faith, our language of prayer allows us to take our lived relationships into our own hands and determine them to the form of godliness. Just as the language of love is inescapably the language of commitment, so that the simple and unremarkable "I love you" is so important in the saying because it carries a commitment, so also the language of prayer is at heart the language of commitment. It allows us not just to dedicate our lives, but to prescribe how our lives shall be before our God.

In our spiritual quest we have had the inescapable sense that prayer was of vital importance to our journey so that it would be inconceivable to be spiritual-hearted without it; in this we have been absolutely correct. But the importance of prayer is not so much in the speaking as in the self-activity it allows us; it structures for us a universe of relationships which have their meaning and value only insofar as we involve ourselves in their unpredictable flux. It is for this reason that our language of prayer allows us, in part, to create ourselves before our God.

In our everyday lives we can make promises of trivial import, but we cannot do this with our vows and commitments. Vows tend to be once-for-all, for life. Commitments are only invoked when a worthy value is at stake. It is for this reason that we do not do these things lightly or casually. Too much of our self is involved, not just at the moment, but down the long-haul of the future. Thus the fact that vows and commitments find a natural home in prayer is simply a concrete demonstration that our praying is one of the most self-involved of all our activities as well as the most demanding.

Perhaps the reason why we often find prayer difficult or irksome lies here: our praying makes such demands on us, not just in terms of the exertion of our energies but, more important, in the active creation of our selves. This we can never do lightly or casually, and simply gearing up our energy to look seriously on our own selves is no easy task. Unless, however, we are completely involved in what we are doing our prayer falls flat and empty.

### Prayer: First-Person Language

In this sense, prayer can never be trivialized to the status of a spectator sport, so that, despite our ways of speaking, there is an inherent and unresolvable contradiction in thinking that we can merely "hear Mass," "attend the Eucharist," or "say our prayers." The language of love and the language of vows are irretrievably first-person language; no one can say or do these things for us. Just as we must speak our own vows, we must say our own prayers, and the worth of what we do is completely determined by the sincerity and integrity of our self-involvement in what we do in our speaking.

In this way, as we have always claimed, only God and the soul know what goes on in prayer; only God and the soul experience the relationship into which prayer permits us to enter. No external sign and no objective test can identify for us the one who is praying. But we will always know the prayerful one by the godly way in which he lives and moves and has his being. If, therefore, our praying is in the form of vows and commitments, then of necessity we are forsaking our sin, foreswearing our deliberate failures, and placing a restraint on our waywardness. These things take great effort; more important, they take great will. It is in our praying that we find the will.

### Methods and Techniques Are Instrumental

Just as there exists an endless variety of ways for the making and speaking of our love, so also there exists a multiplicity of ways of praying. From our long spiritual tradition certain methods of prayer have become systematized and are presented as standarized forms of prayer. What these accepted methods of prayer really tell us is that for certain types of people at given times they have been successful; in no way do they stand as a guarantee that they will be successful for anyone at all who uses that particular method. We seem to be always haunted by the thought that for something as important as prayer there must be an accepted procedure which can stand as a norm and a standard. The sheer number and diversity of the different styles and techniques of prayer should be an unmistakable clue that there exists no single correct or true way of praying.

A sincere beginner, a place where the great majority of us stand most of our lives, can be overawed by the solemnity of the list: meditation, mental prayer, contemplation, private prayer, public prayer, and so on. A simple guideline here should defuse our anxiety: every method and every technique of prayer is only that—a method or a technique. These are simply instruments and have but an instrumental value. As long as they are serviceable in bringing us into the relationship of praying they have a practical value. The methods and the techniques, however, are not ends in themselves. The mere use of the method does not insure that we are praying. We should not feel disconcerted if we find a method cumbersome or—dare we say it—boring. We should not get so wedded to a particular method that we lose touch with the various other forms of prayer which can be much less artificial. Let us remember always to keep instruments in their proper place, simply as tools. The end of our praying is the faith-relationship which is ourself-in-God, and the means to achieving this are so intimately personal as to defy method and technique.

Since the faith-relationship is so uniquely personal to each of us we should be willing to trust our own religious intuition. What, for example, are the methods and techniques of making love? If we are uninitiated we may peruse a current manual that outlines a procedure for love-making. To actually make love by following the textbook, however, would be to treat this activity as if it were something that could be programmed into a machine. One of the secrets of love-making is surely spontaneity and creativity, and this no manual or method can teach.

Since our praying is our faith-love relationship to the God of love, the same personal spontaneity and creativity should be our intuitive guides. When we have prayed well we will know it; when we have prayed badly, we will know that too, and why.

## The Social Relationships of Prayer

Up to this point our focus on prayer has been almost exclusively personal and individual. The obvious reason for this is that the relationship of prayer is one of the most intensely personal and deeply intimate of our human activities. Our self-involvement in prayer is the final judgment on the value of what we have done within ourselves and with our neighbors. Although each of us begins, however, with the sacred privacy of our own self, we do not end there. The intensity of our own self-experience is made possible to us by the freely-bestowed relationships of others and universe and God which provide the environment out of which this personal self emerges.

Each of us is a uniquely creative synthesis of relationships which preceded us and fostered us, and we hold our selfhood only in interchange with these gifted relationships. We are inescapably indebted to the universe, from the air we breathe to the love that gives us meaning. Even our most private, secret, and internal of activities is simply our way of making decisions about how we will cope with, respond to, and enter into the relationships which are given by the universe and its inhabitants. Thus we are irrevocably social in our being and absolutely everything we do will have an effect beyond ourselves.

## The Social Self

Even to focus on the personal self in its struggle to become is to see also that self as it exists within a universe and makes a difference there. Such a view explains the timeless wisdom of our Scriptures which always see the human person only in a social context, related not only to other human persons, but also to the earth itself. We do not exist alone, nor do we become a self alone; there simply is no such thing as life which is not shared. As we grow into our own identity, part of our maturity can be measured by our acknowledgment that we have been allowed to grow by the grace of others, and much of the shape we have taken has been made possible for us by others. Furthermore, our very existence in the universe is to have an effect upon it and upon others. As we mature in a sense of our own sociality we grow likewise in our acknowledgment that our abundance of life is afforded us by others, and, more important, the living of our lives is essentially a living outward toward others.

If our consciousness is funded by our Scriptures, then we will both be haunted and informed by the mystery that the God who is love is likewise the one who enjoined upon us: "Love your neighbor as yourself" (Mt 22:39). The following of this directive is not set out before us as a task; it is rather the essential and formative principle by which we live and through which we hold our being. In this light, anything that we do to ourselves in our praying will have an effect on all those others who constitute our world, and as we ever deepen the meaning of prayer we will come to understand what it means to love our neighbor and our God.


### Because You Were Slaves in Egypt

Our Old Testament history can stand as a reminder and an admonition of what our God expects of us. The content of the exhortations spoken from God are always the social relationships which had already come to healing within their own midst. In the Exodus story, we find a prayer of praise which begins with an admonition to remembrance. Recall that the exhortation begins, "Because you were slaves in Egypt" (Ex 22:20). Notice how the force of this exhortation rests completely upon the Hebrew awareness of their own experience: because you were slaves, because you were oppressed, because you were denied your rights and treated as less than human.

Because you have suffered and endured these things you know full well what they are, you know their evil and their destruction. It is out of this knowledge that it is demanded that you do not perpetrate these death-dealing activities upon others.

In due measure much the same perspective can be applied to our own lives. We in our own way have been slaves in Egypt. Each of us knows what it is to be unloved; we have felt this lostness in ourselves. Each of us knows what it is to be lonely, as each of us knows what it is to be unwanted, unappreciated, alienated, and misunderstood. In varying degrees these have been part of the grim experience of all of us, and we each know their inner torment and terror which is beyond our telling. It is this forbidding quality of our own self-experience which demands of us that we struggle mightily against the deliberate imposition of such experiences upon others.

## Accepting Less Than Good

Perhaps it is a sign of our human and social failure that we are willing to accept such experiences as part of the taken-for-granted quality of life in an imperfect and fallen world. But to take this attitude is to trap ourselves within our own self-fulfilling prophecy. Our Gospel is a sustained protest against the taken-for-grantedness of such experience, and even to take this attitude is to be already captivated by the forces of death. The abundance of life is denied because we are perfectly willing to live with the cancerous germ of death.

Even in our religious tradition there has existed the tendency to sanctify these negativities, to somehow claim that loneliness and alienation, lack of love and refusal of appreciation are in some unknown and mysterious way good for the soul, a force of growth and even a unique token of God's special love. To take such an attitude is the attempt to sanctify abnormalities and canonize negativities, perhaps out of the hopeless despair that we are not large or strong enough to struggle against such evils. Such destructive experiences cannot be viewed as the difficult but necessary hurdles in some spiritual obstacle-course. They are rather the cancers and ulcers which eat away at life itself; even if they do not manage to kill us they will maim us in everything we do.

How can we possibly love well and strongly if from our experience we feel only unloved and worthless? How can we possibly struggle for the abundance of life if we have been willing to accommodate ourselves to the half-life of disease? Why is it that we wish to believe that alienation and imposed pain can be sanctifying? To claim that good can come even from this evil is to miss the point: before a gracious God it must be the case that more good can come from good than could ever come from evil. The Gospels demand that we abandon this banal accommodation with those pervasive forces, both personal and social, which are both death-dealing and a violation of God's love.

Because each of us has experienced these negativities to our own personal degree we have felt our life restricted and our abundance of life denied; we still taste of death. The denial of our own abundance should serve as inspiration enough for us to vow that our lives will be poured out to halt this disfiguring of others. That others are unloved or alienated, that others are oppressed or treated with injustice—this is the effective sign that they have been excluded from the kingdom. It is the kingdom that is less, as well as ourselves. Whatever abundance of life we may have is lessened because these persecuted ones cannot contribute to us of their abundance. Whatever abundance we share is destined to be contaminated by this cancer unless we ourselves root it out. We take this stand against evil—personal or social, institutional or accidental, undeliberate or intended—because of our faith: the faith that the God of love is always the God of life, whose only will is the abundance of life for all.

## The Denial of Abundance

The infinite size of God is but an indication of the magnitude of God's passion for life, a passion which will never be satisfied with less than abundance from all of us. It is our own hunger for abundance which drives us to feed the hungry, our own thirst for richness which impels us to give drink to the thirsty. We do not do these things selfishly nor do we do them for a reward. We do not do these things because they are the right cause or because they are what believers are expected to do. If we try to view our world, even our religious world, from the perspective of causes or of principles, then we always stand in the precarious danger of missing the human face and the human heart which alone justify the cause or the principle. We do these things, rather, because we are lured by that unfathomable challenge to discover what it would mean to love our neighbor as ourselves.

Always it must be our neighbor we love, not the cause; it must be our neighbor we feed, not our own righteousness. Even those whom we choose to see as the enemy, those who perpetrate injustice and foster oppression, those who cheat and starve the little ones—even these have a human face and a human heart. We have not yet learned what it is to love our neighbor until we love such as these. Is it any wonder that so many of us are faint-hearted at the enormity of this task? Need we be surprised that no matter how much we have loved, we can still be indicted for having loved poorly? The road to godliness is not merely long—it is endless. But we know of no other path worth taking.

## The Our Father

It has rightly been said that just as all of us must make our own love, so also all of us must say our own prayers. We have already pointed out the intense self-involvement and personal commitment required of our prayer-life, and we have noted the inability of forms or methods of prayer to do something that can only be done by ourselves. Nevertheless, we have in our Gospel heritage a special prayer which from the very origins of the Gospels themselves has been set out as the true model of all our praying. Every writer of Christian spirituality from the second century on has written a treatise on this prayer as the heart and soul of the spiritual life. This is the prayer which the Gospels speak from the lips of Jesus, the Our

Father or Lord's Prayer. If indeed the Our Father is the perfect model of what our prayer should be, and what we should be in our praying, then it will be worthwhile to see how well our exposition of prayer resonates with the Our Father.

## The Petitions of the Our Father

If the Our Father is to serve as our model for prayer, then an immediate objection can be raised against our entire presentation: the Our Father definitely contains a series of petitions made to God. If one reviews the standard exposition of the Our Father in popular spiritual books, this is often the exact point which is made: the Our Father shows us how to ask rightly of God those things which are necessary to our well-being. The petitions of the Our Father can be set out like the items on a shopping-list, with the proviso that the most important items are listed first, and once these have been purchased we can move on to the items lower on the list. The whole thing is simply a matter of priorities. According to this view, the first requests that we make in this prayer concern the aims and ends of God, not of ourselves. We pray that God's name be hallowed, that his kingdom come, and that his will be done. Perhaps it should strike us as somewhat strange that we pray to God for the accomplishment of his own purposes; nonetheless, these purposes are more universal in scope than our own particular needs.

After we have submitted ourselves to the prior claims of God we may proceed to enumerate our own needs, in particular our daily bread and the forgiveness of sins. We receive the impression that the entirety of the Our Father is a protracted petitionary prayer mapping for us a proper scale of values. Since the Our Father has had such a tenacious hold on our spirituality, there is every indication that it expresses something precious and deep within all of us, and hence our intuitive response to the beauty and worth of this prayer is no mischance. Let us probe to see whether this prayer is possibly richer and fuller in its meaning for our spiritual lives than a proper listing of our petitions.

## Setting Forth a Vision

Rather than focusing our attention in the first instance on the petitions, it might be more rewarding to move back to the very opening words of the prayer, "Our Father." What I wish to suggest here is that this prayer is not at all setting out the proper order of our human needs; it is, rather, establishing the right relationships which properly govern our lives. Rather than presenting us with the proper words to address to God, this prayer sets out the context out of which and because of which we enter into prayer at all. The thrust of the Our Father is to give expression to that reality of our lives without which we would be meaningless and void.

At heart, then, the Our Father is a presentation of our faith. As such, it is neither petitionary nor directive. In the simplest and most concrete of terms it sets forth a vision of faith which is to be concretely embodied as a vision of reality. The wording of the Our Father is attempting to show us how to see—how to see the worth of reality with its persons in the light of the creative relationships which establish their very being.

## Eyes To See

How often in the course of the Gospels does Jesus exhort his listeners, "For those who have eyes, let them see." Have we been so lacking in luster that we have never been even idly curious as to what exactly it was that we were to see, or why is it that we fail to see something which Jesus indicates should be obvious to all? We all have eyes and we all see; we would prefer to have our directions more specific and more detailed than this. Perhaps the Our Father may be taken as Jesus' own answer as to what to see and how to see it.

The Our Father presents to us a vision; this vision recommends to us a way of seeing ourselves, reality, and God, and this way of seeing is rightly understood only when it is acknowledged as the guiding and transforming principle of our lives. In this sense the Our Father does not tell us anything new nor does it reveal something which was previously undiscoverable. Rather it recommends to us how we should hold our lives in the face of a graciousness which already exists and upholds us, whether we acknowledge it or not. In this presentation of a vision, the Our Father can only be understood as a recommendation and a challenge. It recommends that we view the world through the eyes of this vision, and it challenges us to respond with our very lives to what we see.

## Recommendation and Challenge

How would we translate this vision-quality of the Our Father? Let us try reading it as a recommendation: *What would it be like if . . .?* What would it be like if indeed we did realize that God is our Father, uniquely and personally the Father of each of us, of all of us, of literally everything? What would it be like if we lived off the inspiration that all of us were in fact brother and sister, that each of us and everything within our universe somehow shared the same body, the same blood? What would it be like if we knew for sure that all the relationships of the universe were gracious and beneficent, were the relationships of family and not of hostile tribe? What would it be like if we had the confidence that the source and end of all that is, that ineffable Holy One, had within his power only the gentleness and tenderness and loving concern of a gracious Father?

What would it be like if this vision were the norm, if not for all, at least for us, the faithful ones? To see with this vision is to be challenged by it: if this is what the world is really like, then we are challenged to make it so. We are challenged to see each other as true brothers and sisters and to treat each other accordingly, and in no other way. We are challenged to forego our narrow ideas of law, threat, punishment, and fear because these stand as our selfish insults to the graciousness of a loving Father. If we accept the recommendation of this vision, our lives are challenged irretrievably and endlessly; either we will never again be the same, or else we surrender all right to pray "Our Father."

What would it be like if God's kingdom actually came?

What would our world be like if poverty were vanquished, injustice overcome, and the homeless sheltered? What would it be like if we had no more lame since they all could walk, no more blind because they, like us, could finally see, if meekness were as commonplace as sin is now? What would it be like if love and respect were the bonds of the kingdom in which life was enshrined as the only value? What would it be like if . . . ? To speak with this vision is to be challenged by it—not to be told, but to be shown that we are unprofitable servants.

### God's Will Is Love

What would it be like if the will of God were done here on earth as it is already done within God himself? Our first religious task is not to obey the will of God but to discover what that will is, and this Jesus also tells us: God is love. God's will is to love, and because of the very nature of this love God cannot efficiently change the way things are, cannot cause us to be other than we are. Because of this love God can only lure us, entice us, attract us by his unsurpassed beauty and loveliness, which, if we could only see it, would bind our hearts irrevocably. But we do not see it. Thus Jesus points to sparrows and foxes, the mustard seed and the fig tree and gently reminds us that if we do not see the workings of God there we shall never perceive them within our own hearts.

Perhaps it is not our eyes that are at fault, but our hearts, for we do not love the world enough. We are not merely unprofitable, we are ungracious, lacking the good sense to revel in the sheer loveliness of our universe and the ecstatic joy of our presence to each other. We are challenged not to wait for, but actively to seek out, the abundance of God's love already present among us, challenged to stop expecting the abundance of life like a reward for the righteous, but rather to share of our own abundance, like God's rainfall, with the unrighteous and the unrepentant.

Shall we ever find the strength, except in this vision, to testify to this awful truth: *we* are God's will on earth; whatever we choose is chosen for God. If we dare speak with the vision of the Our Father, you and I can never again disclaim that it is we who hold the keys of the kingdom. Perhaps if we had our wits about us, we begin to perceive, it might be easier for us if we discontinued saying the Our Father.

## Daily Bread for All

What would it be like if today's bread were bread for all? All bread is provided by the graciousness of this good earth, and no matter what we may think, we do not deserve it and have no prior right to it. Bread is one of the gracious gifts of God's good universe which is meant to be shared for the life of all. What would it be like if the common sufficiency of our daily bread could do away with the need for greed, avarice, aggrandizement and conflict? What would it be like if the sharing of bread were cause for common abundance of life rather than the occasion for destructive and death-dealing divisions? This is the vision, but it is also the challenge: it is we who must take our bread and share it, we who must heal the divisions by protesting always for life rather than accommodating with the forces of death. The challenge prompts us that, like a loving parent, we have no right to still our own hunger before the hunger of our loved ones.

And, finally, this challenge also indicts us: our very lives, like our bread, are sheer undeserved gift, and the only gratitude which God would ask is that we enjoy these gifts to their fullest, with that enigmatic irony that only in their sharing can they be enjoyed. What would it be like if we, you and I, could share ourselves, as Jesus did, as the bread of the world?

## The Size of Our Vision

This decision to regard the Our Father as the vision of faith has firm support in the practical working out of our lives. Despite our language, we do not live from hand to mouth, nor do we settle for the meaning of our existence with "So it goes."

In even the most common and trivial of our everyday affairs we make our choices out of a spectrum of alternatives because we are enlivened by some unuttered vision of what is worthwhile to us, what values are worth achieving for our own best well-being, what sort of person we are striving to become. However unspoken or unsystematized this version of our ideals, it functions within us by providing the reasons which are the motives for our strivings. For to live is to strive, and once we cease our striving we succumb to death. The objection, therefore, cannot be that we are visionaries because we naively choose to entertain a vision, as if this were a matter of choice.

The only serious question of consequence concerns not the choice, but the size of the vision that inspires us. For it is ultimately the size of our vision that measures the size of our lives. Whatever passion we may be fortunate enough to experience comes out of the passionate struggle itself; whatever fullness of life we may enjoy comes out of the size of the experience we are willing to venture; whatever abundance we share arises from the size of the world we explore.

In this world that you and I experience daily, it is not obvious that God is the Father of all; it is not obvious that his kingdom is in the making; it is not even obvious what his will for us is. The choices we make are rooted in a vision of faith, and it is the Our Father which in an almost final and perfect fashion expresses this vision for us. We dare not neglect to notice the seeming arrogance which Jesus recommends to us— the arrogance of such as you and I bold enough to claim that God is our Father. (Unmoved Mover and First Cause we can accept, for these are impersonal.) Dare we stand in the arrogance of referring to God as our Father unless we are willing to enflesh that Fatherhood in the everyday and ordinary brotherhood and sisterhood of our own lives? In the light of the way we treat each other, our divisions of righteous and unrighteous, moral and immoral, good and evil, dare we live with the arrogant claim that the life-giving and creative relationships of God are love and nothing else?

## Are We Big Enough?

We the sons and daughters are not orphans, for we claim to know who our Father is. Unless our own relationships are informed by compassion, concern, affirmation and challenge we give the lie to our true parentage. Jesus recommends to us such self-assurance only on the condition that the consuming and all-embracing vision which took flesh in him also take flesh in our unspectacular lives. Jesus offers this vision as a challenge to embark on the way to godliness. Thus the spiritual question which should ever disturb our souls is simply: Are we big enough to say "Our Father"? Do we choose to take on the size of the true sons and daughters? Dare we look like Jesus?

Perhaps the single saving grace of viewing the Our Father as our inspiriting vision is this: a challenge is issued only to those who have the capacity to perform it, who are strong enough to receive it. In this sense Jesus has paid us the highest imaginable compliment: having walked with us and shared his bread with us he has said: "You, too, may become the sons and daughters of the Father." How you and I choose to cope with this particular indulgence is the story of our spiritual lives.

## Jesus: Eyes To See

The view of prayer presented here is intended to remove our praying from the notions of routine, obligation, good works performed, or debts paid. We do not say "I love you" (to another person, or to God) because this is expected or required, but rather simply because there is nothing else we can do in the face of this graced relationship. So, also, we do not pray because we are supposed to; we pray because it is the most meaningful and the most personal human interchange available to us. Like our loving, then, there is nothing automatic or mechanical about our prayer; like our loving, our praying is an act of total self-involvement in which only we, who are held within this relational interchange, can test the validity of what we say and do.

Just as we do not say "I love you" in order to bring about the effect of love, so also we do not pray in order that we may have faith. The relationship flows only in the opposite direction: our actual loving prompts us to utter "I love you," and our lived faith inspires us to pray. However, in the mysterious miracle of our existence, once this relationship is brought to awareness, then these two poles feed off each other with the wondrous result that every saying of love is an act of loving, and every praying is an act of faith.

Perhaps we are yet unsatisfied. Where does one find this faith which can have such striking results? In our long religious tradition it has always been claimed that faith is first and last a gift, always a gift. This is true. But likewise in our long human tradition it has always been claimed that love also is first and last a gift, always a gift. We do not think it strange that we do not look to heaven for our earthly loves. We simply look around us, and we find ourselves enamored of the beauty and loveliness which reside within the world. Whatever there is which can be loved and which can be responded to in love is here, in this world, before our eyes and part of our lives. If we do not find love here, we shall never find love at all.

Does it not cause us to wonder that among ourselves we do not all fall in love with exactly the same people? Why should this be? You and I who are the closest of friends fall in love with different persons. Why? Basically it is a matter of how each of us sees the world, how we are geared to look—and we look out of our own particular mix of attitudes, values, emotions and desires. Thus it is that we hold ourselves before the world in uniquely personal ways, and this holding forth of self can trigger a resonance which lures a response from some special other.

The relationship of love is here before us, in our world, in our lives, in our very selves. Our only call is to be sensitive and unselfish enough to respond to this lure when it strikes like grace. All of us, to one degree or another, live with parched souls; the lesson of our lives is that the life-giving rain must be a gift from another and cannot be produced by us. But love, like rain, is always available to us. We need merely the eyes to see, and the good grace to be gracious.

## What Is the Good News?

It may be instructive here to look back at Jesus in the Gospels to judge whether this viewpoint has any validity for our spiritual lives. It was not by mere quirk that the message of his preaching was entitled the good news by some of those who heard it and chose to follow it. The Gospels make it clear that what was disturbing about Jesus was his persistent movement against the organized and legalized religious structures of his day. It was not so much that he stood against the temple, or the law, or the priesthood of his time, for he did not. Rather, he stood against the idea that the life of one's soul could be guaranteed by ritual, by cult, by legal observance, by doctrinal purity. "The kingdom of God is within *you*," he proclaimed, not within the temple, law or priesthood. If you would find your God then look within, for if you do not find God there you will never, never find him anyplace else in all the world.

## Jesus: Proving by Pointing

It is no surprise that Jesus should be challenged for his teachings; he was often asked for authority, evidence, and proof. On those occasions when Jesus is pressed for some authority to back up and give credence to his message, it is remarkable that he does not cite God, or one of the prophets, as his witness. In response to such a challenge, Jesus tends *to point*, and when he does so, he points at something existing within the real world that has been there all along. For example, Jesus points to the obvious and unremarkable fact that the rain falls on the just and the unjust at exactly the same time, or the equally prosaic fact that the sun rises on the good and the bad indiscriminately. It is on such occasions that he invokes the curious dictum, "For those who have eyes, let them see."

What exactly is it that we are supposed to see? What are we looking at that we are missing? Our eyes follow where he is pointing, and we see the rain fall and the sun rise. These things we have seen before; they are commonplace and taken-for-granted. More astounding, however, is that this is the only evidence that Jesus has to offer—evidence which has lain before our eyes all the while. Nothing miraculous here, nothing called down from heaven, no supernatural witness—just the rainfall and the sunrise, the lilies of the field and the fig tree. The question of Jesus is not whether we have seen these things, since we have, but whether the eye of the inner heart has understood what such commonplaces reveal.

The rain falls on the just and the unjust alike, Jesus indicates by his pointing—are we so dull of heart that it has not occurred to us that the Source and End of all that is, the Holy One whom we call Father, is such that he will not withhold his gifts because of what the children have done? The relationships of this God who is Father are always gifted love, free and unmerited on our part so that no matter what we do we do not restrain the bounty of this Giver. Precisely because this Father is love he will everlastingly bestow the gifts that sustain us in being whether we use them rightly or wrongly. The sun will rise on us whether we use the day for good or ill; the rain will come to our parched souls whether we love or hate. We with our actions cannot make this relentless love less warm or tender; we may turn away, but God's love, like the sun and the rain, will not.

Jesus asks us to acknowledge, possibly for the first time, that the very nature of God's universe is such that its relationships are always gracious; it will always hold us in being and sustain our life—regardless of who we are or what we do. This, Jesus insists, is the very nature of the universe itself; graciousness is the very air we breathe, the food we eat, the gravity that holds us in place. The very universe bathes us in sustaining love, and because this is so ordinary we do not bother to acknowledge it.

## What Should the Daughters and Sons Be Like?

This pointing of Jesus, however, is not just at the universe; unremittingly and almost accusingly, it is a pointing at ourselves. For the message of the universe is the message of our very being: if your Father is like this, what should the children be like? Do the daughters and sons, who have been sustained within a universe of loving gifts, relate to each other with the same giftedness? Are the daughters and sons of this Father such that they will withhold their gifts because of what the other has done? Do the children withhold their love from the unjust, restrain their concern for the unloving, turn their backs on the enemy? Are the children so unmindful of their Father that they nurse their love according to the condition of the other, parcel out their free gifts according to the rate of return, ration their concern for those found worthy of it?

If ever there was a revelation from Jesus it must be here, and it stands as an inescapable indictment: if this is how the sons and daughters behave, they are not merely in conflict with the will of God, they are in violation of the very nature of the universe itself. All of created reality is the embodied reflection of the God who is love, and it is this gifted feature which holds us in being. We desecrate the universe with our mean-heartedness and we ravish its giftedness with our malice. The sun and the rain, the sparrows and the lilies stand up to condemn us. The unloving children are an offense not only to God but to the very universe which feeds us and warms us and shows us something about love.

### Faithfulness

None of this is beyond our knowing: for those who have eyes let them see. The evidence for who we really are and what our God is like sits before us with the ordinariness of a seed and the marvel of food. Faith, we have said, is a gift; but it is not an abstract knowledge nor an item of belief about God that will have the power to redeem us. Let us abandon the idea that faith denotes some abstract ideal which it is our duty to possess even though it is a gift. Faith exists only in faithful people and their faithful lives. The gift which they have re-

ceived, Jesus insists, is available to all of us. Perhaps we refuse
to search beneath the wrappings of the world.

We are faithful when we acknowledge the graciousness of
our lives, of our world, of those others who tell us who we are;
we are faithful when we really see that our gratitude is the call
to celebration; we are faithful when we are willing to let the
abundance of our lives be the food for the abundance of the
world. All these things, Jesus reminds us, are before us, before
our very eyes. And if we care to look—at the farmer, the
fisherman, the shepherd, the father in bed with his children—
we will catch a fleeting glimpse of the Gracious One who
always enjoins, "Taste and see."

## Abundance: The Pearl of Great Price

The unquenchable thirst of our lives is for life in abundance. Much of our confusion surely arises from the fact that
the world invites us with a broad selection of enticing versions
of abundance. The world, however, for better or for worse
cannot offer infallibility, with the sad result that to whatever
choice we commit ourselves it is fraught with uncertainty and
liable to disappointment. Like the pearl-merchant of the Gospel, we are inexorably involved in searching out the pearl of
great price. We are so consumed with our passion for pearls
that every endeavor of our lives is devoured in searching out
these pearls. What we discover is an endless variety, large and
small, round and knobby, white and pink. But once our eyes
have feasted on the pearl of great price, all these lesser pearls
lapse into insignificance; what we thought was worthwhile is
trivial and what we thought was valuable is cheap. We are so
driven to possess the pearl of great price that we will sacrifice
all these lesser pearls. Such is the quest of our lives, the
passionate urge to seek out abundance wherever it be found.
What will finally satisfy us? What is ultimately worth striving
for? What is it that in its possession will not betray us? How will
we know that pearl which is true abundance?

## Risk for the Pearl

That great pearl to which Jesus points and which is the abundance of life lies before us and is available to all. Abundance is not found by the achievement of wealth, power, happiness, and prestige. These things are but accretions that can be added like pearls to a collection. We will catch a glimpse of the great pearl when we are enamored of life itself, when we let go of our cheap security and let our identity float loose to be caught up in a web of relationships that come unbidden like dew. Only when we finally see that we have nothing to lose but the quality of our lives will we be willing to risk the safe and the comfortable, will we be willing to let go of all those things that do not enrich by addition but rather serve to tie us down, will we let go of that one final truth which we thought was ours—that our life is our own.

Should we not be obsessed with that strange wisdom of Jesus: if you wish to save your life you must lose it? The quality of our lives lies not in its achievements but in its intensity. The secret, as Jesus shows us, lies not in the exceptional or the supernatural; the pearl lies within. When we seize upon life itself, when we become enamored of the living relationships which grace our lives like sunshine and air, when we are convinced that the quality of life which imbues us with passion lies within the sustaining relationships of our love, when we are willing to risk a death for the intensity of a beauty, then we have unveiled the pearl which has always lain in reach. And because we are becoming godly we will recognize, finally, this pearl as the God of love.

## Selected Readings

In a remarkable and persuasive essay, "Theology as Critique of Expostulation," Joseph Haroutunian deals with prayer in the very human context of the struggle for understanding, acceptance, and relief, in brief, our right to expostulate with God. For several years now I have found this article unusually rewarding. It can be found in *The Future of Empirical Theology,* edited by Bernard Meland (Chicago: The University of Chicago Press, 1969).

A discussion of prayer which comes closest to the model of prayer which I am attempting to develop here is that of Lewis Ford, "Our Prayer as God's Passions," in *Religious Experience and Process Theology,* edited by Harry Cargas and Bernard Lee (New York: Paulist Press, 1976).

Another excellent article by Lewis Ford which deals with the power of God but is relevant to our concept of prayer is "Divine Persuasion and the Triumph of Good," in *Process Philosophy and Christian Thought,* edited by Delwin Brown, Ralph James, and Gene Reeves (Indianapolis and New York: The Bobbs-Merrill Company, 1971).

Since the issue of the social and political commitments of the Christian believer is of major concern today, it is important that we have a clear and accurate understanding of the stance of Jesus in the New Testament. Especially valuable in this regard is John Howard Yoder, *The Politics of Jesus* (Grand Rapids, Michigan: William B. Eerdmans Publishing Company, 1972).

*Scripture Reading*

The Gospel of Matthew Chapter 6: 7–15

The Letter to the Galatians Chapter 5: 16–24

# 8

# Faith and Faithfulness

Even without special reflection we realize that the spiritual life derives the fullness of its meaning only from the context of faith. On various occasions we have already spoken about the intimate and necessary relationship between faith and prayer. Since, however, our traditionally received notion of faith is so much a product of a substance-worldview, it may be helpful if we further search out the meaning of faith and try to discover how it can be a living reality within our lives.

The import of faith is not primarily a set of doctrines or truths to which we adhere for the sake of salvation. The first and last import of faith, rather, is the faithfulness of our lives. The word of the Gospel must become flesh in the life of each of us, and our gradual enfleshment of the Gospel will be the process of putting on Jesus, as Paul enjoins. We are enabled to do this, not by our beliefs, but by our believing practice which is our life of faithfulness. The object of our faithfulness can be specified by the types of commitments in which we engage ourselves; for this reason it will be worth our effort to try to establish what it is that we do in our commitments and for what reasons.

Even though we tend to lean upon our intellects as a fundamental means of guidance and control in our lives, it is not really the rational intellect which has first priority in the determination of our decisions. Most of our decisions are made within a context which is so concrete and particular, so unique in its conditions and unmatched in its circumstances, that a general, abstract principle can be of little help. We find that in the most human choices of our lives we respond much more readily to the appeal of a story than that of a principle. Our Gospel record is very thin on principle but extremely robust in story. In this chapter we will develop the links between faith, commitment, and story as the model of faithfulness presented in the Gospel and established by Jesus.

### The Meaning of Faith

As part of the heritage of a substance-worldview which has shaped our religious tradition we have received a substantive notion of faith. By this is meant that we have the ability and the language to speak about the reality of faith as if it were something objectively real, something describable and definable and, after a fashion, measurable. Thus we can speak of someone receiving the faith or losing it, having great faith or little faith, strong or weak faith, being grateful for or denying the faith. Such noun-language surely gives the impression that there is something objective about faith. It has already been pointed out that faith has the same type of reality as love in that the reality of both of these nouns exists only in a concrete context of relationships. In this sense there is neither love nor faith, but merely loving and faithing between existing persons and, naturally, God.

Associated with this assumption of the objectivity of faith is the tendency to think that faith is something that is done with the intellect. The model of faith has been closely linked to the model of knowledge with the result that the faith came to designate a body of truth or a cluster of doctrines. What distinguished these truths of faith from ordinary knowledge was the fact that they came from God and had to do with God. This assimilation of faith to knowledge perhaps explains why we could so readily speak of faith in a quantitative sense— receiving and losing it, having more or less of it. It will be shown that faith, like love, has a remote but not a primary relationship to the intellect. Every great mystic in our historic tradition, including Jesus, insists that faith has more to do with the heart than with the head. This is surely worth exploring.

The use of noun-language for the notions of faith and love

allows us to describe these realities in objective terms. This objective language makes it possible for us to speak about faith in terms of its doctrines, in terms of its increase or decrease, its presence or absence. In exactly the same way we can use this objective language to speak about love. In both cases, however, the object of our speaking is treated as if it existed outside of ourselves and thus had a describable reality in much the same way as trees or mountains. It is quite conceivable that a scholar could spend an entire lifetime studying either trees or mountains even though he had never seen one. However, we do not talk about love or faith because they are there, external to ourselves. We only speak of love and faith because they are inside; they are part of us. So it is that the proper language of both love and faith is not the language of objects toward which we can take the stance of a spectator.

## The Personal Language of Faith

The only proper language of love and faith is first-person language. We speak the language of love and faith not when we describe something but when we speak for ourselves. All the songs and all the poems about love are crippled and useless when the lover finally has to say for himself in his own words, "I love you." In the same fashion, as tempted as we are to be intellectually interested in the content and meaning of faith, the only proper language of faith is intensely personal when each of us must say for ourselves, "I believe; I trust; I repent; I am forgiven." As in the case of love, no one can say these things for us.

It may perhaps be almost disappointing to search out the language of faith only to discover there that there are no such things as sacred words, or holy words, or religious words. The entire vocabulary of the language of faith is in fact made up of quite ordinary and everyday words, words which we already use practically and meaningfully in the commonplace interchanges of our lives. So it is that words like "hope," "grace," "peace," and "healing" are ordinary words used by us meaningfully in ordinary situations. Each of these words has a particular context, and when one of them is used properly within that context we know what it means. We learn the meaning of the word only when we see it exemplified in the context of its use. As we grow up, for example, we learn in what context "I'm sorry" has its proper meaning, and learning this we know how to use it for ourselves.

With these ordinary words we need simply look at our world and ask: Where does forgiveness happen? Where does repentance happen? Where does love happen? And we learn the meaning of these terms, not from the dictionary, but from the way they are used by the persons involved in these contexts. Thus it is our social community which exemplifies these terms, and it teaches us their use, not by talking about them, but by actually practicing forgiveness, repentance, healing, and love. This should not be at all surprising, for no matter how much we may hear about the concept of love, it is only the actual loving of individuals and community which teaches us what love concretely means.

### The Content of Faith

This first-person quality of the language of faith indicates that the content of faith is not primarily intellectual or doctrinal. The real living content of faith is essentially and necessarily words like hope, trust, love, contrition, forgiveness, and compassion, not in their abstract definition but in their concrete and lived exemplification. We appropriate for ourselves the content of faith only when we learn to use these words properly, and we learn such use only by doing these things for ourselves: I hope; I trust; I love; I repent; I forgive; I have mercy. Thus it is that we learn the living content of faith when we personally appropriate and then speak meaningfully and sincerely this peculiar cluster of words—peculiar because they form the heart of the Gospel and are there used to describe the faithful person. As a result, the content of faith is not at first-hand intellectual; this content refers, rather, to our living and to our relationships, with the curious result that we will be recognized as having the faith, not by what we say, but by what we do.

Noteworthy also is the fact that to invoke these words personally is to invoke also several other things, none of them verbal: the proper use of these words of faith is attitudinal, valuational, appreciative, convictional and emotional. The proper use of "I'm sorry," for example, requires beyond the mere words the attitude of repentance, the conviction that wrong must be righted, the feeling of sorrow, and the value of the dignity of another. All of these terms of faith are so self-involving that a whole spectrum of attitudes, emotions and values must be called into play for the proper use of this apparently simple speaking; perhaps what is being pointed at here is why it is so difficult for us to be faithful.

If we attempt to give a description of these words of faith, that is, if we try to set out the meaning of hope, trust, repentance, and love, we find that we are pointing out those relationships which constitute the deepest meaning of our human world. So it is that the content of faith functions to carry to expression those attitudes and values which we must bring to our ongoing involvement with the world of others, those emotions and convictions which define our engagement with relationships that are inevitable. What we call "having the faith" will in fact be our faithfulness to those activities which invoke from us and from others the qualities of love, trust, hope, forgiveness, and the like. To have the faith is to be engaged with the world in very definite and particular ways, and the Gospel recommends to us these special ways.

## Faith as Lure

Our objective use of the word faith is intended to lure us into an engagement and a grappling with life which is deeply satisfactory; faith is the alluring symbol of life which is intense, rich, full, deep, healing and creative. The first-person use of the language of faith is our attempt to engage ourselves in the fullness of involvement inspired by those qualities—emotional, attitudinal, and convictional—which most create depth in our experiencing. It is within this faithful engagement with life that we experience forgiveness, repentance, trust, and love, and with the experience of these qualities we know what it is to be healed.

What would be the purpose of such salvation? The purpose can be none other than wholeness—not wholeness which we arrive at like an end-point, but the wholeness of bringing the finest qualities of our selves to focus on the integrity of what we do. The language of faith points out those qualities which are essential for such wholeness, which is to say, those qualities that demand the very most of our selves. Thus the strange paradox: self-involvement is both the condition and the product of faith. We have the faith when we speak rightly the language of faith—I repent, I forgive, I have mercy, I love—and we speak rightly only when we are so involved that we could not speak otherwise.

For too long, perhaps, have we tried to identify the faithful by the doctrinal contents of their minds rather than insisting on those Gospel activities which describe the kingdom. If, however, we acknowledge that faith is an active relationship to life, then when we seek to discern the fruits of faith we will not first look for orthodoxy; rather, we will look for the fruits of mercy, forgiveness, patience, meekness, and love. How will we discover who is the faithful person? Let us look for those with wholeness of life, those who bring passion to all their affairs, those who are restless and ill at ease because others lack, not intelligence, but love.

### Passionate Involvement

Note well that the fruit of faith is not happiness in our usual sense, but intensity. Life is not measured by happiness because this is too fleeting and subject to the tricks of fortune not ours to control. It is the intensity with which we experience that gauges the quality of our lives, and it is only intensity that can include fear, doubt, hurt, pain, effort, joy and always,

always passion. Although we often may have little choice as to circumstances and relationships and conditions, we always have a choice which is inescapably ours and ours alone—the degree of passion with which we choose to involve ourselves. Our faith is there to point out what things are worth our passion and to what degree; it serves to indicate what is worth our concern and what deserves our pain. Knowing that, it is for us to involve ourselves with whatever passion we can summon.

On those rare occasions when we take inventory of our lives to search out there whether they were worth the living, how would we decide such a grim question? Why is it that our success is sour and our fame bitter? Possibly because such things can be achieved through self-investment but do not necessarily require self-involvement. Ultimately our self-involvement is measured by the degree of our passion, and the only telling testimony to the worth of our lives is the passion which with it was expended.

We can read the Gospel parables as setting out what it means to be passionately involved. Whatever else Jesus was, he was a spinner of stories, and his tales can only be understood by those who have experienced the passion he is describing. To the almost cynical question "Who is my neighbor?" Jesus responds not with a list, but with a story. Surprisingly, the story of the good Samaritan nowhere invokes the word "love," yet when we have understood the story we have understood also the meaning of love. What sort of passion drove that Samaritan to expend so much energy and concern on this stranger in the ditch? If we do not understand the passion we do not know the meaning of love. We are left with but the simple directive: "Go and do likewise." We will have no trouble finding our own stranger in whatever ditch. Our problem is not a problem of strangers; it is a problem of passion.

## Parables of the Kingdom

We need not be reminded how consistent throughout the Gospels is the theme of the kingdom and how frequent are the parables concerning the kingdom. Less obvious perhaps is the fact that the parables of the kingdom surely do not describe a place or state, nor do they define a condition. The kingdom stories, without exception, simply set out different types of human relationships, relationships so unspectacular and ordinary that they do not demand our notice, much less our comment—a farmer and his seed, a shepherd and his sheep, a widow and her mite, an owner and his barn, a vinedresser and his vines, a father and his sons, a master and his servants, and so many others.

In no way are such parables intended to teach us prudence or to call attention to the workings of the world. They are, rather, simple reminders of the kind of passion and the kind of concern that ordinary people bring to the very commonplace situations of their lives. Inevitably these parables set out relationships which, though common, are by no means unimportant. These, for most of us, will be the best we ever have and hence whatever we make of ourselves will be made out of such stuff as this. When queried about the membership of the kingdom, Jesus gave the almost disappointing reply which referred not to some high religiosity that might at least demand some heroism, but rather to the somewhat undistinguished and almost forgettable and unheroic activities of giving food to the hungry one, drink to the thirsty one, a shirt to the naked one, and a simple visit to the sick one.

It is a blow to our spiritual pride that the kingdom will be peopled only with such prosaically common virtues. These relationships, Jesus insists, are available to all of us; what we bring to them will be the only discernible indication of how we value, not just our neighbor, but ourselves and that intangible bond between us which is our God. To be faithful is to remember with all the passion of our souls that love and justice, mercy and forgiveness, goodness and peace, have their concrete existence only in their enactment. And who will be their actors if not ourselves? Let us take the language of faith upon ourselves; let us learn to say rightly at least one word, for this surely will unlock the rest: "I love."

## Where God Is Found

Certainly one of the gravest difficulties of our spiritual life is that we do not see God nor do we hear him speaking clearly and unambiguously. What we see is ourselves, our neighbor, and our world, but Jesus assures us that these are sufficient. The food of our lives is our relationships with the mundane and the ordinary. It is here and here alone that we can learn how to say "I am sorry," "I trust you," "I believe you," and "I love you." If we do not learn how to do these things properly with ourselves and our neighbors whom we see, then we will have no way of knowing how to do these things in relation to the God whom we do not see.

Has it occurred to us that the first meaning of forgiveness is self-forgiveness, that we must first of all learn to be generous in forgiving ourselves before we can approach God to ask forgiveness? It would surely appear to be an insult to God and a violation of the act of forgiveness to request of God that he forgive something that we had not ourselves forgiven, even if within ourselves. Thus the hard and lovely fact is that this world alone is the breeding ground of faith, that our life with our neighbors will teach us how to be faithful. The poor, the hungry, the lonely, the fearful and the unloved—let us never be so unimaginative and insensible as to claim we do not know where God is to be found or what God wants, or, most important to our spiritual lives, whether we ourselves are godly.

## Solitariness and World-Loyalty

What we have said here simply reminds us that we must be ever heedful of that final mystery of our spiritual quest—in order to find our life we must lose it. If indeed the nature of God is love, then the inevitable tension between self and other lies at the heart of reality itself. The ineffable mystery of God is not his infinity or his power; it is that, his nature being love, he is at the mercy of such as ourselves, whom he would love. Our finest value lies in what we are for God everlastingly, and this is by our own choice rather than God's.

The unavoidable conflict between the inner spiritual struggle of the self toward perfection and the necessary inter-change with a world of others who would both distract and pervert that personal endeavor is the classic battleground of the spiritual life. An other-worldly spirituality based on a dual-istic worldview resolves this tension by placing life's supreme value in another life and another world; and for this reason life in the present world can be removed insofar as possible from all human commerce and worldly temptation. Such a solution seems to do little justice either to the Gospels or to our own experience of passionate love within this world. If our previous presentation has any merit, it serves to take seriously the Gospel injunctions such as love, mercy, forgiveness and peace by making these the very context of our faithful lives rather than an environment to be superseded. The danger of a dualis-tic view of the religious life is that too easily can spirituality denote solely the relation of the individual soul to God to the exclusion of the world and others.

## The Soul in Solitariness

In a remarkable volume entitled *Religion in the Making*, A.N. Whitehead analyzes the nature of religion and its func-tion in our lives. In the early part of this book Whitehead reflects that *religion is what one does with one's solitariness.* Whitehead not only develops this notion, he repeats it on six separate occasions throughout the book. For this reason, this concept from Whitehead is often quoted in defense of the position that religion is a completely private affair, that the relationship between the soul and God is solitary and exclu-sive.

Whitehead, however, continues to expound upon this idea until he eventually comes to the point where he claims: "Reli-gion is *world-loyalty.*" What Whitehead demonstrates is that the initial thrust of religion is the turn within, the effort to determine one's identity and one's goal by an unflinching appraisal in which the self discerns the convictions and com-mitments which are the final arbiter of self-identity. In this sense, as Whitehead points out, unless one is solitary one can never be religious. A strange turn, however, occurs within this process of introspection. The only available language of self-awareness is the language of relationships, with the result that the self can only be discovered as the creative outcome of relationships outside of itself—parents, family, language, country, education, religion and the like.

## The Social Self

As the self in its search for true identity begins to chart these sustaining relationships it is discovered that every named relationship is but the outcome of a larger environment of connections which allow it to be. The final religious awareness is that the entire cosmos is a complex and intricate plot to hold us in being. Thus it is that the intimate value of the self has debts of gratitude which stretch across the entire universe. Surely the proper religious emotion in the light of such awareness is sheer awe at the intricate and elegant grandeur of a gracious reality which will conspire to hold us in being.

The two poles of the spiritual life are thus inseparably joined by Whitehead—the finality of self-value and the absolute necessity of relationships for the creation of this self-value. In Whitehead's analysis, the cosmos itself, finite and limited as it is, is simply the universal context of relationships which defines the experience of God. It is, therefore, in this trinitarian synthesis of self, world, and God that the spiritual quest finds both its meaning and its goal. As a consequence, the personal self is irretrievably social, so that the greater the engendering of social relationships the greater the creation of the self.

In traditional spirituality, the self was considered as social only in the sense that the relationship between the soul and God was fundamental and essential to the soul (but not to God). The weakness of this position was that it was thought that the self could be enhanced by bypassing all relationships except God, and hence the world could be excluded. Besides the sheer physical and psychological impossibility of such a maneuver (How can we abandon the earth's air, sunshine and gravity? How can we possibly forego our language or the conceptual climate which allows us to be rational?), the anti-worldly bias was a denigration of God's good creation, and the fear that worldly loves would derogate from the love of God was an insult to the infinite graciousness of God himself. It is only when the world is rightly appreciated for the value and beauty which is properly its own that we begin to have an inkling of the unimaginable size and marvelous goodness of God.

## Our Shared Existence

If in our solitariness we come to an awareness of our own supreme worth, not just because of, but before our God, then we also begin to appreciate the sacred value of every individual. It is not merely that all of us happen to exist together, individuals before God; rather, because of God we exist in sustaining mutuality like the intricate web of cells within a single body. Our mutual coexistence is our first sustaining environment, and out of it we create one another, enable each other, bestow identities and endow with a personal name. When we delve into our own solitary depths we come to know that the only debt we can concretely pay is to those others who, in their sustaining love, tell us who we are.

There are debts across the universe which we will forever be unable to pay except in the finite and fragmentary intercourse of our everyday lives. This provides the concrete context of faith in which we are willing to entrust our lives to those relationships which have already established us and to which we can contribute everlastingly. It is this world of others, consequently, which is our primary meeting-ground for the presence of God. Unless we are willing to surrender ourselves to the lives of others and offer ourselves as a gracious gift in the cause of life, we will not find our own souls, not even with God. How hard the lesson that it is in defense of our self-identity that we lose our lives! In the patient surrender of love we find both our lives and our selves.

## The Darkness of Faith and Love

The chief difficulty here, as with any spirituality, is that we must live our lives by faith; and faith in this sense also has the meaning that we see through a glass darkly, and so we have no assurance that we see rightly. As with the relationship of love, faith necessarily entails both trust and hope. Both faith and love are a response to gifted relationships, and precisely because of this giftedness there must be trust in the sustenance offered and hope for continued ongoingness and well-being. There is no guarantee that the object of our love or of our faith will in the future continue to grace us with its presence or its allure. Faith, like love, must endure without proof; to demand proof of either is to both misunderstand and destroy the very trust that makes the relationship possible.

We stand before all those matters which count to us the most with a certain fear and trembling—fear of loss, fear of betrayal, fear of uncertain future. We do not possess, cannot possess, the object of faith or of love, and because of this we cannot control. The most we can do is to be open and receptive to this undue graciousness. It is because of such uncertainty that we must have hope, for it is hope which allows us to gather up the tangled mess which is the present in the reliant trust that this alone will provide for us a usable future. Without hope any ideal in the future would be dismissed as irrevelant and we would stagnate in the present. It is only because of faith and love that we believe the future is worth stirving for, sometimes even worth dying for. That we have doubts, that we are uncertain even of ourselves, is but the reflection of how much we do in fact depend upon the good grace of a universe and others to hold us in being.

## The Relationship of Faith and Trust

We often fail to notice that our primordial relationship to the universe is a relationship of trust, that every single relationship out of which we fashion our lives and our reality is a relationship of trust. In spite of our casually used scientific language, there is for us no such thing as objective certainty. We have grown accustomed to large-scale patterns of order, and we like to think of these in terms of laws; what we choose to call natural laws or laws of the universe are simply descriptions of cosmic behavior which we cannot control. Each day we trust that our sun will rise, that our atmosphere will contain air, that rain will come, that food will grow, that gravity will hold. Cosmic eons ago this earth and its conditions were not as they are now; we simply trust that they will hold long enough to sustain us with our short-futured plans.

In similar fasion, every encounter with another human being has its initial foundation in trust, and the growth of a human relationship relies on trust as on its bedrock. Trust is our deeply human way of handling the unpredictability of the unknown future, and without trust we would be crippled, both in thought and in action. If we had no basic trust that our striving could achieve some results of value and of satisfaction we would remain indecisive and be locked in the hopelessness of the present.

Trust is the basic and foundational ingredient that sustains faith, hope, and love, and this is but evidence that these three are inseparably bound together, aspects of one single foundational relationship for which we have no name. Earlier I have called it love-faith, but hope also must be included. More surprising than we care to admit, we trust as inexorably and as consistently as we breathe, and this provides our first, unreflective aspiration of world-loyalty. We live loyally to each other and loyally to the universe because our trust has been fruitful and our provident lives are the evidence we hold. In our religious lives we know full well what is the cornerstone of our trust—it is the unfailing and everlasting God who will not lose even the sparrow or the lily because he loves them too much, whose immutability is the steadfastness of his love in our regard. We discover, then, that without realizing it we have come to trust God because we have already learned to trust the universe and ourselves. Faith and trust are as natural to us as the pull of gravity, and as necessary.

## Our Final Trust

Our ultimate trust, however, is more than trust in the continuing structures of the universe, the reliability of friends and loved ones, or the confidence in at least partial success for our efforts; no, our ultimate trust is much more audacious than this. Our full and final trust dares to crash through the finite borders which restrict the possibilities of our knowing; it dares to hold that the worth of what we do now, the value of our sacrificial struggle, the lovely excellence of our finest achievements—these all become the final and everlasting values within the experience of God. We have the almost impudent trust that what we do now not only counts, but counts everlastingly. We dare to believe, you and I, that we make a difference which is an everlasting difference in the all-encompassing nature of God. We dare never underrate ourselves (nor move toward despair) since only God knows our true worth in the intimacies of his own experience. This is an act of mighty faith and mighty hope; it is this which sustains us in mighty love.

## The Meaning of Commitment

The accelerating changes of our recent cultural history have included a fairly wide-scale distrust of institutions, both political and religious. The healthy distrust of the institutional encroachment upon the personal intimacy of our lives need not be unnecessarily bemoaned since it frees us to make choices out of our own strength rather than by institutional coercion. Rightly or wrongly, however, linked to this distrust of institutions has been a concomitant distrust of the idea of commitment.

Those institutionally sponsored commitments—for example, marriage, religious life, priesthood, celibacy—have suffered the same erosion of credibility, since the new wisdom has maintained that the idea of a long-term or perpetual commitment is inherently contradictory to the experience of an ever-changing, ever-becoming person. The emphasis on the qualitative intensity of experience now precluded any reliable investment in the future. Thus it is that many of us found ourselves within commitments once seriously made—marriage or celibacy, for example—which had now become seriously suspect. We were led to question our own ability even to make a long-term commitment. The very idea of commitment has fallen on hard times indeed. Surely most of us are not about to surrender our commitments this readily; let us see whether our commitments can indeed have a final and lasting claim upon us.

## Commitment as Faithfulness

Almost certainly most of us instinctively sense that there is an essential relationship between commitment and the spiritual life, and the reason for this is quite straightforward: a commitment necessarily requires the qualities of faith, trust, and love, for without these it cannot be a commitment at all. What is our everyday understanding of the idea of commitment? Broadly speaking, a commitment is a choice of value which will be pursued and which will be held fast in spite of changing and unpredictable circumstances which lie yet in the future. When we make a commitment we assert to ourselves: in spite of change, in spite of chance, in spite of unpredicatability, in this particular value-choice I will remain the same; with all my heart, I will persevere in this value. In short, I will be faithful.

What would motivate us to express our present identity in this type of promise toward the future? We are inspired to make a commitment because we perceive a particular value to be of such importance and of such worth that to lose it would be equivalent to losing part of ourselves, to lose part of our identity; this is the driving motivation which compels us to make a commitment that will demand perseverance. The underlying claim that sustains a commitment is the feeling that some relationships are so important that we cannot do without them and life in a very definite sense would not be worthwhile.

Unquestionably the experience of love provides the most compelling instance of why one would wish to commit oneself to another into the indefinite future—the loss of this gracious presence becomes inconceivable. We are so affected by the relational presence of the loved one that we intuitively feel that we would be a different person without this presence. In this way, a commitment involves the awareness of our own enhanced self-identity. A paradoxical relationship, however, is established here: viewed from one side, a commitment is a giving of ourselves over to the pursuit of a value transcending ourselves; viewed from the other side, a commitment is the effort to maintain a present self-identity by means of this same value. This is but another way of perceiving that we are inescapably self-involved in every choice and every activity, so that our proper vested interest is our own most worthwhile self. This is the only self we have to offer to others.

## Commitment: A Pledge to Loyalty

While it is some perceived and experienced value which lures us to make a commitment, what is demanded of us by this commitment is loyalty and faithfulness. A commitment is our pledge that this value, now so attractive and enriching, will continue to be a constitutive and formative part of our lives. Any firm pledge of loyalty requires simultaneously the choice of a worthwhile value and the strength of character to ensure perseverance in this value.

By our loyalty we pledge that out of our strength we will continue in this value-choice even in the face of new and conflicting values; we will remain loyal to this choice in spite of the consequences which at the moment are unknown or dimly seen. What is being pledged by the commitment is our own faithfulness; precisely because we do not know the circumstances and conditions of our future (and most certainly they will be different from the present), we pledge our hearts that in this value we will remain exactly the same.

It is not out of poetry or accident, for example, that the wedding ceremony should contain the words, "for richer or for poorer, in sickness and in health." What is being specified here is that the very unpredictability of the future can be destructive, and only a choice of faithfulness now can override our being turned aside by possible conflicts in the future. The only reason we would commit ourselves to such faithfulness in the face of an unknown future is our intuitive sense that a particular value is so self-enhancing that to lose it would be to lose the important meaning of our lives. I will not be the same because this relationship has enriched me and satisfied me and fulfilled me in a way I will no longer do without. Notice that the only force which draws us and holds us to a commitment is the suasive lure of a perceived value.

Once, for example, I am in love with this particular other, then I also perceive that I can do no other and I wish to be no other than this-one-in-love. I am lured to commitment by the self-fulfillment of the relationship itself. From then on it is the suasive power of the commitment which enables us to endure through the thick and thin of fragile and unpredictable human relationships. It is the commitment which puts the relationship beyond momentary feeling, temporary conflict, unforeseen circumstance. The aim of the commitment is to provide enduring power over tediousness, monotony, boredom, conflict and change.

If the idea of commitment is used in too casual a sense, then we miss its meaning entirely. For we do not pledge our hearts lightly nor do we pledge them to trivial things. That we would pledge the loyalty of our hearts means that we are attracted by something of worth comparable to our heart's deepest desire. We give our allegiance rightly only to that which deserves it. It would be self-destructive to be faithful to the paltry or the insignificant. For the very reason that our heart is involved, we want this to be worthy of our heart's passion. Because of this allegiance of the heart, if we look carefully, we will discover that our commitments are only made to another person, never to an object, or an institution, or an idea. This point must be examined more carefully.

## Commitment: Only to a Person

Even though we talk quite comfortably about being committed to the Church, to marriage, to celibacy, or to principle, it is suggested here that this is not a proper use of the word "commitment" at all; however, since we are so accustomed to this usage we are easily misguided as to the real and lasting worth of our commitments. Because a commitment demands the dedication of the heart to a value which is life-enhancing and which fashions our identity in the world, we must ask where would we rightly give our allegiance so wholeheartedly and lastingly. Is it not evident that we can only pledge our hearts in loving faithfulness to another person, and never to an object or a thing? The final value of our human world is the value of other persons, and nothing else.

To imagine that any non-personal value, whether an institution, a principle, or an abstract ideal, can function as the source of meaning and identity in our lives is to misconstrue our own inherent loveliness. It is a contradiction of our very being to seek fulfillment and satisfaction in the love of anything except persons. Why is it that we look with such disdain on those who commit their lives to the pursuit of power, money, or success? These are non-personal values, and to allow these to give definition to our lives is to reduce other persons to the status of means and objects. How would it be possible to love one's neighbor as oneself if the heart's allegiance were first to a principle and only secondly to people? The sacred individuality of the concrete person is too easily overlooked in an appeal to principle, cause, or institution. It is only persons, our God and those concrete others who make up our lives, who deserve the commitment of our hearts.

## Institutional Commitments

On the other hand, however, it is true that we do make commitments in the name of institutions, principles, and causes. Let us look carefully at exactly what does take place in such situations. It still strikes us as virtuous that one should be committed to the Church, or to celibacy, or to marriage, for example. Such commitments, however, precisely because they are to non-personal objects, can only be commitments if they contain a necessary relationship to a person. Perhaps marriage as an example can clarify this. Even though we may speak of being committed to marriage, we should notice that marriage is simply the formal structure which guarantees commitment to another person—wife or husband, and children. It is only because we are priorly committed to another person that we enter into the institution of marriage which provides the social structures both to make possible and to guarantee at a social level this personal commitment. In this sense, then, marriage is but the concrete means by which the ongoing faithfullness of our lived commitment to another may be maintained.

In much the same fashion, what we call our commitment to the Church is in reality not a commitment to the Church at all, but to God and to the godly life. It is only God who is the final object of our heart's allegiance, but it is the Church which, by providing the instruments of theology, sacrament and moral guidance, is the enabling means which provides the concrete context for our lived commitment. In this sense, the Church is not an end at all, since only God can be our final end; the Church is but one of many means for the faithful living of the godly life.

Our commitment to celibacy can be analyzed in the same light. Celibacy in itself cannot possibly be an end in our spiritual life since there is absolutely nothing inherently sanctifying about having or not having sexual experience. The context for the commitment of celibacy is the Gospel life which is necessarily and inescapably commitment to the love and service of others. A possible means for the freeing of the self for such single-minded dedication and fervid service of others could be the foregoing of overt sexuality and the married state. Two important items, however, must be noticed here. First, celibacy is merely a means, and never an end. A means can never be sanctifying in itself; it is only the end which can be sanctifying. In the case of celibacy, it is the fullest love of God and our neighbor which is the end, and our sanctification will be a measure of our love. Second, there is no necessary connection between celibacy and dedication to God and neighbor. It is quite possible to be celibate without loving either God or neighbor, as it is quite possible to be celibate instead of loving our neighbor.

Celibacy thus is at best an instrument in our lives which receives whatever virtue it has from the end which it helps to achieve. If our celibacy has not been instrumental in enabling our love to reach more persons more deeply, then it has been of little worth. Celibacy is simply the structural form which allows us to be single-minded and wholehearted in our commitment to others and to God.

In all of these cases it should be clear that we should be exceedingly shy in awarding our commitment to anything which is not personal, whether Church, law, principle, or ideal. All of these realities exist only for the sake of the well-being of all persons, and if this well-being is not being served, then this particular means has become self-defeating and humanly intolerable. Only God whom we do not see and our neighbor whom we do see are worthy of the wholeness of our heart's allegiance and the dedicated faithfulness of our very lives. When such things as Church, principle and cause are allowed to claim the consuming commitment of our allegiance, then it comes about that our faithfulness is to something other than persons; worse, and even demonic, persons are evaluated in terms of their relationship to the institution or cause rather than the other way around, and this is to degrade both other persons and ourselves.

Once again we need simply advert to the commonsense wisdom of Jesus. God alone, he reminds us, is worthy of the wholeness of our heart, mind, and soul, and the test of such wholeness is not obedience to law or subservience to institution, but the faithful concern for those least likely ones, the hungry, the thirsty, the poor and the oppressed. It is only persons, if we can believe Jesus, who can and ought to be loved with the wholeheartedness demanded by God. Only persons are worthy of such a commitment for the simple reason that the end of all our loving is God.

## The Fragility of Our Relationships

We do make commitments, however, because we realize full well how fragile and partial our relationships are. Those very relationships which are the most meaningful to us are at the same time the most ambiguous and darksome; and surely our relationship to God is the most darksome of all. We are always uncertain and unclear about our own best qualities, even more so are we unsure of the innermost qualities of others. For this reason, then, the fundamental motive for making a commitment is not at all the stability of the object (or the other person); the commitment is, rather, an attempt to provide for our own stability—we wish to make ourselves stable and self-identified by faithful adherence to that value which informs our very being. Our commitments serve as our way of handling our own instability, unpredictability, and selfishness; they are but the instrumental means of guiding our range of choices by the definite exclusion of those choices which would distract us from the pearl of great price.

## Total Commitment: To God Alone

Here we can discern our intuitively good logic in perceiving that God alone is worthy of the total and absolute commitment of our selves and our lives; any lesser value can only be pursued in relation to this final good. And the purpose of this commitment is to keep ourselves reliable and unfailing in our wholeheartedness to God; the commitment, however, is but the means, and only God is the end. The living out of this supreme commitment (rightly speaking, this commitment is made in baptism) will be the quality of our faithful lives, and the content will be the loving concern by which we esteem and treat both neighbor and stranger as if they were ourselves.

Admittedly, such commitment and such love are a difficult if not an impossible challenge; no doubt this is precisely why we make a commitment. The saving indulgence, however, of our inspired Gospel and of our gracious God is that our commitment will be judged by the sincerity of endeavor and not by some ideal achievement. Let us observe, then, how our commitments serve to define those values which we esteem as the most fulfilling, satisfying, and life-enhancing, those things which alone are worth the investment of our lives. Let us observe also how our commitments do in fact enable us to energetically seek out, and even to achieve, these life-defining values which often demand sacrifice and sometimes demand heroic effort. Even though our achievement may be partial and incomplete, at least our lives are firmly set in the direction of wholeness.

The first and final test, therefore, of the worth of our commitments is always our own committed lives. If our ideals are not gradually enfleshed within us, then it may well be the case that we are not sincerely committed to them. Abstract causes and principles, we should note, cannot take on our flesh; only other persons and that Transcendent Person who embodies all ideals can be enlivened within ourselves. It is God and persons to whom we pledge our hearts and whom we love; because of this love we dedicate ourselves to causes and principles which have but one purpose—the creative possibilities of greater love.

When we embody our commitments, therefore, we show forth our God. Let us leave off speaking for God and let God speak for himself; his speaking is clearly and undeniably "Love one another as I have loved you."

Since we do not see God we must make do with our neighbor. This, indeed, requires both faith and faithfulness. We persevere in such faith in the loving trust that our living faithfully will be the abundance of life itself. We stand on holy ground, for it is here, in this world and before our neighbor, that we meet and love our God.

### Stories on the Way

In our spiritual quest we have the good grace to be able to join that large company of saints and holy ones—both those who have preceded us and those who walk on the way with us. We recognize each other as belonging to the same conspiracy because all of us seek out our direction by telling the same stories. The hero of our stories is always God, but in our stories he can only be dimly discerned as a shadowy and illusive figure hidden behind many images—sometimes a father, then a farmer; now a shepherd, and then a fisherman; a husband, and even a son. What this God looks like, it seems, is not at all important; what should catch our attention is what he is doing.

Each of these storied images is a ray of light cast upon those types of relationships which concern this God—so much so that this mysterious Holy One is not so much discerned in the image as in the relationships themselves. If you would find your God, Jesus seems to caution, look at what is happening before your eyes. In order to draw our attention to those relationships which are available to be the lasting stuff of our lives, Jesus spins out a series of tales and stories, from the humdrum and unexceptional to the startling and rare. With lovely good sense those early witnesses copied their Jesus by retaining and retelling his stories; thus it is that this is the burden of what they have left us of Jesus.

## The Stories Show

These Gospel stories are not primarily designed to instruct us or teach us, and they surely are not intended to entertain us (though they may do all of these things). It is perhaps our own insecurity which demands that they teach us lessons, our own unwillingness to be responsible for ourselves which has us ask what they really mean. These Jesus-stories, as stories, in a very real sense do not *mean* anything. The point of a joke, for example, is not to *mean* anything; it is to be funny. A joke succeeds or fails by virtue of its funniness, and not by virtue of sublimity of meaning.

So also, stories do not *mean;* they simply *show.* And what Jesus shows in these stories is the only clue we will ever get as to what God is up to, what the kingdom is like, how to discern its members, what ground is really sacred. The point of the Gospel stories, therefore, is to simply show us what God and reality are all about, and once having been shown we are challenged to decide for ourselves whether we are willing to see it this way or not. For the most part these stories teach us nothing new, for what they show has been obvious and available to those who would use their eyes to look. This showing of the stories is the challenge to see what is already so transparent and manifest that to deny it would be a strange obduracy, a perverse hardness of heart with which not even God can deal.

By means of such stories Jesus enjoins upon us the relationships and the behavior exemplified in the tales. Rather than being instructions, they stand as challenges. The sort of behavior exemplified by the story is neither unduly heroic nor peculiarly special—the relationships between father and children, shepherd and sheep, landowner and workers, even a widow and her mite. Perhaps we expected more and feel dissatisfied with so little. It is none other than the quality of these relationships which are so simply displayed that is enjoined upon us in a series of verbs.

The injunction "Go and do likewise" is the one and only point behind any of these stories, and the behavior to which it refers is always offered in a series of verbs which we understand in the doing: repent, forgive, show mercy, be patient, have compassion. The stories are invoked by Jesus to show us what this behavior would look like; and once having been shown, all that is left for us is to do likewise. Notice that nothing is ever proved by the use of the story, and no demonstration of the evidence is provided. The story merely presents the case; if we understand the story then we understand also the challenge.

## The Stories Are About Ourselves

It is quite possible that we tend to identify too readily with the figures of goodness presented in the stories—the good Samaritan, the loving father who waits for the prodigal, the caring shepherd. A more fruitful approach might be the admission that these models of goodness are yet but an ideal for us since we have little practice there. If, however, we identify with some of the other figures, then we strike something which does in fact resonate with our own experience. We do know what it is to have squandered our inheritance, to have been slovenly with our gifts, to have wandered from our true home in the selfish search of some greener and easier pasture, to have been stranded in our own emotional or psychological or physical ditch. We know what it is to be found when we thought we were lost, to be loved when we thought we were loveless, to be called by name when we thought no one cared, to be suddenly called into fruitfulness when we thought we were barren. Each of us knows what it is to live with our own failure and our own weakness, as we also know those precious moments of grace when someone touches us, if even briefly, by calling our name or showing a concern. There is no one among us who has not been loved or not been healed by the presence of another.

It is out of experiences such as these that we grasp the true meaning of the parables and know, without it being explained, what is being shown. It is out of this restlessness and unease of our own experience that we are lured to respond to the challenge of these stories—having been lost we are urged to find; having been healed we are called to heal; having been loved we are lured to love. These things the Gospel stories show us, and their only power is the suasion that these things shown are, indeed, better than anything else in all the world. Of such things as these we have already tasted; if we still refuse to see, Jesus sadly reminds us, there is absolutely nothing else to show in evidence.

### Doing the Stories: The Way to Faithfulness

In our spiritual quest it is these Gospel stories which claim our fiercest loyalty, and rightly so. These stories are the most concrete and earthly exemplification possible of a life of faithfulness; after these stories only the deed is possible. The gracious beauty of these stories is that our spiritual quest is this simple and this ordinary; the fearsome challenge of the stories is that there is no ending—after every hungry mouth fed there is another hungry mouth, after every sheep found there is another one lost, after every field has been sown there is a new crop of weeds, never have we forgiven till seventy times seven.

To have faith means to pledge our hearts to God in ultimate commitment, and this commitment requires of us the day-to-day struggle to be faithful. The Gospel stories claim our loyalty because they are our only sure witness to the faithful life. We understand these stories when we take upon ourselves those things the verbs have enjoined—fear not, follow, consider the birds of the air and the lilies, search for justice, love. It is in the doing of such things that we show our faith in God, as it is in the doing of these things that we too become godly. If we can believe Jesus, this is our first taste of abundance, as it is the beginning of resurrection.

### Selected Readings

One of the richest explorations of the notion of faith as the empowering force of our lives, loaded with ambiguity and doubt and fear yet relentlessly compelling, can be found in a delightfully captivating book by John Meagher, *The Gathering of the Ungifted* (New York: Paulist Press, 1972).

A systematic exposition of faith in terms of the faithful lives of committed believers which is amply rewarding because of its personal tone and content is the work of James W. McClendon, Jr., *Biography as Theology* (Nashville: Abingdon Press, 1974).

A fine study of the parables of Jesus as containing an existential challenge to our lives is the work of Dominic Crossan, *The Dark Interval* (Chicago: Argus Press, 1975).

In *Stories of Faith,* John Shea develops the notion of faith in terms of the lived response of our lives within the community of faith. See especially Chapter Two, "The Revelation of God and the Journey of Faith" (Chicago: The Thomas More Press, 1980).

This same theme of the responsibilities of the faithful life of the people on the way is compellingly presented by Paul van Buren in *Discerning the Way*. See Chapter Two, "Together in the Way: Theological Responsibility."

Especially important to the content of this chapter is Paul Holmer's *The Grammar of Faith*. I am much indebted to Chapter Six, "Language and Theology."

*Scripture Readings*

The Gospel of Matthew Chapter 5:1–16

The Gospel of Matthew Chapter 6:25–34

The Gospel of Luke Chapter 16:19–31

# 9

# The God of Love
# and the Abundant Life

As we reach the end of the exploration which we began in the first chapter we discover that we have not reached an end at all. At best what we have at this point is simply a way of looking—at ourselves, our world, and our God. If the perspective developed in these pages serves to illumine to some degree the meaning of our lives in relationship to our Gospel stories, then perhaps we are looking in the right direction. However, we have no way of knowing this for sure and so both the direction of our search and the direction of our first steps are tentative.

As in the Gospels, the only available evidence will be in the fruits, which in this case will be the quality and satisfaction of the lives we lead. No matter which vision we choose to follow or which prophet we feel called to heed, we must remember that we are on the way. The history of our Christian tradition gives ample testimony that this way is not always clear nor is the direction obvious. Only two points on our spiritual map stand out with absolute clarity: God is love and his will is life in abundance. What this will concretely mean in the personal and communal journey of our spiritual lives is the burden of our faith.

This final chapter will draw together some of the themes that have been scattered throughout these pages. While some have been developed more thoroughly than others, all are but seeds. It is hoped that the experience of each one of us will provide the fertile soil. If any of these seeds should take root, we have but one certainty: what grows will be abundantly alive.

## Two Fundamental Affirmations

If we are willing to accept as the cornerstone of our spiritual quest the twofold Gospel affirmation that God is love and his will is life in abundance, then we have also made a decision as to our understanding of the nature and end of human life. If God is love, then to be human is to be a subject of God's love, to be inherently valuable and intrinsically beautiful. This is the creative grace of our existence. And if God's will is life in abundance, then the goal of our human life is the very fullness and abundance of life which is a participation in love. The strengths of this position are likewise twofold: a strong affirmation of this present life and this world, and the consequent demand for full participation in this life and in this world.

Our spirituality must begin with our strengths: we are alive and we are loved. Our natural habitat is this present world, and our only instrument is this personal life. This flesh, this world, these loves—this is the grace with which we are asked to fashion our lives with God. We have not been placed in this world and in this flesh in order that we may work our way out; we have been placed in this world and in these bodies because this is where God dwells. All flesh is holy and all ground is sacred. There is no such thing as existing "outside" of God; everything that is exists within the embrace of God's all-encompassing love. The incarnation assures us that God is no stranger to the flesh.

## The Context of Our Love

If we look upon our gift of life as the supreme symbol of the love of God then our only purpose in this world is to live our lives abundantly. This demands of us a full participation in the reality of self, other, world and God. The abundance of life resides in the quality of living, and this quality is made possible only by our relationships. That relationship which is most godly is love, and hence if God is love, this is what we too are called to be. But the only context of our loving is this world, this self, these neighbors. If we attempt to protect ourselves and refuse to share our lives, then we are headed for death.

We look to our Christ-figure to give us direction and we begin to discern his vision of the world in the words of the Our Father. Jesus was able to see the gracious presence of the Father everywhere—in the mustard seed, in the blossoming fig tree, in the wheat, and finally in the bread. It is not that our world is different from that of Jesus; it is that our sensibilities are pallid and fugitive in comparison to his. We are disinclined to see beyond the surface and reluctant to surrender our self-interest. If we begin to do those things which the Gospel enjoins upon us, we will be amazed at how our sensibilities develop in startling ways. We will hear cries which before fell on our deaf ears, see pain where before we were too preoccupied to notice, discover love in the least and most unlikely of strangers. The entire universe is created anew within the vision of faith.

## Together with God

Such a vision lays demands upon us and this is why we find it difficult to persevere. It is to our grave discredit, however, that we fail to heed the central plea of our Scriptures: whatever it is that the will of God seeks in this world, it will only be achieved by our cooperation; whatever God is doing, he is not doing it by himself. Let us take seriously the language of our Scriptures which indicates the passionate involvement of God in the affairs of this world. This is the tragic and healing truth of the universe: the struggle for life and the struggle for love are as arduous and onerous for God as they are for us. It is not just that we are involved in the work of God; we are involved in the passion of God too, as God is involved in our work and in our passion.

The classic battle of the spiritual life is not so much the conflict between the forces of good and the powers of evil; it is, rather, the struggle of God, the universe, and ourselves for the fullness of life. The spiritual person is not fighting a battle on a different plain or battling foes invisible to the merely worldly-wise. The spiritual person takes this life and this world for its real worth, and this worth is its inescapable God-relatedness. For this reason the spiritual person simply focuses on what is there and available to everyone, the God-relationship, and dedicates all the heart's energies to discovering and embodying this one relationship, since it is the most creative and fulfilling of all relationships.

The Gospels chart both the glories and the difficulties of those who choose this path. We are fortunate to have before us one who has walked well and boldly; he stands as our Christ because his commitment to the abundant life for all has led him through death into resurrection. Whenever we break the bread together, his risen presence is there beckoning us to follow. As is obvious, few of us have the heart to do so.

## Asceticism: God Is the Poet of the World

Of long-standing value in our spiritual tradition has been the notion of *asceticism.* The root for our words "ascetic" and "asceticism" is the Greek verb *askein,* and this word denotes the *artful shaping of a material.* This is perhaps the gentlest and truest of images for spirituality that we will ever discover. The spiritual person is ascetic precisely because the spiritual person is the one who is interested in and dedicated to the artful handling of the world, the artful shaping of one's own self, and the artful forming of one's life into something beautiful. The beautiful is the supreme attraction of the spiritual person, and hence his or her energies are committed to the creation of the beautiful in life, the beautiful in the world. The only material available for this artful shaping is life itself, and thus it is that the spiritual person takes life in hand to inform it with the transcendent beauty of God.

The power of God is the suasive lure of his ideal beauty which calls us to fashion our selves and our lives artfully in response to his ideal vision. In accord with this aesthetic view of artful fashioning, Whitehead has left us this kindly line in *Process and Reality:* "God is the poet of the world, with tender patience leading it by his vision of truth, beauty and goodness." This artful fashioning of life cannot be done by coercion or regimentation; it is only achieved by virtue of spontaneous desire and passionate pursual. Asceticism in this sense is not something that happens to us; it is rather something we take upon ourselves because we wish to fashion the most beautiful self that God could love.

In a more traditional way we have tended to use the term "asceticism" to indicate the giving up of things we liked or the undergoing of hardship—all, somehow, for the love of God. Nonetheless, this second meaning of asceticism rests on an intuition which is essentially correct: to be ascetic means to set priorities; it means to determine a hierarchy of values. To be ascetic means to determine which value will be the controlling value to set the form and shape after which all lesser values will be fashioned. This selection of the pearl of great price will demand that we be willing to forego lesser values for the attainment of the greater, ready to sacrifice worthwhile things for the sake of supreme worth.

In this meaning of asceticism we do give things up, make sacrifices and deny ourselves, but these things are done only in the service of life and their only goal is to make life more gracious. What we do we do out of love, and what we renounce we renounce in the service of love. As always, such renouncings and denials are but means for the greater good of life and hence can never be regarded as ends; our spiritual growth cannot be measured by the size of the things we gave up, only by the size of the life we have artfully fashioned.

## Suffering and Love

To deliberately choose suffering or pain simply because they appear to have ascetic value is to mock God. Our God is the God of love and of life, so that suffering and pain are a mockery and a hindrance to the abundance which is his only will. Because of the fragmentation of our half-lived lives there

will inevitably be suffering and pain which is more than sufficient for most of us, and we can only make sense out of such
negativities if they can be of service in the cause of life itself.
We already know from experience that suffering can engender
a passion for life which did not exist before, and pain can
provide moments of exceptional growth. Undeniably such
things can be used in the service of life, but they can never be
intended as ends in themselves. There is nothing inherently
sanctifying about pain and suffering; it is how we incorporate
these in order to enlarge ourselves which makes the difference.

### The Symbol of the Cross

It may well be the case that all sincere love will include
suffering, but suffering in itself is not love and cannot be
substituted for love. Rather than seek out suffering, love attempts to overcome it. Sufferings of whatever sort which will
occur in our interchange with others and with our unpredictable relationships to the forces of the universe can be utilized
for growth and enlargement. There is no doubt that a certain
largeness of personality can be born of the patience taught by
suffering; a depth of character emerges from the tolerance
learned from suffering; a certain gentleness is the outcome of a
new sympathetic awareness of the suffering of others. But
these after-effects of suffering, as splendid as they are, cannot
serve to justify suffering. The insistent prophetic call of the
Scriptures is that we strive with the wholeness of our strength
to diminish and overcome all suffering. With our Scriptures we
believe firmly that God also suffers. But for God who is love
and for ourselves who strive to be loving, suffering represents
a failure which only love can overcome.

On this particular score, even that central symbol of our
faith, the cross, cannot be viewed as some ideal end to which
we should all conform. The cross, to our everlasting shame,
was a means which Jesus incorporated into a greater cause. It is
our faith that Christ would have been resurrected no matter in
what way his life had ended, but it is to our human shame that
it had to end on the cross. In our persistent emphasis on the

abundance and fullness of life we, at the risk of our souls, dare not forget the message of the cross: all love is inexorably suffering love. Even more, it is only the strength and passionate commitment of love which will give us the enabling power to lay out our own suffering and our own lives as the means for the abundant life for those many others who enjoy less of life than we.

The cross is the unforgettable symbol that our most passionate loves will be the occasion for our greatest suffering; it is likewise the final testimony that what is out of love and because of love is the only redemption we will ever know. We know without being told that we are willing to suffer the most, give up the most, and endure the most pain for those whom we love most intensely. In such cases it is the degree and depth of love which draws from us a willingness to sacrifice and suffer to an extent we had previously deemed impossible and would never have deliberately chosen. But it is the love itself which draws such sacrifice from us, and whatever is suffered or endured is done so only in behalf of the loved one. Whatever meaning such sacrifice may have for us, it can only be bestowed by the depth of the love relationship itself and hence can only be performed in the name of that love. This is simply to say that suffering and pain can only be embraced for the good of others and never for their own sakes.

On the other hand, however, the cross remains a living reminder that the degree to which we open ourselves to others in love is the degree to which we become vulnerable to pain and suffering for the sake of that very love and those loved ones. Perhaps we are slow and shy to move out in love because we already know that the price of the consequences can be very high. But, again, the cross testifies that not even death is a price too high in a world in which God is love.

Our asceticism, then, must be an asceticism in the service of life, a fashioning of our own lives into the stuff of great love and great beauty. The price of such beauty and such love can only be discovered in the fashioning and thus can never be legislated beforehand. We should be wise enough in the ways of wordly life to realize that pain and suffering enough will be there for us and we need never go out looking. The abundance of life which we seek, however, will derive its passionate quality from the effort and struggle with which we pursue its risky adventure.

## The Meaning of Discipline

It has been customary to speak of the disciplines of spirituality, as if spirituality were a matter of rigid technique and tightly-controlled exercises. Our word "discipline" has the same Latin root as our word "disciple" and thus denotes simply the learning from and hence the following after another. The only true discipline of spirituality can be but the learning of the ways of the abundant life, and the following after is entering vitally into the web of life which is ours to share. Any other discipline, whether of prayer, meditation, or asceticism, can at best be a means or an instrument in the service of a richer life.

As means and instruments, however, these disciplines can be picked up and put down, used for a time or disregarded; at no time can they be taken as a measure or a sign of one's spirituality. If such disciplines do not have a discernible result in the quality of our own well-being, then they should be abandoned. The merit of these disciplines is that over the course of the years they have been of service to certain persons at certain particular times. It is the peculiar milieu of our contemporary world from which we should seek to draw whatever exercises can be usefully employed for the development of our consciousness of the qualities of life. We have so much yet to discover, both about life and the means of achieving its beauties, that we dare not be satisfied with the well-used but time-worn usages of the past.

## To Imitate Jesus

The determining discipline of our lives can only be the following of Jesus as we know him through our Gospels and as we see him followed by our spiritual heroes. The supreme challenge of the Gospel to us is to imitate Christ, though not in the narrow and cheapening sense of artificially trying to reproduce his words and actions in the attempt to make our lives look like his.

On the contrary, to imitate Christ is to be challenged to do exactly what he did—to become the Christ. It is perhaps high time that we let go of that rather pedestrian notion of a cookie-mold version of humanity and of spirituality—that somehow God would be supremely pleased if all of us looked exactly alike, acted alike, spoke alike. Let us admit to the self-destructive inhumanity implied in the idea that God would be pleased by the suppression of all individuality and all uniqueness. The one unremittable claim that each carries within us like a holy grail is the claim to sacred uniqueness and individual distinctness. Each of us is loved by God, not as a member of a class, but as a completely novel and surprising self, capable of achieving for God a unique quality of experience and a distinct individuality of love never before experienced by God.

In our sinfulness we do not rob God of what someone else could also give to him; we steal away, rather, what would have been his from us and us alone. Are we willing to be large enough for the power we have over God, such that the quality of love which either you or I deny to him is denied to him everlastingly? The response to the call to follow Jesus is to heed the challenge that salvation lies within our own hands and nowhere else, to let our individually unique lives be the incarnation of God in this time and in this place. Each of us must wrestle with our own individual angel and perhaps our devil too, but the conflict is personal to ourselves and God must await the outcome. In this sense also, no one can die for us; each of us must do our own dying and accomplish our own death, and however our death is achieved it will be but the mirror-side of our living—something so uniquely personal that it is the one gift we can give to God that he has never before received. This, surely, is both our burden and our glory.

The total and only point of all of our asceticism and in each of our disciplines is the quality of our service to the God of love; and such service can only be our loving lives and nothing else. There is absolutely nothing which can be substituted for the uniquely personal act of love that is the heart of our lives and the soul of our relationship to God. Too easily can we be distracted by the production of surrogate activities which are intended to procure some vicarious satisfaction for a God who despises our sin. But the only satisfaction worthy of our God is that we leave our sin and embrace the love which has never left us. The tale of our sinfulness is not so much the list of commissions and omissions which we can draw up on our spiritual tally-sheet; our sinfulness is in our compromises with death as we settle for less than the fullness of life. Almost to our despair, this is so easy to do.

## Sin: Missing the Mark

The Greek root for the word "sin" (*hamartia*) is based on an archery image, and it means to miss the mark. Each of us knows already that it takes no talent at all to miss the mark; we can miss unconsciously, semi-consciously, or unreflectedly. To hit the mark takes both talent and effort, and rarely do these come to us without patience, practice, determination and desire. The spiritual discipline called for here is the will to learn of the Gospels where our neighbor is and what is his need, and our asceticism is the stepping from our own appointed path to attend to needs that interfere with our own.

To miss the mark by selfishness requires no training and no talent, but each movement away from such selfishness is also a movement in direction of the proper mark, which is love. The very personal nature of such skills requires lifelong attentiveness and ever-renewed devotion because the target, who is both God and our neighbor, is ever moving and ever new. It is from our partial successes that we receive the emotional energy which will be our only sign that this discipline is worth the effort. We are fortunate in that we have our sacramental liturgies in which we may both renew our motivation to this priceless cause and taste of the supper which is God's good gift to those of us who will recognize him in the breaking of the bread.

## To Change Our Heart

As we strive to make of this world a more human habitat and to shape our societies with a more humane face, we rest this demanding enterprise on one single surety: this is the work of God. In the light of the state of the world in which we live, it may at first glance appear that we are charged with an impossible task. Yet if we hearken to Jesus we will know that God's demand is not first that we change the world or convert our societies; his first sweet call, rather, is to each of us by name that we turn within and change our hearts even before we change our ways.

With a change of heart the first thing we acknowledge is that holy presence within us, aware perhaps for the first time that the first good news is our very selves. It is not at all a matter of receiving through some miraculous gift something which we had heretofore lacked; on the contrary, it is the acknowledgment and then the proclamation that we are alive because we are of the body of God, and that we do not enter or leave that body, but, rather, by personal choice, become healthy or ill and thus infect our human context with the contagion of grace or sin. The challenge is that we are responsible for so much; the comfort is that we are already graced in strength by the gifts of so many.

The tidings of Jesus are that we may start with the simple and humble ways of repenting, showing mercy, forgiving, and offering bread and water. As these become our habit we have no way of knowing beforehand what our hunger for justice and thirst for peace will demand of us. All that we will know is that we believe firmly that our own abundance lies in our faithfulness because we have tasted of a love that grows both more precious and more intense as it becomes the consuming passion of our heart.

## Letting Be

In these several pages we have simply been examining from various angles our dominant theme: that the first and final effect of the spiritual life is our own very selves and the quality of our lives in the world, and the consequence of our prayer is that we become prayerful in every action and in every relationship available to us. The quest for our spirituality is the reclamation of that singular freedom which alone establishes us as the very image of God: we freely make choices which are choices made for God. Our long history is the often sad story of freedom stolen and freedom surrendered, of responsibility abrogated and responsibility relinquished. As in the requirement that we each must make our own love, so also it is contradictory that we allow our choices to be made by any but ourselves.

We must have the strength to take charge of our own lives, realizing that institutions and legal systems, churches and moral codes, are but the social context in which we each learn how to choose. As in our loving where, for good or ill, we are fully responsible for the quality of our love and can lay no blame at a further doorstep, so also in the matter of our lives the choices out of which we create ourselves and which are the mode of our relationships to others must unremittingly be, for the sake of our very personhood, our choices entirely. To be willing to take less than full responsibility for the quality of our choices would be to delegate our loving of God to another, something which is not just impossible, but also meaningless. In this matter of love, the sole responsibility for our success or failure is our own.

If we reflect on the creative activity of God as portrayed in Genesis we notice that the language of creativity appears there as "Let there be." In its Hebrew form this phrase is couched in a verb-form which reflects not a command but a permission. In this orderly sequence God is calling the various items of reality into being by allowing them to become. "Let there be light, growing things, animals, etc." represents God's encouragement to the forces of chaos (the spirit hovering over the waters) to emerge into forms of definiteness by choices of order. Only if these passages are understood as God's call and permission do the subsequent repetitions "He saw that it was good" have any meaning at all, for this phrasing reflects a

degree of surprise on the part of God. The creative responses
to the lure of his call had formed into definite patterns of
goodness both surprising and pleasing to God.

According to Genesis it is by virtue of God's ideals and the
encouragement of his suasive lure that reality takes the definite forms which we experience within the universe. The long
and checkered story of cosmic evolution as we now know it
describes the lengthy and tortuous path by which the very
atoms and molecules which are the driving power of our stars
gradually organized and congealed into this precious form
which you and I know as ensouled flesh. This, we should
believe, was a precious and lovely surprise even to God.

The power which is described in Genesis should be the
selfsame power which describes our spiritual lives. The first
and irreversible thrust of our spirit is letting ourselves be, and
the story of our lives is but the configuration of the various
choices by which we allow ourselves to become. Neither Genesis nor the Gospels give any reasonable warrant for the imposing of strictures nor the laying down of censures on the
gracious possibilities for our becoming.

Because of our social history we are a law-conscious people, and our relationship to the larger social context is highly
defined by the legal, so much so that we tend to assume that
without benefit of the strictures and obligations of law we are
doomed to return to disorder, chaos and destruction. It should
be to our surprise and shame that we have calmly accepted
this situation as normal, even God-inspired. We claim to have
our roots in the Bible with its grand Wisdom tradition of the
divine creativity and responsibility which is the distinguishing
characteristic of the human, as well as in the divine vision of
Jesus which would reduce the near-infinite complexity of law
to one single invitation.

### A Basis of Trust

A spirituality which is based on the Scriptures must be a
spirituality based on trust. There must first of all be trust that
God's suasive power is finally reliable and trustworthy and

overwhelming in its lure. Secondly, there must be trust in ourselves, trust that Genesis speaks rightly when it claims that we are made in the image of God. If this bestowal of the image of God is the primal covenant which establishes our very existence, then we must be faithful and loyal to the only powers we ever really know, the powers of our own being.

To exist as God's image surely must mean that our deepest strivings, our most sincere efforts, our wholehearted desire to know, our fierce loyalty to our own intuition—such qualities as define the deepest meaning of our personal lives—cannot be out of tune, or misguided, or predestined to futility. Our faith in this primal covenant is our faith in the wisdom of a God who does all things well, so that our natures are not awry, our wills bent or our intellects askew.

That God would do so poorly is to misread both our Scriptures and our own experience. That we are created out of and for the love of God is the first and final thing we know about ourselves. We must learn to work against our own desperation to affirm our own goodness, our own rightness, our own beauty. *That* we are loved by God is ineradicable faith; *how* God loves us is determined by our trust in the gracious possibilities which reside within us.

The God who is love willingly "lets us be" because the quality of our love must be freely chosen, sincerely desired, and fashioned with passion. We must allow ourselves to move forward toward ideals which transcend us; to move outward toward visions which, though not clear, are yet forceful in their lure; to let go of the comfort of the present because our life is yet in the future. Our God is large enough to allow us to go our way; he can only trust us, since it is not within his power to coerce us.

If by some perverse chance God could coerce us, then we would have but the cold comfort of knowing that we are not loved and neither is our God. If we reject such obduracy then perhaps we can strive to focus both our eyes and our energy on the grand possibilities before us: we are endowed with life and the only end of life is life in abundance. Just as lovers devote themselves to seeking out the endless ways in which their love can be expressed, to discover anew each time that this novel expression between them is also a novel quality of their love, so also those who believe in life entrust themselves to the discovery of the infinite variety of ways in which life can be enhanced, to be rewarded in turn by a new cause for celebration of their own lives.

### The Cause of Life

It is the cause of life which is the basis and motive of our prayerfulness. Before the inexhaustible mystery of life with its perplexing conflict and its allowance of death we must hold ourselves in prayerfulness. Desire as we may the fullness of life for ourselves and those beloved by us, we exist in doubt, in anxiety, in perplexity, in the near despair of the feeling that we are finally lost since all life leads inexorably to death. Our prayer is the holding before us of our doubt, our confusion, our anxiety and even our despair with the full awareness that this is the most urgent stuff of our lives and that all our future will be fashioned out of these wounds and these scars. But what makes this prayer rather than self-pity is the radical trust that this also is the stuff of our lives that has been redeemed.

Our prayer is not the request of a miracle that new life will be ours, but the faithful trust that this wounded life can be better than it is because our fragile lives are held up by an infinite web of gracious relationships which demand our cooperation and our refusal to surrender. We are sustained by prayer if we refuse to seek answers or cures and seek only to endure in our passionate involvement. Our Gospel faith is that we will endure if we but persevere in the simple faithfulness of ordinary bread and water, unspectacular justice and homely love.

### What Are We Willing To Settle For?

Whenever we seek to discern those final values toward which we strive and out of which we fashion our lives we are engaged in that search for meaning which is the soul of the spiritual quest. Although there are numberless ways of posing these questions—What is the meaning of life? What is life for? What is the final end of life?—they are all fundamentally the same question. Let us reformulate this question so that it points first of all to ourselves: *What are we willing to settle for?*

We can look upon the irreversible ongoingness of our lives as a complex web of choices which are ours to make, moment by moment, day by day. Some of our choices are made out of habit, some out of emotion, some out of sheer acquiescence. The reasons for our choices are as varied as the values of the universe, but if we are willing to weigh our reasons to discover the implicit hierarchy which controls much of our choosing we will get a fair and reliable indication of what indeed we are willing to settle for. Perhaps we will discover that we are ready to make any kind of choice as long as our subsistence is guaranteed, or perhaps we find that our choices are highly geared to the projection of our public image, so that reputation has high value, or possibly our choices are determined by the self-assurance given by money or power. In such cases, despite our lofty claims, our actions reveal the quality of those things we are willing to settle for.

It is to our disgrace that the high ideals of our religious life do not in fact countermand our concrete settling for security, for safety, for power, for deferred salvation. While the religious question which charges the struggle of our lives is *What are we willing to settle for?* the only religious answer which is the radical content of our faith is: *We are not willing to settle for anything less than the abundance of life.* Nothing else is finally worth settling for—none of the rewards of life, none of its decorations, none of its assurances, none of its idols. Life and life alone is what we will live for, and there is absolutely no substitute for the fullness of life itself.

The first and final issue is the size of our lives, and that size will be defined by the quality of our self-investment in those transcendent ideals which draw us to transcend our own selves. These ideals will leave us always restless and hungry, since life feeds upon life and engenders more life. We will not settle for anything which restricts us, or keeps us safe, or would have us conform rather than risk. Any hint of abundance which we may be fortunate enough to enjoy is but a foretaste of the richness of our resurrection if we but make it so.

### The Size of God: Infinite Passion

This same question may be mirrored in its complement: *What is the size of our God?* The reason for this form of the question is simply that the size of God will mirror the size of our own lives. It has been the burden of our faith to assert, in one fashion or another—infinity, absolute power, supreme perfection—that our God is of very great size. But if the majestic size of our God is translated for us into terms of law, or obedience, or sin, then we have made of God but the gruesome reflection of our own smallness. Is our God so small that he must demand of us our obedience, that he can only rule by law, that legal infringements must be satisfied after the fashion of debts, that he would demand a pound of flesh? If we so believe about our God, then our lives will be passionless and safe, risk-free and drained of vitality. We do an ungracious injustice to the One who has called us not servants, but friends.

If we but reassert the rights to our Gospel heritage we must trust the tender truth that our God is love. It is the love of God which demands that the passion of God be infinite. Thus the infinite size of our God is defined by the infinite passion of the One whose passionate involvement for life will never be satisfied and whose passionate involvement in love can never be stilled. Our God is that Holy One who will never settle for less than the fullness of life. No matter how much we struggle, no matter how much we give, no matter how much we do, our God will ask for more. The infinite size of God is that passion for life and love which can run into everlastingness and never be exhausted. Thus it is that the controlling relation to God is not obedience or conformity, but rather creativity and challenge, the lure to taste of the passion which is the restless heart of God.

Nothing is of supreme value for us except the love of the God of love. Nothing is worth our total commitment except supreme love. This is our faith, and we live on this by faith.

The spiritual ones believe, in the face of a world that believes otherwise, that the nature of God is indeed love and nothing else. Out of our experience of a broken world with its irrefutable evidence of cruelty and oppression, this is indeed a difficult faith and few can bear it. It is easy to settle for power or law or good order.

Our primary task is not so much to demonstrate to others that God is love and that the nature of his creation is loving; it is rather to ask of ourselves and to so act as to make sense out of our asking: What would it look like, what would it look like in us and in our world, if indeed love were our ultimate commitment? How would we appear to others, and what would happen to our world? What would life look like for all? This is the "what if" question which is at the heart of religious faith, enshrined for us in the Our Father. In the infinite mystery of God, the answer to this "what if" question lies not in God but in ourselves. What if we were to become like God? What if we were to become godly? We will never know these things until we try.

Those Gospel people who have so tried have left ample testimony to the graciousness created for the rest of us. We are ungrateful to them, to our heritage, to our God if we do not try. The size of our lives and the size of our loves is something we hold within our own power. The quality of our lives is something which is created within the context of our sharing life with others, as the quality of our love is something which is created out of the gifted relationships to which we respond. We have within us the power to become greater than we dared dream, for we contribute everlastingly to the size of God.

## Conviction and Celebration

By and large we are inspired by good will and the sincerity of our best efforts is usually beyond question. Nonetheless, we find the efforts of our spiritual life difficult and the self-doubt irksome. We are unsure of our guides, uncertain of the results within ourselves, unconvinced of the possibilities of endurance. In our moments of quiet we are drawn by the beauty of our ideals, but in the day-to-day commerce of our worldly affairs we are worn down by the tedium of friction and recalcitrance. There is the strong temptation to separate our spiritual world from the secular, to partition off our sacred times from the profane places. To our sad despair, the secular and profane will always overwhelm us by sheer weight of numbers and wear us down by brute attrition. For every hour in prayer there are sixty in the marketplace. Our spirit recedes into a vague ghost.

In the light of this, one of the fundamental problems of the spiritual life is a matter of energy for perseverance. Where do we get the motivating power to struggle against all odds to be our best and finest when so much of what surrounds us demands that we compromise with the cheap and easy? The problem here is not so much a problem of belief; for the most part we believe rightly concerning God and the highest goals of our life. The problem is, rather, one of conviction. Our belief has not sunk into our very roots and infected us with a restless dissatisfaction with the way our lives are and the way all things are. What we know and what we are convinced of, unfortunately, can be two separate items.

Whereas we profess to know our true goals and our proper striving, it is difficult to be convinced in the face of a world whose counter-example is so persistent and so pervasive. Perhaps an example will be helpful here. Picture a couple who have been married for a good number of years. The first romance is long gone, the children are for the most part grown and departed, the early anxieties over survival have been overcome with job security. The marriage has apparently done what marriages are supposed to do, but there is little flavor and little zest—only the taken-for-granted patterns and the tedium of expecting nothing new. What is it precisely that has vanished from this marriage, the presence of which would be an occasion of vitality and renewed commitment?

What has vanished from this marriage is something which initially had been spontaneous and essential: celebration. If we but examine the early stages of our love relationships we will see how great a part is played by simple celebration, how much time is spent doing things which are just enjoyable for their own sakes, how much shared activity is but an excuse for the joy of shared presence. These spontaneous acts of celebration serve to highlight the joy of the shared relationship as well as to intensify the qualitative depth of the relationship itself. Any love relationship which is to endure the test of time can only do so by a consistent fueling of such moments of celebration; otherwise the relentless dreariness of the ordinary and expected will wear down and finally exhaust the sublime joy of stimulation which was the first felt emotion of being in love.

### The Source of Conviction

Our spiritual life is burdened by the same psychological and emotional demands. To take on the pressures of life at any level can be demanding and exhausting, but to approach life with the stance of responsive love can be sheer romanticism unless fired by the emotional conviction that is able to draw the self into a commitment. Perhaps we have a difficult time standing by our beliefs because the very oppressiveness of the tasks at hand precludes the levity of celebration. Thus it is that our prayer and our liturgies take on the same pallor of oppressiveness as the causes we struggle against.

In prayer and liturgy we ceaselessly remind ourselves of evil, oppression, inhumanity and death. Are not realities such as these pervasive and burdensome enough without making of them also the content of our prayer and the basis of our emotional conviction? Finally we cannot be defined by those things we are against; we take our identity only from those things which are the positive fuel of our self-growth. The very seriousness of the causes which are oppressive and destructive of life compels us to include them as the focal point of our deepest religious striving—we are against war, poverty, oppression, racism, and cruelty of any sort, and so our prayer and our liturgies are dominated by these themes. We come away reinforced in our antipathy for such things, but not necessarily revitalized with an exuberance for the marvelous splendor of life itself.

We must be ever wary of the constant temptation to use our prayer and our liturgies for purposes beyond that of worship. Are we so naive that we assume God is unaware of the injustices we are pointing to? While such negative emotions as hatred for evil and repugnance at injustice may have a short-term effect of focusing our energy in a single direction, in the long-term they are corrosive and dehumanizing.

## Worship Is Celebration

To be properly worshipful, our prayer and our liturgies must be acts of genuine celebration and nothing else. We need not be afraid to admit that our life, in spite of the bitter-sweet mix afforded by the world, is good, that we enjoy immensely our own well-being, that we draw pleasure from the worldly gifts that are ours to enjoy even though others may lack them, that our shared loves have given moments of unspeakable passion. These intimations of abundance are the root-cause for our conviction that life is worthwhile and for the consequent commitment to the sharing of such life as our true purpose. To celebrate, however, the graciousness of the good that is already within our midst is to be grateful in our entire attitude of gracious acceptance.

Our liturgical celebrations are intended to be our grateful acceptance of the goodness of life expressed in the intensity and vigor of our mutually shared joy. Let us not use our liturgies for some purpose extraneous to sheer celebration; let us do nothing with our liturgies except enjoy ourselves, enjoy one another, enjoy our life with God. Before God our liturgies are nothing more than the invocation of the goodness and beauty of what God has already done in our midst and will continue to do. By our prayers and our liturgies we add nothing to God and pay no debts; we simply, in our gratitude of joyful acceptance, enable God to be ever more gracious, because always grace grows upon grace.

What is suggested here, however, is that it is exactly the emotional depth, the sense of satisfaction, the experienced joy, the suasive attraction of our shared presence and our mutual goodness which establish the deep emotional base that will create a conviction of sufficient fervor and passion to maintain us in the long-haul struggle with the ordinary, the trivial, the evil and the sinful.

### We Are the Good News

As spiritual persons we are finally described as the people of the good news. The news must be good first of all to those who hear it; otherwise it cannot enhance their lives. Our first good news is surely not what we say, what we preach, what we proclaim in our demonstrations. Our first good news is ourselves. In a very real sense we cannot speak the good news; we can merely show it forth. And it will be shown in the quality of our own lives, in the passion we bring to one another, in the joy we show in shared presence, in the love we offer to those least likely. It is the intent of our prayerful and liturgical celebrations to enflesh us with the good news, to fashion us by participation into the living symbol of what God can do, to draw us into godliness by tasting of the bread which is the source of all life.

Only when the conviction of our own worth and our own goodness breaks into celebration will the convictions of our faith grab hold of us with awesome power so that our very presence to others will be good news indeed. If we are enamored of life it will show in everything we do, everything we say; it will show in our attitudes, in our values, in our relationships, and most of all in our love. Only when others first respond to our presence will they ask us who we are, and then we, the people of the good news, will begin to tell our stories and show to others that it is possible to say Our Father.

### Our Journey and Its Company

As we walk together on our spiritual quest we take good comfort from each other's company. Nevertheless we always walk with a degree of doubt, uncertainty, even anxiety. When the gentle Master said "Come and see," we were not convinced that this journey would take a lifetime. And yet what has already occurred in our midst and within our own selves in the course of our journey has been sufficiently attractive to have us believe that the quest is worthwhile. We do not really know a better way to go.

One thing those of us who are serious about the quest do know is that we have been seized by our glimpse of a grand vision that has already fired many a saintly hero and heroine whom we would gladly emulate. Perhaps we did not realize it at the time, but once we have caught this vision, we will never see the same; indeed, we will never be the same. Whether we choose to follow this vision with the wholeness of our hearts or not, it will still be there; it will not go away and it will not leave us. We know for sure that this is not a dream which, upon opening our eyes, will disappear.

We are grateful for the loyal company with whom we walk. At our times of rest we celebrate those gracious moments which have bound us together and which give meaning to our mutual quest. Other than this, the stories we tell are all familiar with repetition, so we find that we look at each other's lives also. That one is patient and this one is meek; this one is forgiving and that one is loving. It is good to walk with such as these; the more we walk the more we come to look like our companions. Out ahead we hear the voice of Jesus: "Come and see. God is love." We have abundance enough. This journey of our hearts is worthwhile.

### Selected Readings

That this emphasis on the maturity and responsibility incumbent upon each of us to take charge of the shape and quality of our own lives has a strong biblical foundation is convincingly demonstrated by Walter Brueggemann in *In Man We Trust: The Neglected Side of Biblical Faith* (Atlanta: John Knox Press, 1972). See, for example, Chapter Two, "The Trusted Creature."

A very humane and appealing discussion of the splendor and wonder possible to our everyday lives is that of Sam Keen in *To a Dancing God*, Chapter Two, "Education for Serendipity."

A fine analysis of the notion of asceticism which can be appropriate for today is done by Margaret Miles in "Toward a New Asceticism" (*The Christian Century*, October 28, 1981), pp. 1097–98.

The emphasis of this work on the abundant life compels us to take a second look at some of the current notions about poverty. A remarkably revealing work on this topic is that of Michael Guinan, O.F.M., *Gospel Poverty* (New York: Paulist Press, 1981), in which he demonstrates that the biblical view of poverty is that it stands as an affront to God and is something to be overcome rather than joined.

The works previously cited by Paul Holmer, Paul van Buren, and John Shea all have material relevant to this chapter.

*Scripture Reading*

The First Letter to the Corinthians Chapter 13:1–13

The Gospel of Matthew Chapter 5: 43–48

The Letter to the Romans Chapter 12:14–21